The Vision of Matthew

Theological Inquiries

Studies in Contemporary
Biblical and Theological Problems

General Editor
Rev. Lawrence Boadt, C.S.P.

PAULIST PRESS
New York • Ramsey • Toronto

The Vision of Matthew

Christ, Church, and Morality
in the First Gospel

John P. Meier

PAULIST PRESS
New York ● Ramsey ● Toronto

Nihil Obstat:
Myles M. Bourke, S.S.L., S.T.D.
Censor Deputatus

Imprimatur:
Joseph T. O'Keefe
Vicar-General, Archdiocese of New York

November 10, 1978

The Nihil Obstat and Imprimatur are official declarations that a book or pamphlet is free of doctrinal or moral error. No implication is contained therein that those who have granted the Nihil Obstat and Imprimatur agree with the contents, opinions or statements expressed.

All abbreviations for biblical books and theological tools conform to the style sheet of the *Catholic Biblical Quarterly* and the *Journal of Biblical Literature*.

Library of Congress
Catalog Card Number: 78-70820

ISBN: 0-8091-2171-9

Published by Paulist Press
Editorial Office: 1865 Broadway, New York, N.Y. 10023
Business Office: 545 Island Road, Ramsey, N.J. 07446

Printed and bound in the
United States of America

Contents

PART THREE
REMODELING MORALITY:
THE ESCHATOLOGICAL DEMAND OF CHRIST

To my parents

Paul Ulrich Meier
and
Elizabeth O'Reilly Meier

who first taught me the meaning
of the gospel message

INTRODUCTION

Why Another Book on Matthew?

The present work was called forth by two totally different yet highly significant publications: Jack Dean Kingsbury's *Matthew: Structure, Christology, Kingdom* (Philadelphia: Fortress, 1975) and the report, *Human Sexuality* (N.Y.: Paulist, 1977), submitted to the Catholic Theological Society of America. One might wonder how two books so diverse in content and purpose could unwittingly conspire to produce the present volume. I hope the reader will indulge me as I give a few words of autobiographical explanation.

On the one hand, Kingsbury's splendid work raised two basic questions in my mind: (1) Is the title Son of God *the* central title in Matthew's Christology, as Kingsbury claims; and (2) How does the church fit into this Christological concern of Matthew? Both questions are handled by Kingsbury with great skill, and yet I am not totally convinced by his answers. The pages that follow, and especially Part II, are an attempt on my part to find more satisfying answers. Contrary to Kingsbury, I would consider Son of Man just as central to Matthew's Christology as is Son of God. And I would also see the bond between Christ and his church as *the* characteristic mark of Matthew's Christology.

But, on the other hand, an investigation of the nexus between Christ and church in Matthew's gospel necessarily leads one to the moral teaching that rests upon this nexus as its foundation. Here lies the connection with the other work, the CTSA report on *Human Sexuality*. Part of the report attempts to summarize and interpret the teaching of the New Testament on sexual morality.

1

The intentions of the authors are excellent and I applaud their desire to break new ground in a sadly neglected area. But, along with other Catholic exegetes, I am disturbed by the small space given to the New Testament data, the sweeping generalizations made about the data, and the tendency to dismiss certain rigorous demands with the magic phrase of "time conditioned." I think the New Testament data on morality—and certainly not just sexual morality—deserve more detailed and serious treatment. Furthermore, I must confess myself uneasy with a tendency to dismiss as time bound any rigorous demand that offends the spirit of the moment. At times it may be we ourselves, rather than the New Testament, who deserve the warning label of time bound. The problem with the criterion of instant relevance is that it may not always do justice to the prophetic and eschatological nature of the moral demands in the New Testament. Perhaps we should listen most attentively to those passages of the New Testament which on first contact strike us as offensive or difficult. It may be especially at such pressure points that the wholly other Word, the eschatological Kingdom of God, is breaking into our hermetically sealed modern lives. At least we should not ward off or neutralize a potentially explosive encounter with God's Word by using the all-purpose lightning rod of the "time conditioned."

Of course, I do not pretend that the present work encompasses the whole moral message of Jesus or the New Testament. Nor does it answer all the moral problems raised by the text or by modern man. But it is, I hope, at least one step toward an exegetically responsible weighing of some key New Testament texts bearing on morality. And, thanks to the impulse from Kingsbury's seminal work, this weighing takes place not in a vacuum, but in the larger context of Matthew's overarching theology of Christ and church. It is one of the contentions of this book that only in such a framework can the moral message of Matthew be properly understood.

Christ, church, and morality: these, then, are the three major concerns of this book. The book itself divides into three parts. Part I seeks to introduce us to Matthew, to his time and place, to his church and its problems. What makes Matthew and his gospel so relevant to the modern church is that he was not working in an ivory tower, but in and for a church racked by problems of faith and morality in an era of transition.

After this introductory overview, Part II undertakes the major task of proving a central point: the special characteristic, the specificity, of Matthew's gospel, is the nexus between Christ and church. The problem with proving such a thesis is that it is all too easily provable if the author is free to choose which sections of the gospel will be treated to verify his point. Almost any position on any book in the Bible can be proven if the defender of the thesis is free to choose which passages from the book will be considered. All the favorable data will be marshaled, and all the unfavorable data will be ignored. The only way to establish my thesis honestly and convincingly is to present a mini-commentary on the whole of Matthew's gospel, showing that my view on the nexus of Christ and church is verified consistently throughout the gospel, and not just here and there. As will be seen, along the way I also make some subsidiary points about Matthew's Christology, especially the central importance of the title Son of Man and the unique sense in which Christ is a teacher of morality.

Having established the Christological-ecclesiological nexus, and having already seen some of its impact on discipleship and morality, we then turn to some key moral questions in Part III. The general consideration of the relation of Christ to the Law in Matthew 5:17–20 provides an introduction to the specific moral questions of murder and anger, adultery and internal impurity, divorce and remarriage, oaths and vows, retaliation and legal action, and hatred of enemies in 5:21–48. This by no means exhausts the moral problems of the New Testament or of Matthew's gospel. But I hope that this synthetic treatment of specific morality in the wider context of Christ and his church will provide one possible model both for future studies on morality in the New Testament as well as for continuing redactional work on Matthew's Christology and theology in general.

Thanks are due to many people who made this book possible. The Rev. Msgr. Myles M. Bourke first guided my studies in Matthew, studies which bore fruit in my first book, *Law and History in Matthew's Gospel* (Rome: Biblical Institute Press, 1976). Much of the material in Parts I and III is based on that monograph, and scholars who would wish more detailed argumentation might wish to consult it. For stimulation and criticism I owe a great debt to the Catholic Biblical Association's Task Force on Matthew, of which I was a member from 1973 to 1977. Its other members, Joseph Comber, Lamar Cope, Douglas Hare, Daniel Harrington, Jack Kingsbury, James Reese, Donald Senior, and William Thompson, have all contributed to the formation of my own position, though I must take responsibility for what is said here. In particular, the outstanding work of Jack Dean Kingsbury has created a new period and set a new agenda for Matthean studies in the United States. If I take issue with some of his positions in this book, that should be construed simply as a tribute to the great catalyst his own work constitutes. It has been a pleasure to work with Dr. Kingsbury, who is both a first-rate Matthean scholar and a true Christian gentleman. I also wish to express my gratitude to the Rev. Kevin Lynch and the Rev. Lawrence Boadt of Paulist Press; their patient editorial work has made the publication of this volume possible. Finally, I wish to thank my friends, Norbert and Shelley Dickman, for their hospitality during the final days of work on this book. I marked the end both of my stay with them and of this work by baptizing their second son Matthew.

PART ONE

REMODELING THE FORM OF GOSPEL

From Mark to Matthew

CHAPTER ONE

Matthew and the Task of Remodeling

I.   REMODELING AS AN HISTORICAL PROCESS

Christians who are concerned with the burning moral issues of the day or with their personal spiritual growth may be annoyed when, upon turning to Part I, they see that I am delving back into the dusty documents and vanished communities of the first century A.D. I can hear the cry now: spirituality, *si*; archeology, *no*. It is a cry often heard in seminaries. Why bother with hypotheses about the historical origins of Matthew's gospel? Why not just take it as it stands, listen to the Word of God speaking to us today, and apply what it says to the problems of our times?

Such an approach is not without support in some areas of modern literary criticism. According to some, a literary work should be savored for its own intrinsic beauty and goodness, apart from questions of the author's life, intentions, or historical situation. This approach, which might be given the vague label "esthetic," has found proponents in Scriptural research, especially in the study of the parables of Jesus.[1] One expression of this a-historical approach is "structuralism." This method prescinds from the conscious intention of the author in order to seek the "depth structures" which belong to the literary work as such, insofar as it is one expression of a larger literary category.[2]

It should be stressed, however, that many practitioners of

---

[1]See, e.g., the various articles in the fascicles of the experimental journal *Semeia*, Volumes 1 and 2.

[2]On this, see the exposition of D. Patte, *What Is Structural Exegesis?* (Philadelphia: Fortress, 1976).

structuralism see it as complementary to the more historical approaches to Scripture. Certainly, to go to Scripture with no knowledge of its historical context would be rank fundamentalism. While a non-historical approach may be quite legitimate for a lyric poem, it would be inadequate, not to say disastrous, for a study of the Declaration of Independence or the Gettysburg Address, however much one may admire these documents as literary works. One might object that the gospel of Matthew should not be compared to such political or constitutional works. But, as N. Perrin pointed out, the gospel of Matthew may be viewed as a "foundation myth,"[3] narrating the past sacred events of the life of Jesus which provide a basis for the present time of the church. As can be seen especially from the gospel's interest in the church, the gospel of Matthew does have a certain "founding" or "constitutional" character which makes an a-historical approach highly questionable. This approach becomes all the more questionable if we decide—as we shall—that Matthew's gospel is a conscious reworking and remodeling of an already existing document and literary form: the gospel of Mark.

But our basic reason for insisting on historical backgrounds goes beyond the unique character of Matthew's gospel or of its primary source. Unlike many religions, Christianity has as its basis an historical revelation centered on and incarnated by an historical person, Jesus of Nazareth. Any attempt to avoid the anchorage of the Christian faith of every age in the Christ-event of the first century turns Christianity into a timeless gnostic myth or a "supreme fiction." This is not to say that we should ignore the need to reinterpret the first-century event for twentieth-century persons. After all, even in the New Testament, we find Christians of the latter part of the first century reinterpreting traditions about Jesus from the earlier part of the first century. It is the constant and ultimate task of hermeneutics to ask: What *does* the text say to us today? But before that question can be asked with any clear understanding and direction, we must ask the prior question of exegesis in the narrow sense: What *did* the

---

[3] N. Perrin, *The New Testament: An Introduction* (N.Y.: Harcourt, Brace, Jovanovich, 1974) 164. Needless to say, I do not equate "myth" with "unhistorical fable."

text say to its author and original audience? On the basis of the author's original intent in his historical situation we can raise superstructures of reinterpretation. To build the superstructures without the basis would be to construct hermeneutical castles in the air.

Hence, our first concern is to recapture, as far as we can today, the original situation in which Matthew spoke to his church, with the hope that it will help us understand how he speaks to our church. Needless to say, our concern with Matthew and *his* intention, *his* message, does not mean we are skeptical about or uninterested in the teaching of the historical Jesus. Jesus certainly stands at the origins of Matthew's gospel. But the gospel tradition as we have it is the result of a long process of tradition and reinterpretation, of "remodeling," stretching from the original oral teaching of Jesus, through the oral teaching of the early church, through the first written documents, down to Matthew's gospel. Thus, what we have before us today, the gospel of Matthew, is the end-result of this whole process. This gospel—and not any hypothetical oral traditions and documents prior to it—is the inspired text the church has canonized and proclaims, the primary datum before us asking for interpretation, and the primary tool scholars have for ascending to the earlier stages of the tradition. If we are ever to understand the teaching of Jesus and the early church correctly, we must begin with the concrete and complex record we have before us. There is no magic pipeline to A.D. 30. And so, I must emphasize at the start that the purpose of this book is to understand the message of Jesus *as proclaimed by Matthew*, that is, the word of God as it has concretely come to us in the words of one particular inspired author. To think that we can bypass him to get directly to the "authentic message" of Jesus betrays a poor understanding of both historical revelation and historical research. More precisely, it is foolish to think we can apply Matthew's moral message to our time if we do not even know what that message meant to say to his own time.

II. THE SOURCES THAT WERE REMODELED

Matthew is a creative author and theologian. To study him is to grow continually in respect for his intellectual ability and achievements. But creativity in the first-century church was not the same thing as literary creativity in the twentieth century. Matthew's situation places him under the constraints of a normative tradition. This is important to realize when we look for signs of Matthew's own creativity and theological stance. He is not creating or theologizing in a vacuum. He is a servant, a guardian, and a reinterpreter of an already venerable tradition, which has existed for decades in his own church. This insight is the perduring contribution of the form-criticism of the 1920's: the evangelist is the recipient of various forms of a tradition which he must respect.

Yet, as the more recent (post-World War II) discipline of redaction criticism has taught us, the evangelists were not simply mechanical collectors of individual traditions, mere robots who pasted together disparate units without imposing upon them any overarching theological viewpoint. By adding, subtracting, reordering, rewriting, the evangelists were able to make the old traditions speak afresh to changing conditions in their communities. Naturally, various traditions allowed for various degrees of liberty and creativity on the part of the evangelist. The infancy narratives, which had not been part of the earliest normative proclamation (which ran from the baptism of Jesus to Easter), gave the most room for creativity, though here too traditions exercised their influence.[4] Paradoxically, then, the infancy narratives, which offer the greatest difficulty from an historical point of view, form one of the richest fields for detecting the evangelist's theology, since he is operating here with relative freedom.[5] Once the public ministry begins, the limits of creativity narrow, though hardly disappear. One need only compare the ministry of Jesus in Mark, Matthew, and Luke to see how the same basic events can be reordered and reinterpreted to suit the message of each au-

---

[4]See, for example, R. Brown, *The Birth of the Messiah* (N.Y.: Doubleday, 1977).

[5]One of the weaknesses of the truly great work of H. Conzelmann, *The Theology of St. Luke* (N.Y.: Harper and Row, 1961), is that it does not take seriously the importance of Luke's infancy narrative for investigating the redactor's theology.

thor.[6] Even the passion narrative, though necessarily fixed in its flow of events, allows for theological reinterpretation and shifts of emphasis.[7] With the resurrection appearances, we return to a situation vaguely reminiscent of the infancy narratives. While the basic event is known in the tradition, there is no one normative narrative describing the event in detail. Consequently, the contribution of the individual evangelist will loom large.[8]

Once we realize that the evangelist is operating within the shifting limitations of various traditions, we see how important it is to find out what sources, written or oral, the evangelist was using, and where in his gospel he used them. Obviously, Mark, Matthew, and Luke are connected by strong literary links. The great amount of common material, expressed in much the same order and much the same wording, forces us to the conclusion that one evangelist must have known and used the work of some other evangelist. But who copied from whom? This is the nub of the so-called "Synoptic Problem" (Mark, Matthew, and Luke being designated as the "Synoptic Gospels"). Almost every imaginable solution has been proposed. St. Augustine of Hippo's view that the order is Matthew-Mark-Luke held sway for centuries and still finds proponents today, though often with a modification: Aramaic Matthew (a totally hypothetical entity) is prior to Greek Mark, which in turn is prior to our Greek Matthew.[9] That very modification betrays the difficulties of the position; moreover, there are no solid reasons for supposing an Aramaic Matthew ever existed. On the other hand, William Farmer, an American scholar, is a zealous apostle of the theory of the eighteenth-

---

[6]For a perfect example in Matthew's gospel, see G. Bornkamm's "The Stilling of the Storm in Matthew," in G. Bornkamm-G. Barth-H. Held, *Tradition and Interpretation in Matthew* (London: SCM, 1963) 52–57.

[7]For Matthew, see the magisterial work of D. Senior, *The Passion Narrative according to Matthew* (Louvain: Leuven University Press, 1975).

[8]The precise weight to be assigned to tradition and/or redaction in the resurrection appearances is a delicate question. For the special case of Matthew 28:16–20, see my article, "Two Disputed Questions in Matt 28:16–20," *JBL* 96 (1977) 407–424.

[9]Cf. B. Butler, *The Originality of St. Matthew* (Cambridge: Cambridge University Press, 1951).

century scholar, J. Griesbach: Matthew wrote first, Luke used Matthew, and finally Mark abridged and reconciled the two.[10]

We could go on listing endless developments and Byzantine variations on these and other proposals. Suffice it to say that the theory which has received the greatest acceptance in international circles is the so-called "two source" or "two document" hypothesis.[11] According to this theory, Mark is the earliest gospel. Matthew and Luke both drew on Mark and on another document, a loose collection of sayings of Jesus, labeled "Q." The Q document has not survived, but can be more or less reconstructed from a comparison of material Matthew and Luke have in common, once Markan material is subtracted.[12] Finally, differences in the treatment of such passages as the infancy narratives, the sermon on the mount (or plain), and the resurrection appearances suggest that Matthew and Luke did not know each other. The major written sources of the Synoptics can thus be diagramed as follows:

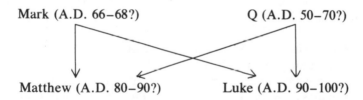

Mark (A.D. 66–68?)   Q (A.D. 50–70?)

Matthew (A.D. 80–90?)   Luke (A.D. 90–100?)

Diagrams are helpful, but reality is never simple. Even after written documents were composed, oral traditions were still alive and influential. We must think of Mark and Q as floating in a sea of oral tradition. And these oral traditions would tend to be "worked into" Mark and Q during their constant repetition, application, and celebration in the liturgy, catechesis, and preaching

---

[10]W. Farmer, *The Synoptic Problem* (N.Y.: Macmillan, 1964); *idem,* "Modern Developments of Griesbach's Hypothesis," *NTS* 23 (1976-77) 275–295.

[11]For arguments in its favor, see the standard New Testament introductions, e.g., W. Kümmel, *Introduction to the New Testament* (Nashville: Abingdon, 1975) 38–80.

[12]For a reconstruction of Q and comments on it, see R. Edwards, *A Theology of Q* (Philadelphia: Fortress, 1976).

of the local churches. By the time Matthew came to write his gospel, Mark and Q were probably encrusted with all sorts of oral traditions, sanctioned by the usage of his church. These various oral traditions (and, no doubt, some written ones too) receive the general label of "M." "M" is not another document; it is simply a convenient designation for all the individual traditions that are joined to Mark and Q by either Matthew or his church before him. A perfect example of this M-material is the so-called "formula quotations" found throughout Matthew's gospel. At a certain point, Matthew will pause in his narrative, reflect back on how this narrative fulfills a particular Old Testament prophecy, and then introduce the explicit Old Testament quotation with a solemn formula like: "Now all this came to pass that what was spoken by the Lord through the prophet might be fulfilled, saying . . . . " Examples are especially frequent in the infancy narrative (Matt 1:23; 2:15; 2:18; 2:23).¹³ How much comes from Matthew and how much from his tradition is difficult to say. It may be that there was a lengthy tradition of scholarly activity in Matthew's church (a "scribal school"),¹⁴ and that Matthew has taken over and imitated a technique already employed by the school. The point is clear: since Matthew is a teacher of his church and a guardian (though also reshaper) of its tradition, it is often difficult to decide what comes from the creativity of the evangelist and what comes from his tradition. We shall see how important this point is when we come to some of Matthew's moral teachings.

III. TIME AND PLACE OF WRITING

(a) When did Matthew write his gospel? If we accept the two source theory, Matthew wrote after Mark, and indeed a fair time after, since apparently Mark had come to enjoy a revered position in Matthew's church. Mark was probably *the* liturgical lectio-

---

¹³Which Old Testament citations in Matthew qualify as formula quotations is still disputed by scholars. See the discussion by G. Soares Prabhu, *The Formula Quotations in the Infancy Narrative of Matthew* (Rome: BIP, 1976) 18–41.

¹⁴Cf. K. Stendahl, *The School of St. Matthew* (second edition; Lund: Gleerup, 1968).

nary for Matthew's church. No doubt, Matthew's work was, among other things, a revision of the lectionary. If Mark was written shortly before or after A.D. 70 (the consensus of most scholars), then we must push Matthew's gospel toward the 80's, if not later. Individual passages confirm this view. In Matthew's parable of the great supper, which he shares with Luke (Matt 22:1–14 = Luke 14:15–24), Matthew introduces a strange motif, hardly in keeping with a story about a feast already prepared which has been refused at the last moment. The king sends his armies and destroys the murderers of his servants and *burns their city* (22:7). In this jarring addition to the traditional parable, Matthew seems to be depicting the fate of Jerusalem in A.D. 70. And one does not exactly get the impression that Matthew is writing on the morning after the destruction of Jerusalem.

Other characteristics of the gospel reinforce this impression. As we shall see, Matthew's church had been strongly Jewish-Christian in origin, but is now becoming increasingly Gentile. In fact, the gospel ends with a commission to *baptize* all nations (Matt 28:16–20—note the lack of any reference to circumcision as the initiation rite). The lack of concern about circumcision is matched by a declaration of freedom from Jewish food laws (Matt 15:11). As we might suspect from such statements, Matthew's church has already separated from the synagogue (see below in point 4). The ending of the gospel also shows a lack of concern about the delay of Christ's second coming. In Matthew 28:20, the final verse of the gospel, the emphasis is on the continued presence of Jesus all days. Instead of a fiery expectation of an imminent second coming, Matthew presents a carefully drawn up outline of salvation-history, with the sacred past of Jesus' own life leading up to a new and different epoch, the time of the church (see below in point 7). All these developments no doubt took time, and so a date between 80–90, perhaps closer to 90, is indicated. Yet we must not push Matthew into the second century. At the beginning of the second century, he is already being used by St. Ignatius of Antioch.[15]

(b) *Where* did Matthew write? In the first century A.D., the ordinary language of most Jews and Jewish Christians in Pales-

---

[15]Ignatius seems to quote Matthew 3:15 in his letter to the Smyr-

tine was Aramaic, a Semitic language akin to Hebrew. Yet Matthew wrote in Greek, indeed in a Greek which improves upon Mark's Greek and introduces some well-known Greek plays-on-words. In fact, some of his word-plays could simply not be reproduced in Aramaic. Add to this the fact that Matthew does not seem to be writing for an intellectual elite (say, the Greek-speaking Hellenists in Jerusalem), but for his church as a whole. His gospel is meant to be a public lectionary, catechism, and manual of order to be proclaimed in and read by his entire church. We can therefore safely conclude that Matthew is writing not in Palestine, but in a place where the general run of Christians would speak Greek as their first language, or at least as a good second language. On the other hand, we detect definite Jewish and Semitic traits in various words and phrases, in rabbinic argumentation and debates on the Mosaic Law and Jewish customs, and in an emphasis on Old Testament prophecy—an interest which is backed up by a phenomenal knowledge of variations in Old Testament texts.[16]

Consequently, Matthew's church seems to be situated somewhere between Jewish and Gentile spheres of cultural influence, with a foot in each camp. The community might at one time have been bilingual, and perhaps some of its members still are. As we shall see below, Matthew's church probably started out as strongly Jewish-Christian, but then became more and more Gentile in composition as the destruction of Jerusalem, the scattering of Jewish-Christian communities in Palestine, the final break with the synagogue, and the triumph of Paul's view on circumcision and food laws converged to give the Christian church progressively greater Gentile coloration.

Where can we find a church that can match this description?

---

naeans (I, 1) and Matthew 10:16b in his letter to Polycarp (II, 2). Since Matthew 3:15 appears to be Matthew's own redactional creation, it is unlikely that Ignatius is quoting stray oral tradition. He knew our written gospel. He also seems to give us the earliest exegesis of Matthew's story of the Magi in his letter to the Ephesians, XIX, 2-3.

[16]Cf. R. Gundry, *The Use of the Old Testament in St. Matthew's Gospel* (Leiden: Brill, 1967).

A likely region is Syria north of Palestine, for it was a great point of meeting between Jew and Gentile and (as we know from the Acts of the Apostles and Galatians) between Jewish Christians and Gentile Christians. In fact, Acts 11:19-20 tells us that Antioch in Syria was the scene of the first major mission to the Gentiles on the part of Jewish Christians. Later events narrated in Acts and Paul's letter to the Galatians would seem to indicate that the mission to the Gentiles at Antioch ran into some opposition from strict Jewish Christians. The strict group seems to have gained the upper hand, at least for a while.

Since the rural areas of Syria would have been largely Aramaic-speaking, the choice of Syria almost necessitates an urban center of Jewish-Greek culture like Antioch, a culture on which Greek-speaking Jewish Christianity could build. By A.D. 90, the church at Antioch would have had enough time to develop the scribal traditions we see reflected in Matthew. It may be no accident that Ignatius of *Antioch* is the first Father of the Church to use passages from Matthew. Naturally, absolute certainty is not to be had in these matters. It is possible that some commercial city on the coast of Syria was the place of origin. But Antioch remains the most likely choice.

IV. IS MATTHEW'S CHURCH STILL UNITED TO THE SYNAGOGUE?

Scholars today are very much divided on the question whether Matthew's church, admittedly Jewish-Christian in origin, was still united to the Jewish synagogue at the time of the gospel's composition. One noteworthy proponent of the view that the bond with the synagogue had not yet been severed is R. Hummel.[17] He holds that, while Matthew's church is engaged in a struggle with Judaism and no longer participates in synagogue liturgy, it has not yet broken its ties with the synagogue once and for all. Judaism still wields authority over the Jewish Christians,

---

[17]R. Hummel, *Die Auseinandersetzung zwischen Kirche und Judentum in Matthäusevangelium* (second edition; Munich: Kaiser, 1966).

and Matthew would prefer to avoid a final break. In support of his view, Hummel points to texts like Matthew 23:2-3: "The scribes and the Pharisees inherited the teaching authority of Moses. Therefore, do and observe everything they tell you." For Matthew, says Hummel, such instructions are a matter more of practical policy than of profound theory; they are intended to prevent the final rupture with Judaism.

But such isolated sayings as Matthew 23:2-3 cannot carry the day against the weight of evidence indicating that Matthew's church is already an independent institution separated from the synagogue. In Matthew 18:20 ("Where two or three are gathered together in my name, there am I in their midst"), we get a picture of a church gathered around the person and teaching of Jesus, not the Mosaic Law. This saying is especially important, since it parallels yet contrasts with a rabbinic saying about the divine presence dwelling among those who study the law.[18] The power to bind and loose, comprising both teaching authority and the power to admit or excommunicate members, is conferred on Peter as "chief rabbi" of the whole church in 16:18-19 and on the local congregation in 18:18-19.[19] The church's celebration of its own Christian rituals (baptism for all nations in 28:19, eucharist in 26:26–29), its rejection of both food laws (15:11, 17-18) and Pharisaic teaching in general (15:12–14; 16:5–12) all indicate that it has broken with Judaism.

D. Hare emphasizes two further arguments in favor of the break, both from additions made by Matthew to his sources.[20] First, whenever the word "synagogue" does not clearly refer to an institution or group set over against Jesus and his disciples, Matthew adds the qualification "their," to stress that, for him,

[18]The rabbinic parallel is found in a number of writings, e.g., *Pirke Aboth* 3:3 and 3:8.

[19]Power to teach seems more prominent in 16:18-19, while power to excommunicate is more prominent in 18:18-19; but the two powers cannot be totally separated. On these two passages, cf. G. Bornkamm, "The Authority To 'Bind' and 'Loose' in the Church in Matthew's Gospel," in *Jesus and Man's Hope, Volume I* (D. Hadidian *et al.*, eds; Pittsburgh: Pittsburgh Theological Seminary, 1970) 37–50.

[20]D. Hare, *The Theme of Jewish Persecution of Christians in the Gospel according to St. Matthew* (Cambridge: Cambridge University Press, 1967) 104-105 and 151–158.

"their synagogue" is something opposed to the author and his church. While, for Luke's Gentile church, the synagogue was always a foreign institution, for Matthew's church it has become a foreign institution. This shift is underlined by Matthew's usage. Second, Matthew reveals his view of Judaism and the church by a telling addition to Mark's parable of the evil tenant-farmers in the vineyard (Mark 12:1–12). In Mark's version, which makes the vineyard represent the people Israel, only the religious leaders are directly attacked. Matthew changes this perspective by adding to his version (Matt 21:33–46) a key verse which shifts the interpretation (Matt 21:43): "Therefore, I say to you that the Kingdom of God will be taken away from you and given to a people bearing its fruits." Thus, Matthew makes the vineyard represent not the people Israel but the Kingdom of God. The Kingdom was once given to Israel. But, because Israel has rejected the Son of God, the Kingdom has been taken from her and given to the new people of God, non-Israel, the church. Notice, by the way, that Matthew never calls this new people of God a "new Israel" or "the true Israel." There is only one Israel, the historical Israel which rejected Jesus and has thus lost her privileged position as the chosen people. Consequently, Matthew does not urge any special mission to Israel as a special group—though individual Jews would still be included in the mandate to make disciples of "all the nations" (Matt 28:19).[21] The Jews are one among many nations; they have been removed from the classification of "chosen people." Needless to say, this teaching of Matthew on the relative status of the church and Judaism could hardly reflect the situation of a Jewish-Christian church which was still bound to the Jewish synagogue and its teachers.

V. WAS MATTHEW HIMSELF A JEW OR A GENTILE?

Up until the last few decades there was virtual unanimity

---

[21]Here I would disagree with D. Hare and D. Harrington, who hold that this final mandate aims at "all the Gentiles," to the exclusion of Jews; cf. their article, "'Make Disciples of All the Gentiles' (Matt 28:19)," CBQ 37 (1975) 359–369; my reply appears in "Gentiles or Nations in Matt 28:19?" CBQ 39 (1977) 94–102.

among scholars that Matthew himself was Jewish in origin. His Jewishness was variously conceived. Some thought of him as a conservative legalist (B. Bacon), a converted Pharisee and rabbi (E. von Dobschütz), or a provincial Jewish-Christian schoolmaster (M. Goulder). Others saw something of a "Hellenistic" coloration in Matthew's Jewishness (Kilpatrick, Stendahl, Hare, and A. Kretzer). But all pointed to the Jewish tone of the gospel, its rabbinic ways of thinking and arguing, its great interest in Jewish Law, customs, and rituals, and its contacts with the Hebrew language as proofs of the Jewishness of the author. Hare even thought that Matthew's fierce anti-Pharisaism and his pessimism about Israel's fate reflect a Jewish Christian who has seen his church persecuted and its mission to Israel fail.

But for the last three decades or so, there has been a growing minority-position which holds that the author is a Gentile Christian. In 1947, this startling view was proposed by K. Clark in a seminal article.[22] In 1958, P. Nepper-Christensen wrote a monograph defending Gentile authorship.[23] But perhaps the writer who has argued the Gentile position at greatest length and most effectively is G. Strecker.[24] Other scholars such as W. Trilling, R. Walker, S. van Tilborg, W. Pesch, and H. Frankemölle have joined him in this opinion. There are some clear aspects of the gospel's general orientation which favor this view: in particular, the apparently unrelenting rejection of Israel and the withering denunciation of the Pharisees (chaps. 15, 16, and 23). It is difficult to imagine anyone of Jewish birth inserting into the passion narrative a picture of "the whole people" of Israel crying out: "His blood be upon us and upon our children" (Matt 27:25). To these general observations, however, more precise arguments can be added. It appears that in at least two passages in the gospel Matthew makes a glaring error about things Jewish—the kind of error no learned Jew or Jewish Christian would make. Now there

[22]K. Clark, "The Gentile Bias of Matthew," *JBL* 66 (1947) 165–172.
[23]P. Nepper-Christensen, *Das Mätthäusevangelium. Ein judenchristliches Evangelium?* (Aarhus: Universitetsforlaget, 1958).
[24]G. Strecker, *Der Weg der Gerechtigkeit* (third edition; Göttingen: Vandenhoeck & Ruprecht, 1971).

is no disputing Matthew's learning and intelligence. The most likely explanation of these errors, then, is that Matthew is a learned Gentile Christian, not a Jewish Christian. His erudition and scribal training had enabled him to master a good deal of the Jewish-Christian traditions of his church, as cultivated by the Christian scribal school. But in two notable instances his lack of direct familiarity with Jewish matters and rabbinic learning becomes obvious.

The first instance is his lack of knowledge about the Sadducees. The Sadducees were a group of Jews, concentrated among the leading priestly families of Jerusalem. Their theological positions are not all that easy to discover, since they are known largely by the unflattering reports of their adversaries, both Pharisees and Christians. It seems, though, that they rejected the Pharisees' attempt to place oral law on the same level with the normative Law of Moses enshrined in the written Pentateuch. Since no developed ideas of life after death or resurrection are to be found in the Pentateuch, the Sadducees rejected the Pharisees "newfangled" ideas about eschatology. The two groups also differed on ritual matters, though the Pharisees seem to have forced their views on the Sadducean priests. Politically, the Sadducees were much more willing to cooperate with the Romans and to defend the status quo. The Pharisees, with more developed Messianic expectations, intensely disliked Roman rule; and from their extreme right wing came the Zealots who led the revolt against Rome and, incidentally, helped wipe out a good number of the Sadducees. After the disaster of A.D. 70, the few Sadducees who survived lost any sort of leadership position in mainstream Judaism to the Pharisees, who had the Sadducean denial of the resurrection officially condemned. The presence of both Pharisees and Sadducees in mainstream Judaism (to say nothing here of more esoteric sidestreams) is a reminder that, before A.D. 70, there was no such thing as one normative Jewish orthodoxy. Such normative uniformity as was imposed after A.D. 70 by the Pharisees was made possible only by the disappearance of the Sadducees as an effective opposition. Neither before nor after A.D. 70, then, would any Jew dream of speaking of the Pharisees and Sadducees as having one common doctrinal stance. They were divided before A.D. 70, and after A.D. 70 the Pharisees had Sadducean doctrine condemned.

What, then, are we to think when we take a look at Christ's warning about leaven, as reported in Mark 8:14–21 and refashioned in Matthew 16:5–12? In Mark, Jesus warns about "the leaven of the Pharisees and the leaven of Herod" (note the separation of the two groups by the double mention of leaven). Whatever the symbolism may be in Mark (the corruption of false Messianic expectations?), Matthew both changes the symbol and supplies a clear interpretation. The leaven becomes the leaven of the Pharisees-and-Sadducees. There is only one mention of leaven, and the Pharisees and Sadducees are modified by only one definite article. At the end of the narrative, Matthew, true to form, refuses to have the disciples remain puzzled or blind. Contrary to Mark, Matthew insists that the disciples do come to understand Jesus' parabolic saying. And what the disciples understand is that by leaven Jesus had meant not the leaven of loaves, but *the* teaching of the Pharisees-and-Sadducees (Matt 16:12). Here the exact Greek text is important: Matthew speaks of *the* doctrine or teaching (*tēs didachēs*) common to the Pharisees-and-Sadducees (*tōn Pharisaiōn kai Saddoukaiōn*, the two nouns being modified by the one definite article). Matthew shows himself ignorant of the doctrinal conflicts which separated the Pharisees and Sadducees into two rival parties.

And this is not just a slip in one verse. We find the same lack of understanding at the beginning of the narrative in which the Sadducees ask Jesus about the resurrection of the dead (Matt 22:23). Both Mark (12:18) and Luke (20:27) correctly identify the Sadducees as that group which can be defined by its denial of the resurrection: "The Sadducees, who say there is no resurrection, came to him and asked him, saying. . . ." Since this position of the Sadducees is confirmed by the Jewish historian Josephus and by the Talmud, it must have been common knowledge among Jews, Jewish Christians, and even some Gentile Christians (Luke, dependent on Mark) in the first century A.D. Yet Matthew, surprisingly, garbles the Markan tradition he inherits. In Matthew 22:23 we read: "On that day, there came to him Sadducees, *saying* there is no resurrection; and they asked him, saying. . . ." The first participle "saying" (*legontes*) is no longer in the attributive position, acting as a definition of a group called the Sadducees. In Matthew it is in the adverbial or predicate position, and simply records what these particular Sadducees were saying as they approached Jesus. Our suspicion seems confirmed: Matthew, unlike Mark and Luke, has no idea of the Sadducees as a party defined by doctrinal differences with the Pharisees. This ignorance is almost impossible to reconcile with the supposed Jewish origin of this learned evangelist.

A second instance of Matthew's mistaken use of matters Jewish is his treatment of the entrance of Jesus into Jerusalem and of the Old Testament citation he sees fulfilled in the event. In this narrative (21:1–9), Matthew is clearly taking over Mark's account (Mark 11:1–10). His major change is the insertion of a formula quotation (v. 5) along with an emphasis on the quotation's literal fulfillment (vv. 2 and 7). In verse 2, Jesus orders two disciples to find "a donkey tied and a colt with her." The disciples are to bring them, and if anyone objects they are to reply that the Lord has need of *them*. All this strikes one as a strange alteration of Mark, where the disciples are told to find simply a donkey, and they are ordered to bring *the* donkey to Jesus. All the stranger is the actual scene of the triumphal procession. In Mark, the disciples put their clothing on the donkey and Jesus sits on *it* (Mark 11:7). In Matthew, the disciples bring the donkey and the colt to Jesus, they place their clothing *on them*, and Jesus sits *on them*! What has occasioned this surprising change and unimaginable scene? The answer lies in the formula quotation, which Matthew wants to see fulfilled literally—in fact, too literally. The quotation in Matthew 21:5 is a mixture of Isaiah 62:11 and Zechariah 9:9. Zechariah speaks of a Savior-King coming to Jerusalem, "riding upon a donkey, and upon a colt, the son of a beast of burden." Now, for Zechariah, this means only one animal. Zechariah is using the most ordinary form of poetic expression in the Hebrew Old Testament: parallelism. In Hebraic parallelism, the same thought is expressed twice in different terms. So here: the one animal is described poetically with two different phrases. But Matthew misunderstands Zechariah; he thinks that two different animals are being mentioned. And Matthew is intent on seeing Scripture literally and exactly fulfilled in the life of Jesus. So, no matter how improbable or unimaginable the scene might be, if Zechariah predicts that the Messianic King will come to Jerusalem mounted on two animals, then Jesus *must* be mounted on two animals. "Now this came to pass in order that what was spoken through the prophet might be fulfilled, saying. . . ." (Matt 21:4).

Admittedly, both Jewish rabbis and New Testament authors could play loose and free with Hebraic parallelism when breaking up the parallel expression into two different objects served some theological purpose. For instance, the rabbis would see two different animals in Zechariah 9:9 when they wanted to see two different Messianic figures in the text. When they were not interested in the two different Messiahs, they saw only one animal. It all depended on the theological ax they were grinding at the moment. The important thing to remember in Matthew 21:2 and 7 is that Matthew has no theological ax to grind except that of literal fulfillment. If he inserts a second animal into Mark's story, it is because he wants a literal fulfillment of what Zechariah prophesies. And this means he understands the literal meaning of Zechariah's prophecy to refer to two animals. And this in turn means he misunderstood the Hebraic parallelism of the Zechariah text.

Where now is Matthew the converted rabbi, the learned conservative Jewish Christian, a former disciple of that leader of post-A.D. 70 Judaism, Johanan ben Zakkai? That Matthew indeed is a learned scholar is clear from his masterful structuring of the whole gospel and especially from his editorial work on various Old Testament textual traditions. But these mistakes about matters Jewish incline us to think that he is a learned Gentile scholar, not a learned Jewish scholar. Of course, certitude is a commodity hard to come by in exegesis. I readily concede that none of the arguments I have presented is so compelling as to force assent to the view that Matthew is a Gentile. I do think these arguments tip the balance of probabilities in favor of my position. But I grant that the majority opinion, that Matthew is Jewish Christian, cannot be absolutely excluded. In that case, however, we would have to understand Matthew to be a Greek-speaking Diaspora Jewish Christian who has rejected particularistic prejudices and is sympathetic to a universal mission to the Gentiles, without the burden of circumcision and food laws. Really, such a type of Jewish Christian would not be all that much different from the learned Gentile Christian I propose, and I could certainly "live with" that kind of Jewish-Christian Matthew. Nevertheless, I think the theory of a Gentile Christian meshes better both with the facts we have examined and with the material we shall be studying in the rest of this book.

Everything we have seen up until now leads us to an unavoidable conclusion about this man we call "Matthew." If he is a learned Gentile author writing outside Palestine around the year 90, it is impossible to identify him with the "Levi" or "Matthew" mentioned in the gospels of Matthew, Mark, and Luke. He is not one of the "twelve apostles." Actually, this decision is not based simply on our view that Matthew is a Gentile Christian writing toward the end of the first century. The gospels themselves raise doubts about the idea that an eyewitness called Matthew-Levi wrote our "first gospel." Three difficulties in particular can be mentioned.

(1) If we accept the two-source hypothesis, we must hold that the evangelist "Matthew" is dependent for his basic narrative on the evangelist Mark. Now, Papias, the earliest Father of the Church to identify "Mark" as the author of our "second gospel," states explicitly that Mark was not an eyewitness of the earthly ministry of Jesus. Consequently, if we identified the "apostle" Matthew as the author of the first gospel, we would have an eyewitness dependent, for his narrative, on a non-eyewitness. A strange relationship, to say the least. This relationship becomes especially intolerable in the case of the story in which Jesus calls Levi (or Matthew) to discipleship (Mark 2:13–17 = Matt 9:9–13). Matthew's narrative is clearly dependent on Mark's. If this is an autobiographical story experienced by the author of the first gospel, why would he have to copy and edit the story out of Mark's gospel?

(2) The identification of the two names "Levi" and "Matthew" as two alternate names for the same historical person

creates a problem. Mark 2:14 and Luke 5:27 refer to the person called to discipleship by Jesus as Levi. It is Matthew's gospel and his alone which calls this man "Matthew" (and only "Matthew," not "Levi") in the same story (Matt 9:9). The problem is, Jews of the first century A.D. could have two first names if one were Semitic and one Greek or Latin (e.g., Saul-Paul). They could also have a first name and then a last name formed by using their father's name (e.g., Simon bar Jona). They could be further defined by their place of residence or origin (e.g., Joseph of Arimathea, Mary Magdalene, Philo of Alexandria). But, as stands to reason, it would be hopelessly confusing for any Jew to have *two* Semitic first names, which could be used interchangeably. Both Levi and Matthew (for Mattayahu or Mattanyahu) are Semitic first names. Thus, to suppose that there ever was one historical disciple of Jesus called both Matthew and Levi is a priori difficult.

(3) The different lists of the "twelve apostles," which contain some variations, only compound the difficulty. In the list of Matthew (Matt 10:2–4), verse 3 mentions "Matthew the tax collector." This obviously refers to the tax collector Matthew who is called to discipleship in Matthew 9:9–13. But Mark, Luke, and Acts, in their lists of the twelve, do list a "Matthew," but do not call him a tax collector. And, of course, Mark and Luke-Acts know only of a tax collector named Levi, whom they never call Matthew and whom they do not list among the twelve. It is not easy to sort out these facts to decide why the names differ. A possible explanation is given by R. Pesch.[25] He notes that the first gospel tends to identify the group called "the twelve" with the group called "disciples." Now, since the Levi found in Mark 2:14 is called to discipleship and yet is not found in the list of the twelve apostles (a list which could not be changed at will), the author of the first gospel preserves his equation of disciple = one of the twelve by renaming the tax collector of Mark's story "Mat-

[25]R. Pesch, "Levi-Matthäus (Mc 2:14/Mt 9:9; 10:3): ein Beitrag zur Lösung eines alten Problems," *ZNW* 59 (1968) 40–56.

thew," a name found in the list of the twelve.[26] Later church tradition noticed the difference in the first gospel, and drew the unlikely conclusion that this tax collector, the apostle Matthew, was the author of the gospel in which "Matthew" replaces "Levi" in the story of the disciple's call.

Having seen the situation which prompted Matthew to remodel the form of gospel, we can now turn to the major theological tool he used in his remodeling, namely, his new vision of salvation history.

---

[26]But why choose this name Matthew rather than one of the other names in the list? Pesch suggests the possibility that this Matthew may have been the source of or authority behind the special traditions of the first gospel. While that remains a possibility, we have no New Testament evidence that the apostle Matthew was active in Antioch or Syria in general.

CHAPTER TWO

Remodeling Salvation History

I. WHY DID MATTHEW REMODEL THE
GOSPEL FORM?

Purpose

The form-critics of the early part of this century taught us to
see the various units of tradition in our gospels as reflections of
and answers to different needs and problems in the Christian
communities. This sociological "setting in life" is what is meant
by the German phrase *Sitz im Leben*.[27] Too often *Sitz im Leben*
has been narrowed down to one activity, such as "preaching,"
which nevertheless remains distressingly vague.[28] When dealing
with the complex and finely woven whole of Matthew's gospel,
we must realize that the situations calling forth such a many-
layered document were themselves many-sided. Matthew's gospel, from one angle, is a "revised lectionary," improving and
expanding Mark and Q for liturgical reading and preaching. The
wording of the formulas for baptism (28:19) and the eucharist
(26:26–28) probably reflect the liturgical practice of Matthew's
church. From another angle, the neat patterns discernible
throughout the gospel (e.g., the five great discourses) and the

---

[27]Unfortunately, the sociological question was not rigorously pursued by the form-critics. It is only recently that sociology has been
applied to New Testament questions with anything like full earnestness;
cf. J. Gager, *Kingdom and Community* (Englewood Cliffs: Prentice-Hall,
1975).

[28]This is the case with M. Dibelius, *From Tradition to Gospel* (N.Y.:
Scribner's, no date).

careful lining-up of topics within a discourse (e.g., the instructions on almsgiving, prayer, and fasting in the sermon on the mount, 6:1–18) indicate an interest in catechesis. Jewish converts, but even more so Gentile converts, were in need of this fundamental Christian instruction. But instruction is also aimed at the church leaders as well. Chapter 18 in particular contains directives for the shepherds of the church and for the whole church assembly on the proper use of authority. That Matthew was especially concerned that Christian leaders not adopt Jewish signs of hierarchical superiority is clear from the all too relevant warnings in Matthew 23:1–12 (avoid distinctive clothing, special seats, and special titles such as rabbi, father, and teacher).

Furthermore, Matthew's interest was not simply centered on the internal society of the church. The external society of prospective converts, Jews and Gentiles alike, was also a concern of the gospel (rabbinic argumentation, proofs from Old Testament prophecy, Jesus' indication of his concern for the Gentiles). At the same time external polemic against the leaders of Pharisaic Judaism had to be carried on (cf. the various controversy stories and the woes spoken against the scribes and Pharisees in 23:13–36). Liturgy, preaching, catechetics, church order, missionary propaganda, polemics—all these interests have had a part in the formation of Matthew's gospel and must be included in any consideration of *Sitz im Leben*.

But the "setting in life" of Matthew's gospel can be understood in a still wider sense: namely, the various tendencies and pressures which were causing the Christian church and Christian thought to develop and change toward the end of the first century A.D.[29] That this was a time of transition, upset, and confusion in Matthew's church seems obvious from the sermon on the mount (7:21–23: charismatics whose showy deeds mask a failure to do the Father's will), the church-order discourse (chapter 18: scandal of the little ones, weak sheep going astray, lack of forgiveness

---

[29]In this context, I purposely avoid the word "trajectory," which can give rise to the misleading image of a neat, smooth line which can be plotted from its start because it moves according to inherent mathematical laws. Historical reality is much more complex.

among the brothers), and the eschatological discourse (chapter 24: false messiahs and prophets; persecution by all the nations; betrayal within the community; love growing cold because wickedness is abounding; falling-off of zeal and watchfulness).[30] At times, however, Matthew is using in these passages both previous sources and stock apocalyptic figures. And so we must beware of painting too detailed a portrait of Matthew's particular community from traditional and widespread Christian motifs. But the concentration of such themes in Matthew does indicate that the evangelist is addressing a community in crisis, torn apart by external persecution and internal strife.

What gives special sharpness to the crisis of the Matthean community is that Matthew's church is a church in transition. That is to say, Matthew's church is a Christian community which is being molded—and shaken—by its experience of a basic shift in its Christian existence. The many problems involved in this transition can be boiled down to one central crisis: a once strongly Jewish-Christian church is becoming increasingly Gentile in composition. This shift in the Church's makeup demands a reinterpretation of many of the venerable Jewish-Christian traditions which had been handed down in Matthew's church. A remodeled church needs a remodeled gospel. Matthew, the faithful servant of the tradition, wishes to affirm, not reject, his Christian past. But he knows that *his* situation is different and that consequently the tradition must be understood in a new light.

Indeed, Matthew may be giving us a self-portrait and a summary of his program at the end of the parable-discourse, when Jesus addresses the disciples who understand his teaching: "Every scribe who has become a disciple in the Kingdom of heaven is like a householder who brings forth from his storehouse things new and old" (13:52). Significant here is the desire to present both the eschatological newness and the traditional truth contained in

[30]For detailed treatment of these passages and the picture of the Matthean church which arises from them, see in particular the works of W. Thompson: *Matthew's Advice to a Divided Community* (Rome: Biblical Institute Press, 1970); "An Historical Perspective in the Gospel of Matthew," *JBL* 93 (1974) 243–262; and (with co-author E. LaVerdiere) "New Testament Communities in Transition: A Study of Matthew and Luke," *TS* 37 (1976) 567–597.

Christ's teaching. At the same time, however, Matthew carefully mentions the new before the old, to stress that the eschatological Christ-event gives the definitive interpretation to the Law and the prophets of the Old Testament. Christ himself, in his person and in his teaching, is *the* hermeneutical principle by which the Old Testament is judged. Judged, yes—but not thrown away. Matthew's desire to preserve the Old Testament revelation is shown perfectly in 9:17. In the Markan parallel, the emphasis is clearly on the incompatibility of the old and the new dispensations: new wine will burst old wineskins (Mark 2:18–22). Matthew keeps this basic message, but modifies it in the direction of continuity, balance, and preservation of the venerable Old Testament tradition: ". . . but they pour the new wine into new skins, *and both are preserved*" (Matt 9:17—the italics indicate Matthew's "remodeling" of Mark). Matthew acknowledges the radical newness and normative nature of Christ's teaching, appreciates the inevitable tension between it and older traditions, and yet wishes to preserve a sense of continuity by reinterpreting the old in the light of the new. To use a modern phrase, he wants to "retrieve the tradition."[31] Specifically, he wants to preserve the traditions of the Jewish-Christian forebears of his church[32] while understanding them in and for the new situation which is opening up for his increasingly Gentile community.

II. WHY DID MATTHEW REMODEL SALVATION-HISTORY?

To solve this tension between the past and present situations of his fellow Christians, Matthew develops a new view of salvation-history. Here we must be careful about defining terms.

---

[31]For a notable present-day attempt to "retrieve the tradition," see D. Tracy's *Blessed Rage for Order* (N.Y.: Seabury, 1975). What makes Matthew an especially relevant gospel for our times is precisely this central problem of reinterpreting venerable tradition in new circumstances.

[32]No doubt there were still a good number of Jewish Christians in Matthew's church even as he writes; the Jewish-Christian churches did not change from a Jewish to a Gentile constituency overnight.

By salvation-history we mean a schematic understanding of God's dealings with men that emphasizes continuity-yet-difference. Insofar as the theologian, reflecting on saving events, sees the one and the same God acting faithfully and consistently within the flow of time, he perceives continuity, a basic horizontal line (though not always a straight one). Insofar as the theologian sees the different ways in which God acts at different times and the different ways in which man responds, he perceives the lines of demarcation which delimit the distinct periods of this history—the vertical lines of division, as it were. Difference within continuity, the various stages within the one divine economy: this is the basic insight on which any outline or pattern of salvation-history is built. It is by constructing such a schema of difference-within-continuity that Matthew is able to accept the Jewish-Christian traditions of his church and insert them into a higher synthesis, a higher viewpoint. Salvation-history is the tool Matthew employs to formulate his higher synthesis, his new vision meant to help a once narrowly Jewish-Christian church over the rough ground of transition. Remodeling salvation-history allows him to remodel the gospel message.

The main lines of Matthew's remodeling of salvation-history can be grasped by a quick comparison of three key texts—10:5–6; 15:24; 28:16–20—all of which appear only in Matthew's gospel.[33]

(1) The passage 10:5-6 is found at the beginning of the missionary discourse, the instruction to the twelve apostles as they start off on their temporary mission during Jesus' public ministry. The very first command Jesus gives them is: "Do not go to the Gentiles, and do not enter a Samaritan city. Go rather to the lost sheep of the house of Israel." The sense of the order is clear: the apostles are limited in their mission to the land and people of Israel.

(2) In 15:24, Jesus tells the Canaanite woman who is pleading for her daughter's healing that the same restriction is imposed on him: "I was not sent except to the lost sheep of the house of

---

[33]For a more detailed treatment of Matthew's schema of salvation-history, see my article, "Salvation-History in Matthew: In Search of a Starting Point," *CBQ* 37 (1975) 203–215.

Israel." The repetition of the key phrase, "to the lost sheep of the house of Israel," indicates Matthew has worked into his gospel (indeed, into two scenes he had received from Mark and Q) some stringent statements which probably come from narrow Jewish-Christian circles opposed to a Gentile mission in the early church.[34] The important thing to note in 10:5-6 and 15:24 is that Matthew takes over these narrow traditions and affirms them instead of rejecting them. He can do this because he fits them into *one* period of his schema of salvation-history. He is able to say of these traditions: yes, that is true—but only during the earthly life of Jesus. The public ministry was subject to geographical and ethnic restrictions which fall away after the death and resurrection.

(3) This is clear when we come to 28:16–20. Here the very same Jesus who ordered the disciples not to go to the Gentiles orders that very same group to undertake a universal mission to all the nations. In fact, this mission to all nations has baptism, not circumcision, as its initiation rite (v. 19). This mission teaches the commands of Jesus, not the Mosaic Law, as the norm of morality (v. 20a). And this mission has the constant presence of the risen Jesus as its mainstay and energizing principle (v. 20b). Obviously, such a universal mission could never be affirmed by a narrow Jewish-Christian rabbi zealous for the Mosaic Law. If you allow that the true people of God can be formed apart from circumcision, you have dealt a death-blow to Judaism. One must therefore be very careful about designating Matthew's gospel as a Jewish-Christian gospel. Matthew does take over stringent Jewish-Christian material (23:2-3, which enjoins complete obedience to the teaching of the scribes and Pharisees, would be another example). But, in the very act of taking over these traditions, Matthew modifies them by inserting them into his "higher synthesis" of salvation-history. They are true—but only of the public ministry of Jesus. The time after the death and resurrection is

---

[34]This does not necessarily exclude the possibility that some form of these statements ultimately goes back to the historical Jesus. What I am interested in here is the immediate source of Matthew's material and the group most likely to have been the bearer of this particularistic tradition in the early church.

ruled by a different economy. Already, we might begin to ask whether questions of law and morality are affected by this schema of salvation-history.

I should point out immediately, however, that this schema is not as simple as might first appear. Matthew loves to anticipate, to point forward, to indicate early in the gospel what is going to happen later. A perfect example is the series of infancy stories in chapter 2, which really form a proleptic[35] passion narrative: Jesus, the Son of God, the true Israel, the second Moses, is rejected and pursued unto death by the false rulers of Israel, while the Gentiles accept him. A number of proleptic signs of the universal mission can be found throughout the gospel: the adoration by the pagan Magi (2:1–12), the healing of the centurion's servant (8:5–13, into which Matthew inserts a Q-statement about many coming from east and west to feast in the Kingdom), the healing of the daughter of the Canaanite woman (15:21–28), the exorcism of the Gadarene demoniacs (8:28–34), the change of residence to Capernaum (4:12–17, with the prophecy of Isaiah about "Galilee of the Gentiles"), and even Jesus' association with tax collectors and sinners (since Jewish-Christian tradition considered these non-observant Jews as bad as Gentiles; cf. 5:46-47 and 18:17). The universal mission hinted at in these passages becomes a reality after the death and resurrection of Jesus.

There is only one problem. Up until now, I have been taking for granted that the death and resurrection of Jesus is the critical turning point in Matthew's outline of salvation-history. In fact, I would even say we should rather speak of the death-resurrection of Jesus as one eschatological event, in which the new age definitively breaks into the old. But can this view of the death-resurrection as the pivotal eschatological event be substantiated from key texts in Matthew's gospel? I think it can. An examination of Matthew's treatment of the traditions of Jesus' death (27:51–54), the empty tomb (28:2-3), and the appearance of Jesus to the disciples (28:16–20) will show that Matthew has carefully clothed these scenes with apocalyptic images and allusions, thus

---

[35]"Proleptic," a word that often appears in discussions of Matthew, means "anticipatory," "describing by way of anticipation something which is still to take place."

making the death-resurrection of Jesus *the* apocalyptic event ushering in the Kingdom of heaven in a new, decisive form. Let me demonstrate my position by examining each of the three texts.

III. THE SIGNS AT JESUS' DEATH (Matt 27:51–54)

In 27:51–54 (the events immediately following upon the death of Jesus), Matthew indicates that the death of Christ (a) spells the end of the sacrificial cult of the Temple; (b) marks the earth-shaking beginning of the new age; (c) causes the resurrection of the dead; (d) brings the community of Gentiles to the Easter faith that Jesus is the Son of God. I may seem to be claiming a great deal for four verses, but Matthew's redaction justifies the claim.

(a) Matthew 27:51a, the rending of the Temple veil, is reproduced from Mark's text. The symbol is ambiguous and has been interpreted in different ways: the sacrifice of Jesus throws open ready access to God, who was hidden in the old dispensation behind the veil, in the Holy of Holies; or the destruction of Jerusalem and the Temple in A.D. 70 is prophesied as the punishment for the crucifixion of Jesus; or, simply, Jesus' death puts an end to the Temple cult. In any of these interpretations, the death of Jesus and the end of the sacrificial ritual in the Temple are somehow related as cause and effect. And, for the pious Jew, the Temple cult, along with the Mosaic Law and good works of kindness, was one of the props of creation. The death of Christ pulls that prop out from under the old world, which begins to dissolve.

(b) Matthew 27:51b, added by Matthew to Mark, begins to describe the dissolution of the old order. The rending of the Temple veil is accompanied by an earthquake, an apocalyptic motif Matthew adds to other passages in his gospel as well (8:24; 28:2). In the Old Testament and later Jewish apocalyptic writings, the earthquake is a sign of God's appearing ("theophany") to judge his enemies in wrath and rescue his faithful people by establishing his rule on earth. This is now being done definitively at the death of Jesus. Far from being just a general eschatological motif, then, this earthquake at the death of Jesus "denotes specifically the invasion of the realm of the dead by the divine Victor."[36] Death is vanquished and must yield up its captives.

(c) This becomes even clearer in 27:52-53. The earthquake is not an isolated sign. It sets off a chain reaction: the earthquake splits the rocks, the splitting of the rocks opens the sepulchers, and the opening of the sepulchers permits the dead to come forth. One could not imagine a more striking—and daring—symbol of the truth that the death of Christ is *the* eschatological event, which includes the general resurrection of the dead. The saintly dead of Israel's past rise at the death of Israel's Messiah. At last the stirring vision of the prophet Ezekiel is fulfilled: the valley of dry bones, i.e., the dead house of Israel, rises to new life (Ezek 37:1-14). Especially significant here are verses 7 and 12-14 in the Greek translation: "And it came to pass that, as I prophesied, behold, there was an earthquake. . . . Thus says the Lord: 'Behold, I open your tombs and I shall lead you from your tombs and I shall lead you into the land of Israel. And you shall know that I am the Lord when I open your tombs to lead you, my people, from your tombs. And I shall give my spirit to you, and you shall live, and I shall see you in your land, and you shall know that I the Lord have spoken and will do it,' says the Lord." The resurrection of the dead, prophesied by Ezekiel, takes place in principle, proleptically, at the life-giving death of Jesus. Nothing could be clearer than that the death of Jesus is *the* decisive eschatological event, and nothing is clearer than that Matthew has skillfully tied together the death of Jesus with his resurrection by using both the motif of the earthquake (occurring again in 28:2) and the motif of resurrection.[37] It is not reading into Matthew, therefore, to speak

---

[36]G. Bornkamm, "Seiō, seismos," *Theological Dictionary of the New Testament, Volume VII* (Grand Rapids: Eerdmans, 1971) 200.

[37]In fact, some critics suggest that this scene of the resurrection of the holy ones originally went with the story of the resurrection of Jesus and that, when Matthew moved the resurrection of the holy ones back to the death of Jesus, he inserted the phrase "after his resurrection" in 27:53 to preserve the primacy of Jesus as the "first fruits of the dead." Be that as it may, the eschatological message of 27:52-53 in its present position could not be clearer. For a full treatment, see D. Senior, "The Death of Jesus and the Resurrection of the Holy Ones," *CBQ* 38 (1976) 312-329.

of his presenting the death-resurrection of Jesus as one apocalyptic event, in which the new age decisively breaks into the old.

(d) The new age will be marked by the saving event being received in faith by the Gentiles, and so it is at the foot of the cross. Here Matthew makes some noteworthy changes in Mark's text. In Mark 15:39, only the centurion makes a profession of faith. In Matthew, the centurion *and those standing guard over Jesus with him* proclaim their faith. The Gentile community has become believers. And what they believe is the Easter faith which marks true disciples. At the end of Matthew's story of Jesus' walking on water, the disciples are not left baffled and bewildered, as in Mark (Mark 6:52) but rather fall down in worship and proclaim with the later church: "Truly you are God's Son" (Matt 14:33). Now, at the cross, at the apocalyptic turning of the ages, the uncircumcised Gentiles can join the original Jewish disciples in this Paschal proclamation: "Truly this [dropping Mark's 'man'] was God's Son." The universal mission commanded at the end of the gospel by the risen Lord (28:16–20) is realized by way of anticipation at the cross. Thus, the union of death and resurrection as the one decisive event is again stressed.

IV. THE EMPTY TOMB (Matt 28:2–3)

As has been already mentioned, Matthew continues to clothe the Markan material with apocalyptic imagery when he edits the story of the empty tomb. While Mark's version provides some basis for Matthew's apocalyptic imagery (the white garment of the young man, the fear), Mark's narrative, like most of the resurrection narratives in the canonical gospels, is remarkably lacking in the more blatant types of apocalyptic imagery. Moreover, in his desire to "apocalypticize" the empty tomb tradition, Matthew faced a special difficulty; the mainstream Christian tradition seems to have contained a tacit prohibition against portraying the resurrection-event itself.

In keeping with that stricture, Matthew pours his apocalyptic images into the ready container of the mysterious young man and the mysteriously removed stone. In Matthew, the stone is not simply already lying to one side, with the young man sitting within the tomb. Instead, Matthew begins the chain of events with his beloved earthquake—this time, "a great earthquake" (Matt 28:2). Just as the earthquake introduced the raising of the dead at the cross, so now it introduces "the angel of the Lord descending from heaven" to announce the resurrection of Jesus. It is this New Testament version of the Old Testament *mal'ak Yahweh* (messenger of Yahweh) who performs the mighty feat of rolling back the stone. And then, instead of entering the tomb, he sits upon the stone: a perfect symbol of God's triumph over death—the death of Christ and of all men—by Christ's resurrection. As at the cross of Jesus, so at the tomb of Jesus, the power of *Sh'eôl* (the realm of the dead) has been broken. Lest anyone miss the apocalyptic point, Matthew describes the angel of the Lord in the traditional images we meet in the book of Daniel, the accounts of Christ's transfiguration, the Revelation of St. John, and many other apocalypses:[38] "His appearance was as lightning, and his garment white as snow" (28:3). The reaction of the guards is also a stock theme of apocalyptic: shaken by fear, they become as dead men (28:4; cf. Dan 10:8,16). There is an interesting contrast here with the guards at the cross. At the cross, the guards (*hoi . . . tērountes*) see the earth shaken (*eseisthē*) and the dead rise, and this leads them to fear (*ephobēthēsan*) and faith. At the tomb, after the dead Jesus has been raised to life, the guards (*hoi tērountes*) are shaken (*eseisthēsan*) by fear (*phobou*) and become as dead men. Once again, we see that Matthew carefully weaves together the events of death and resurrection by common words and themes.

---

[38]See, for instance, Daniel 7:9; 10:5-6; Matthew 17:2 (and parallels); Revelation 1:14–16; 10:1. In connection with Matthew's empty tomb story, the gospel of Peter 35–44, 50–57 is often cited, as though it preserved an earlier tradition Matthew uses (so states X. Léon-Dufour in his *Resurrection and the Message of Easter* [London: Chapman, 1974] 105). But since the gospel of Peter probably comes from around the middle of the second century and since it exhibits the tendency of later traditions to move from an appearance of an angel to an appearance of the risen Christ himself, use of this apocryphal gospel to explain Matthew is questionable.

V. JESUS COMES TO HIS CHURCH
(Matt 28:16—20)

Only when we have fully appreciated the death-resurrection as the apocalyptic turning point which ushers in (proleptically) the general resurrection of the dead can we come back to 28:16–20 with a complete understanding of what this final pericope says. Perhaps this finale of Matthew's gospel is best seen in contrast to Luke's conception of the events after the resurrection. Luke has a number of appearances to various disciples (in Acts 1, throughout forty days). This series of resurrection-appearances culminates in an ascension, a sort of parousia written backward. Just as the Son of Man is to come on a cloud with his angels, so Jesus goes away on a cloud while the angels explain that he will come again in the same way he departed. In the interim, he will send upon the disciples the Holy Spirit to supply for his absence, and to guide and energize the church during the long haul of history.

By contrast, Matthew has only one resurrection appearance to the eleven disciples. And there is no question of Jesus ascending at the end of the appearance. Rather, the whole point of 28:16–20 is that the risen Jesus comes *to* his church, to remain with it all days until the end of this age. Thus, what Matthew portrays is not just a resurrection appearance, but also a "proleptic parousia": the exalted Son of Man comes to his church with cosmic power, to inaugurate his universal reign. This is the sense of Jesus' announcement of his power, which in turn grounds his worldwide commission: "All power was given to me [at the resurrection/exaltation] in heaven and on earth. Going, *therefore*, make disciples of all the nations." In these words of majesty we have an allusion to the description of what happens when the Son of Man comes on the clouds of heaven in Daniel 7:14: "And power was given to him, and all the nations . . . shall serve him." We have here the fulfillment of what the Matthean Jesus prophesied at his trial: "*From now on* you will see the Son of Man seated at the right hand of the power and coming on the clouds of heaven" (Matt 26:64).[39]

---

[39]The vital modification, "from now on" (*ap'arti*), is added by Matthew to the Markan form of the saying (Mark 14:62).

That promise is now fulfilled. The Son of Man, exalted by the resurrection to God's right hand,[40] comes to his church in proleptic parousia. During his earthly life, Jesus indeed had power *(exousia)*. But now he comes as the cosmocrator, with *all power,* to establish his universal reign by a universal mission.

VI. SUMMING UP

To sum up: Matthew uses apocalyptic motifs to reinterpret the traditional Christian message of the death and resurrection of Jesus. He presents it as the decisive event which breaks through the old barriers of territory, race, and Law and unleashes the mission to all nations as the visible effect of the new age invading the old. We must not be carried away, however. The old age still perdures, as the phrase "until the end of the age" in 28:20 reminds us. In this in between time, when the new age has invaded but yet not fully destroyed the old age, both the church and the world remain a "mixed bag" of good and evil (see the explanation of the parable of the wheat and the tares in Matt 13:36–43, and the man without a wedding garment in 22:11–14). There remains a need for a final division of the good and the bad, the sheep and the goats at the end of time (cf. the scene of judgment in 25:31–46). Hence Matthew does not disregard the hope of a final coming of Christ in glory. But the final parousia has definitely receded on the Matthean horizon. In 28:20, the emphasis is certainly on "behold I *am* with you *all days*" (opening up an indefinite future), rather than on "until the end of the age." Matthew does not have as fully "realized" an eschatology as John, but he is moving in that direction.

Consequently, Christian existence is eschatological for Matthew in two ways. First, the death-resurrection as turning point in salvation-history has brought the believer into a new age, free of the old barriers of nation, race, and Mosaic Law. The present is

---

[40]For Matthew, the resurrection *is* the exaltation. There is no separate act of exaltation labeled "ascension" or "being taken up," as in Luke.

eschatologically conditioned by the saving past. Second, the Christian and the church as a whole still await the coming judgment, a judgment to be passed strictly according to whether Christians lived according to the teachings of the earthly Jesus, who will judge them in the end as Son of Man. This awaiting of the final judgment still molds present Christian existence as eschatological existence. The difference is that, in Matthew's gospel, stringent judgment, rather then temporally proximate judgment, is the main motive force behind Matthew's moral exhortation.

We see, then, how Matthew's peculiar brand of salvation-history and eschatology form the framework, set the stage, for his moral teaching. And we see equally well that this moral teaching cannot be separated from the moral teacher, Jesus Christ, who will judge as he taught. We must now investigate more closely who Jesus is in the first gospel and how he not only teaches Christian living but also proves to be the very basis of that living.

PART TWO

REMODELING THE MESSAGE OF GOSPEL

A Mini-Commentary on the Gospel of Matthew

CHAPTER THREE

Christ and Church as the Basis of Morality

I. FIVE THESES ON CHRIST AND THE CHURCH

At the end of Part I, I stated that, for Matthew, Christian morality is inseparable from the Christ who teaches it. Jesus is not just another messenger from God, a messenger who can deliver his message and then disappear behind it, a messenger who is dispensable once he brings the indispensable message. Consequently, if the title "teacher" is to be applied to Jesus, it must be done with provisos.

Any human teacher you or I have ever had was—in principle—dispensable or interchangeable with someone else. The algebra teacher I had in high school could have easily been replaced by other algebra teachers, some better, some worse. But the basic content of the algebra course, as well as its perduring truth, validity, and usefulness, would have remained the same, no matter who taught me algebra. The content taught to me was not essentially tied to the unique person teaching me. And once my teacher had taught me what he knew, I had no further use for him—at least, not in his capacity as an algebra teacher. By the very act of teaching me what he knew, he put an end to our relationship, at least on an academic level. Put bluntly: once I learned what was to be taught, the person of the teacher became irrelevant. Of course, I might also have struck up a personal relationship with him, but that relationship was not an essential part of the teacher-student relationship, a relationship which was bound to pass.

Such a temporary and tenuous relationship between teacher and student cannot, of course, be transferred to the relationship between Christ the teacher and his disciples. Matthew seems to sense this, as he goes about presenting Christ to us as a teacher of morality. Christ is a teacher in a unique way, for what he teaches depends on his own person for its truth, validity, and permanence. Teacher and teaching become inextricably bound together. You do not fully understand what the teaching is unless you understand who the teacher is. You cannot fully accept the teaching as true unless you accept the teacher as your Lord, as Son of God and Son of Man. In short, accepting his teaching involves following him in the path of discipleship, permanently. Throughout the rest of this book, we shall be exploring the ramifications of this welding together of teacher and teaching. More precisely, in this chapter I propose to set forth five basic propositions or theses which form the foundation of Matthew's approach to morality. The five theses move from the more general to the more specific, and from Christology, through ecclesiology, to morality.

1. Jesus is a teacher of morality; in fact, he is *the* teacher of Christian morality.

2. Jesus not only teaches Christian morality. He embodies and grounds the life he teaches. The new existence to which he calls the disciple is a new existence he himself makes possible, especially by his death-resurrection.

3. This Christological dimension of morality is inextricably bound to an ecclesiological dimension. Indeed, the nexus between Christ and his people, between Christology and ecclesiology, is the specific message of Matthew's gospel.

4. The function which Jesus entrusts to his church in matters of morality is the commission to teach and interpret all he commanded during his earthly ministry.

5. Finally, by way of corollary: the connection between the teachings of the earthly Jesus, the turning point of Jesus' death-resurrection, the commission of the risen and reigning Jesus to his church, and the coming of Jesus to judge at the end of the age—

all these interlocking Christological and ecclesiological dimensions of Christian morality suggest that the overarching concept of Son of Man is vital to Matthew's Christology and total message. It is just as important as the title Son of God.

It is one thing to state these propositions; it is another thing to prove them. Faced with the problem of demonstrating these five theses, I think a convenient distinction can be made. The first proposition, on Jesus as teacher, enunciates a fairly obvious truth; a very cursory reading of the gospel would be sufficient to support it. The truth becomes all the more apparent when one observes how Matthew structures the body of his gospel around great blocks of teaching material. Accordingly, I shall first deal with proposition number one. In a sense, it will mean exegeting the obvious; but it will give us an initial orientation with regard both to the structure and to the content of Matthew's gospel.

After this initial sounding, we will be faced with the more difficult and debatable propositions, numbers two through five. One might be tempted to prove these positions by selecting a few key pericopes from the gospel (Peter's confession at Caesarea Philippi, the parable of the evil farmers, the trials before Caiaphas and Pilate, the death-resurrection, the final commission) and by showing how the propositions are verified in these pivotal examples. The problem with that method is that almost anything can be proven by an exegete if he is free to choose a few pericopes to sustain his position. Naturally, he will select the passages which will exemplify his own view most strongly. The question will remain: Does the whole gospel, or at least the greater part of it, sustain these views? Is it a case of a motif which surfaces now or then, or of a sustained melody which runs throughout the composition? And how do the various key themes or melodies interact with one another as they move through the gospel toward the finale? Only a careful reading of the whole gospel will answer these questions. And so I propose to test propositions two through five by moving through the whole gospel, section by section.

The result will be something of a mini-commentary. But I should like to stress the prefix *mini*. Obviously space does not allow for a full commentary on the gospel. Nor would that serve our purpose, since many interesting problems in the text would only divert our attention from the propositions under investigation. Therefore, as we read the gospel section by section, we shall carefully focus our attention on those matters which bear on the questions we are raising. We shall be on the alert for those statements on Christology and ecclesiology which have an impact on the moral life of the disciple. Christ, church, and morality: that is the optic with which we shall read the first gospel and so provide the basis for Part III, dealing with specific moral questions.

II. JESUS AS TEACHER OF MORALITY

Our first task is to deal with the simplest of our five propositions, proposition number one: Jesus is a teacher of morality; in fact, he is *the* teacher of Christian morality.

The very structure of Matthew's gospel makes this point clear. In the Markan gospel he inherited, Matthew found only two lengthy discourses to the disciples (and, in part, to the crowds): Mark 4, the parables, and Mark 13, the eschatological discourse. As usual, Matthew takes his cue from Mark and builds upon what he finds there. In this case, Matthew expands the discourse materials to the point that the formation and placement of the discourse material becomes a key structural element in his gospel. The whole of the public ministry is divided into a pattern of narrative-then-discourse, narrative-then-discourse, by the careful allocation of the five great discourses addressed to the disciples and, in part, to the crowds.[1] Matthew skillfully creates this alternating pattern by avoiding any bunching together of the discourses. They are placed at the beginning, in the course of, and at the end of the public ministry: the sermon on the mount (chaps. 5–7); the missionary charge to the twelve disciples (chap. 10); the parables discourse (chap. 13); the church order discourse (chap. 18); and the eschatological discourse (chaps. 24-25). Each dis-

---

[1] One reason why chapter 23 should not be counted with the five great discourses is that, despite the "crowds and his disciples" mentioned in verse 1, most of the discourse (vv. 13-39) is addressed to the hypocritical scribes and Pharisees and to the condemned Jerusalem.

course is clearly marked off from, yet joined to, what follows by a set formula: "And it came to pass, when Jesus had finished these words [or commands, or parables]. . . ." This formula occurs in Matthew only at the end of the five discourses (7:28; 11:1; 13:53; 19:1; 26:1). In fact, Matthew's intention to enumerate and demarcate the discourses is made abundantly clear by his addition to the last formula, in 26:1: "And it came to pass when Jesus had finished *all* these words. . . ."

What is more, each discourse fits the narrative material around it. For instance, after the baptism and temptation of Jesus (3:13–4:11), the public ministry begins with narratives of Jesus' movement to Capernaum (4:12–17), his call of the first disciples (4:18–22, thus supplying the necessary core group for the sermon on the mount), and a summary of his ministry (4:23–25). This summary is most interesting, since 4:23 is repeated almost word for word in 9:35, thus providing an inclusion for chaps. 5–7 (the sermon on the mount: Jesus as teacher) and chaps. 8–9 (narratives, notably nine miracle stories:[2] Jesus as miracle-worker).[3] Taking a closer look at 4:23, we notice first of all the order of Jesus' actions: "teaching in their synagogues" is put first, before "proclaiming the gospel of the Kingdom and healing every kind of disease." Then we notice that "teaching," unlike "proclaiming" and "healing," has no direct object. *What* Jesus teaches is to be explained in the sermon on the mount that follows and, in a

---

[2]Often the number is given as ten; but Matthew 9:18-26 (the raising of the ruler's daughter and the healing of the woman with the flow of blood) was already one dovetailed narrative in Mark. Matthew has streamlined and compressed the narrative, giving us even more reason to count it as one story. What results, then, are three "trios" of miracle stories in chapters 8-9. Each trio is marked off from what follows by some non-miraculous "buffer" pericope, involving some saying of Jesus. As often in Matthew, these "buffer" pericopes have a Janus-like quality: they look back and conclude even as they look forward and introduce. In a way, this is true even of the great discourses.

[3]This Christological "diptych" in chapters 5-9 is often referred to as "Messiah of the Word" and "Messiah of the Deed." This is not an altogether happy division, since Matthew, vis-à-vis Mark, stresses the word of Jesus in the miracle stories. This powerful word of Jesus, which possesses divine *exousia* (power, authority), is what binds together the sermon on the mount and the catena of nine miracle stories.

wider sense, in all the five discourses. It is to all this teaching that the risen Jesus refers in the final commission of 28:16–20: "teaching them to observe all whatsoever I commanded you" (28:20).

The point, then, is clear. From the beginning of the public ministry, Matthew makes teaching a main function of Jesus and gives examples which fit the narrative context. After Jesus has begun to attract large crowds by his proclamation of the Kingdom (4:23–25), it is only fitting that he speak on the law of discipleship in that Magna Carta of the Kingdom which we call the sermon on the mount (chaps. 5–7). After Jesus has shown himself to be teacher (chaps. 5–7) and healer (chaps. 8–9), it is only fitting that he respond to the pitiful and pressing needs of the scattered sheep of Israel by sending his twelve disciples out on mission (chap. 10, the missionary discourse). The disciples are commissioned to be for the people what Jesus has already been: preachers and teachers.[4] But the negative response of the people and especially of their leaders to the preaching of Jesus and his disciples (chaps. 11-12) moves Jesus to withdraw into the mysterious speech of the parable (chap. 13).

The parables form a line of division. Their riddle-like expressions are meant to punish the people for their willful lack of understanding, while Jesus continues his ministry of teaching by giving the inner group of disciples explanations of the parables.[5] After chapter 13, Jesus devotes himself more and more to the formation of the disciples, the embryo from which the church is to come. The Kingdom which will find its earthly manifestation in the church is the main concern of chapters 14–17. It is no accident that here Peter plays a prominent part (14:22-23, the walking on the water; 16:13–20, the confession near Caesarea Philippi; 17:1–13, the transfiguration; and 17:24–27, the paying of the Temple tax). It is only fitting that this most ecclesial section of the

---

[4]Note that Matthew does *not* include in the commissioning of chapter 10 the function of teaching. Only at the great commission, given by the risen Jesus at the end of the gospel, are the disciples ordered to teach (28:20). During the public ministry, only Jesus is the legitimate teacher.

[5]A comparison with Mark is very instructive here. In Mark 4:12, Jesus speaks in parables *in order that* the people may not understand. In Matthew 13:13, Jesus speaks in parables *because* the people do not understand.

develop ix

gospel should be followed by the discourse on church life (chap. 18), which emphasizes a church order based on love, the avoidance of scandal, care for the lost, and forgiveness of one's sinful brother. These are what give "order" to the church or assembly (*ekklēsia*) of Jesus.[6] Finally, at the end of the whole public ministry, as the climax of a strife-filled Jerusalem ministry, after parables of judgment, controversy-stories, and woes pronounced on scribes and Pharisees, Jesus delivers his eschatological discourse. Mark's weaving together of the themes of judgment on Jerusalem and the coming of the Son of Man at the end of the world tend to become separated in Matthew. Matthew adds a number of parousia-parables to teach (1) that there will be a delay before the final judgment and (2) that the final judgment will be strictly according to what men did during their lives, and not according to any presumed privilege or group affiliation. After this apocalyptic discourse, there is nothing left to narrate except the apocalyptic event of the death-resurrection (chaps. 26–28), that turning point of the ages which we studied in Part I of this book.

To press home our point about Jesus as teacher, we could go on to examine the many individual pericopes involving teaching that are scattered throughout Matthew's gospel: Sabbath controversies, disputes over laws of ritual cleanness, rejection of the teachings—and even the authority—of the Pharisees, etc. These pericopes, however, are best seen in context and will therefore be treated in our mini-commentary. What we have already seen is sufficient to convince us that Christ's teaching activity has been purposely highlighted by Matthew as he goes about restructuring the Markan framework. Christ's teaching activity is carefully made the warp and woof of the first gospel. If the title is properly understood and is cleansed of any overtone of diminishing Jesus' status, Matthew is quite willing to affirm that Jesus is *the one* teacher of Christians. Jesus alone fulfills that office in its true and complete sense: "One is your teacher . . . your instructor is one, the Messiah (23:8, 10).

---

[6]Interestingly, the word *ekklēsia* occurs in Matthew only in 18:17 and 16:18, another confirmation of the fact that the ecclesiastical discourse is tied to the ecclesiastical narratives which precede it.

Only when we understand fully how intent Matthew is on Christ's teaching can we appreciate the strange fact that Matthew never allows full disciples to address Jesus as "teacher" (*didaskalos*).[7] That address belongs rather in the mouth of the unbeliever, or at least someone who is not fully committed to discipleship. A good example is Matthew 9:11, where the scandalized Pharisees ask "his disciples": "Why does *your teacher* eat with tax collectors and sinners?" The connotations of distance, unbelief, and hostility are clear. Similar cases occur in 12:38; 17:24; 19:16 (the rich young man will fail to follow Jesus); 22:16; 22:24; and 24:36.

The same overtones are attached to the Semitic address, *Rabbi*. A perfect example occurs in Jesus' prediction of his betrayal at the last supper. Each of the startled disciples asks in 26:22: "It isn't I, is it, Lord (*kyrie*)?" By contrast, in 26:25, Judas, "the one who betrayed him," asks: "It isn't I, is it, *Rabbi*?" Matthew supplies the perfect answer to Judas' question when he narrates how "the one who betrayed him" (26:48) comes up to Jesus in Gethsemane and marks him out for arrest by saying: "Hail, *Rabbi!*"

Thus, in Matthew we are faced with a paradox. Matthew never tires of presenting Jesus as teacher; Jesus even designates himself as such (23:8, 10). Yet the title "teacher" or "Rabbi" is addressed to Jesus only by those who are hostile to him or who, at the very least, seem to lack the stamina to become full disciples by following Jesus at all costs.[8] The problem with all these people

---

[7] Matthew 8:19 might seem to be an exception. But the address is placed in the mouth of a "scribe," and the stern reply of Jesus may indicate that the scribe does not really become a disciple, or at least that he does not yet possess a true disciple's understanding at the moment of his profession of devotion.

[8] Note that we are treating cases where *men* use these words as titles addressed to Jesus. From these cases must be carefully distinguished the instances where Jesus speaks of himself as a teacher in the third person: 23:7-10; 26:18; and more indirectly 10:24-25. Here Jesus simply uses the noun to express what he says with the verb in 26:55: "Daily I sat in the temple teaching." Matthew himself uses the verb of Jesus in 4:23; 5:2; 7:29; 9:35; 11:1; 13:54; 21:23; and 22:16 (in the mouth of Jesus' adversaries). It is clear, then, that there is nothing inherently evil for Matthew in the title "teacher." The evil lies in the fact that it is used by men who see in Jesus nothing but a human teacher.

is that they recognize in Jesus only a human teacher, a teacher whose word does not possess the divine authority (*exousia*) needed to overturn the letter of the Mosaic Law or to demand total commitment at any and all costs. The title "teacher" is inadequate because it carries the idea of *merely* a teacher, *only* a human being, who does not have in himself the sufficient authority and basis for the superhuman claims and demands his teaching makes on men. What is lacking in all these people is the insight of faith, the understanding which Matthew, unlike Mark, is willing to attribute to the disciples during the public ministry. The inadequate address "teacher" expresses for Matthew the blindness of most Jews to *who* Jesus is and therefore to *why* his teaching carries unique authority. The teaching of Jesus is through and through a Christological problem. To understand Matthew's presentation of Jesus' moral teaching one must first understand Matthew's Christology, his estimation of the person of Jesus, and the relation of that person to his church. It is with this goal in mind that we shall now review the whole gospel.

Admittedly, we might be tempted at first glance to think that plowing through the whole gospel is not necessary, that Matthew's Christology is readily available. For apparently all we have to do is to contrast the title "teacher" in the mouth of unbelievers with the title with which the disciples regularly address Jesus: "Lord" (*kyrie*). Faced with this one fact, we might jump to the facile conclusion that Matthew's Christology is one of Jesus as Lord.

Yet, as J. D. Kingsbury has pointed out so well,[9] Matthew does not develop a detailed Christology based on the title *kyrios*. Most of the instances of *kyrios* in Matthew occur in the vocative case, as direct address. They obviously express the attitude of a believer, the faith of Matthew and his church. But the title Lord, in itself, does not inform us as to the detailed content of that Christological faith. Clearly, "Lord" is a title of majesty, used to designate Jesus' more-than-human status. But what exactly that status is (and why therefore Jesus can be the basis of his own teaching) is "fleshed out" by Matthew with the aid of two other

---

[9]Kingsbury, *Matthew: Structure, Christology, Kingdom*, 103-113.

titles which bear the content that *kyrios* lacks: Son of God and Son of Man. It is because Jesus, in his teaching, is both Son of God and Son of Man that his teaching has binding, superhuman authority, superseding both the letter of the Mosaic Law and the self-centered interests of would-be disciples. It is my contention that, to understand how Matthew grounds the teaching of Christ in the person of Christ, one must examine these two main Christological titles[10] and their relation to each other, as well as their relation to the church and the problems of Christian morality. For this, we must move on to our mini-commentary.

---

[10]In what follows, I am especially indebted to Kingsbury; for a shorter summary of his views on Matthean Christology, see his *Matthew* volume in the *Proclamation Commentaries* series (Philadelphia: Fortress, 1977) 30-57.

CHAPTER FOUR

Commentary on the Prologue and Book I (Matt 1:1—7:27)

I. THE PROLOGUE (MATT 1—2): INFANCY AS PASSION NARRATIVE

Matthew's prologue (chaps. 1-2) is made up of the genealogy of Jesus Christ (1:1-17) and the four narratives of the annunciation to Joseph (1:18-25), the adoration of the Gentile Magi in the face of Jewish indifference and hostility (2:1-12), the flight into Egypt with the massacre of the infants (2:13-18), and the return from Egypt (2:19-23). The two chapters are so stuffed with titles and place names relating to and defining Jesus that K. Stendahl has entitled these chapters "Quis et unde?"—who is he and where does he come from?[11] The titles and place-names are by no means scattered indiscriminately. Perhaps that is more obvious in the case of the place-names. The four narratives[12] trace out an itinerary for the Son of God: from Bethlehem of Judea to Egypt, back to Judea (land of Israel), and then up to Galilee, specifically

---

[11]K. Stendahl, "Quis et Unde? An Analysis of Mt 1-2," in *Judentum, Urchristentum, Kirche* (ed. W. Eltester; Berlin: Töpelmann, 1960) 94-105. If it be true that Matthew's infancy narrative is also a proleptic passion narrative, then we might add a "Quo?"—where is he going?

[12]Strictly speaking, the place-names do not begin to be mentioned until Matthew 2:1: "Bethlehem of Judea." But we can presume that, in Matthew's mind, the setting for 1:18-25 is also Bethlehem. Matthew, unlike Luke, seems to think that Joseph and Mary are natives of Bethlehem.

Nazareth. The path of the infant Son of God is marked out beforehand in prophecy, just as the way of the Son of Man is likewise prophesied and fulfilled as it leads through the ministry to death and resurrection. In both cases, the Son obediently makes the journey willed by his Father and reaches the appointed goal, even though it means passing through persecution and danger of death. Thus, the infancy narrative becomes a proleptic passion narrative.[13]

The great number of titles for Jesus in the infancy narrative may obscure the same sort of purposeful movement toward a goal, but even here Matthew arranges the titles so that they aim at a climactic revelation of who Jesus is. The titles begin with a heavy emphasis on continuity with and fulfillment of the Old Testament: "Jesus Christ, the son of David, son of Abraham" (1:1). To begin with, then, Jesus is the anointed Messiah of the royal line of David, the fulfillment of the promise made to Abraham, that in him all the tribes of the earth would be blessed.[14] Then, using an apocalyptic pattern of three periods of fourteen generations, Matthew shows that the whole of Israel's salvation history tends toward and finds its fulfillment in Jesus Christ. Tracing the genealogy of Jesus through the reigning kings of Judah,[15] Matthew shows the believer that, when you "add up" the meaning of history, the "bottom line" is Jesus Christ, the son of David.[16] The emphasis on the royal Messiah of the house of

---

[13]This is not so much the case in Luke's joyful, lightsome infancy narrative, though the dark shadows of the cross are not totally lacking (Luke 2:34-35; perhaps 2:46-47).

[14]Possibly there is an inclusion here with the final commission of the risen Jesus: "Going therefore make disciples of all nations" (28:19).

[15]Luke, on the contrary, chooses descendants of David who were not reigning kings. Possibly Matthew includes the names of Asaph (v. 7) and Amos (v. 10) to involve psalmists and prophets, as well as kings, in the ancestry of Jesus. The implication would be that all three parts of the Old Testament witness unto Christ. On the whole question, cf. M. Johnson, *The Purpose of the Biblical Genealogies* (Cambridge: Cambridge U.P., 1969).

[16]It may even be that Matthew is using an esoteric system of interpretation which gave Hebrew letters numerical value ("gematria"). It is true that the numerical value of the Hebrew consonants spelling the name of David adds up to fourteen $(D+W+D = 4+6+4)$.

David, and hence the element of continuity, is very strong.

Yet, in his gospel Matthew is forever joining together continuity with discontinuity. So it is here in the infancy narrative. Already, in the genealogy, we find mentioned not the famous wives of the patriarchs, but rather four women who represent some "holy irregularity" in salvation-history: Tamar, Rahab, Ruth, and Bathsheba. But the supreme holy irregularity is recounted in 1:18-25, which acts as a "footnote" to the quick mention of the virginal conception in 1:16.

The annunciation to Joseph in 1:18-25 makes a number of statements about Jesus: he is virginally conceived; his name signifies that he will save "his people" from their sins;[17] his throne name is Emmanuel, God with us.[18] But the major thrust of this pericope is not here but in the final verse. Despite the fact that Jesus is virginally conceived and is God with us, he qualifies as son of David because Joseph, the son of David (v. 20), accepts him as his son and so places him in David's royal line. The first title of Jesus in 1:1, son of David, has remained the main interest throughout the chapter.

Chapter 2 of Matthew's gospel opens on this same Messianic note: the King of the Jews is born in Bethlehem of Judea. But now the horizon widens, and the results of the whole gospel are played out beforehand. Rejected by his own people, the King is adored by the Gentiles, the Magi. They have received some re-

---

[17]In Matthew's perspective "his people" (1:21) are equivalent to "my church" in 16:18. Already there is a glance toward the saving death-resurrection of Jesus which will constitute the new people of God, the church.

[18]At first glance, it may seem puzzling that Matthew has the prophecy concerning Emmanuel comment on the name Jesus. Obviously one point of connection is the mention of a virgin in both Matthew's narrative and the Septuagint form of Isaiah 7:14. But Matthew may also be hinting that sin is precisely what separates God from his people and that therefore Jesus, the savior from sin, is the one who makes God present to his people again. The throne name Emmanuel would thus be a further explanation of why and how Jesus is savior. Yet we must not weaken Emmanuel so that it simply says that in Jesus God draws near to his people. Contrary to his usual style, Matthew takes pains to translate Emmanuel so as to stress its force: Jesus *is* God with us. How he is God with us will be explained in 2:15: he is God's Son.

mote guidance from their own natural religion; but to reach the King of the Jews, they must come into contact with the old people of God and be directed by the Old Testament prophecies.

The horizon widens even further in the story of the flight into Egypt. At the end of the story of the flight (v. 15), Matthew anticipates the return, so that he can insert a formula quotation which is the theological and Christological climax of the infancy narrative: "Out of Egypt I called my son" (Hosea 11:1). Two important Christological statements are contained in this citation. First, Hosea 11:1 in its original context obviously refers to the people Israel in its exodus from Egypt. Matthew therefore sees Jesus as the new and true Israel, recapitulating in himself the experience of the Israel of old.[19] This point will be continued in the baptism and temptation narratives. Second, the Hosea quotation gives us the highest and climactic title of Jesus in the infancy narrative. Though Jesus is indeed son of David (and therefore Messianic king) and son of Abraham (and therefore the promised one of the nations), though he is the virginally conceived son of Mary and the adopted son of Joseph, he nevertheless transcends any and all of these sonships. Ultimately, he cannot be defined adequately by any earthly filiation. Through Old Testament prophecy Yahweh himself[20] solemnly proclaims that Jesus is "my Son." And, while Israel of old or Israel's king could be called God's son in an adoptive sense, the virginal conception by the

---

[19]Contrary to the title of W. Trilling's justly famous book, *Das wahre Israel* (The True Israel), I think that, for Matthew, only Jesus is the new or true Israel. Matthew indeed sees the church as the new people of God, but he never calls the church Israel. Applied to a whole people, the word "Israel" in Matthew always refers to the people tied to the Old Testament and Judaism. What Israel was has now been absorbed into the person of Jesus.—I do not mean to deny that A. Vögtle is correct in seeing in the infancy narrative an element of Moses-typology (cf. his *Messias und Gottessohn* [Düsseldorf: Patmos, 1971] *passim*). Yet the plain fact is that Matthew does not use any formula quotation which directly refers to Moses, while he does use Hosea 11:1, which clearly refers to Israel. I would therefore firmly maintain against Vögtle that Matthew is working here with an Israel-typology, whether or not one wishes to see the influence of the Jacob-Laban legend witnessed in the later Passover Haggada.

[20]This is the force of *kyriou*, "Lord," in 2:15.

power of the Holy Spirit makes clear that Jesus' sonship is not to be understood in this weak, metaphorical sense. His sonship is transcendent and unique, however much he may share it with his disciples. He will later speak to the disciples of "my Father" and "your Father." He will even teach the disciples to say the "Our Father" as *their* prayer (not his). But he will never use "Our Father" as an umbrella-term to designate globally a relationship to the Father which the disciples share equally with him. He is the only one who can be addressed in the singular as "*the* Son of the living God" (16:16). It is this unique divine sonship which will be publicly manifested after the baptism at the Jordan and which will be put to the test by the devil in the wilderness.[21] But in 2:15, God himself already reveals the truth to the readers of the gospel.[22]

---

[21]Kingsbury is quite right in emphasizing the continuity of this Son-of-God Christology from infancy narrative to baptism and temptation. However, I do not think he is correct when he takes over E. Krentz's view that the prologue of the gospel extends from 1:1 to 4:16, the baptism and temptation thus belonging structurally to the infancy narratives rather than to the public ministry (*Matthew: Structure, Christology, Kingdom*, 8). Kingsbury puts too much weight in his argument on the weak and ambiguous particle *de* in 3:1 (*ibid.*, 13). While it can act as a connective, it can just as easily have a disjunctive force. The context is what decides. And the context here is a jump of about thirty years, the introduction of a new character (the Baptist is not included in Matthew's infancy narrative, as opposed to Luke's), and a new eschatological event introduced solemnly by the unique phrase "now in those days." Moreover, in 3:2, Matthew shows his special theological view by placing John the Baptist in parallel position to Jesus. He proclaims word-for-word what Jesus will proclaim in 4:17 (supposedly across the great structural divide): "Repent for the Kingdom of heaven has drawn near." I would therefore hold that 3:1 marks the end of the prologue and the beginning of the body of the gospel.

[22]Because of his structural views, Kingsbury misses the full force of the climactic nature of 2:15. He claims that in 2:15 the sonship is stated only in the words of the ancient prophet. "At 3:17 . . . Matthew brings just such an open assertion of the divine sonship of Jesus, and this by none other than God himself" (*Matthew: Structure, Christology, Kingdom*, 15). But the Old Testament words of 2:15 are said to be "spoken *by* the Lord *through* the prophet." On this whole matter, cf. R. Pesch, "Der Gottessohn im matthäischen Evangelienprolog (Mt 1-2)," *Bib* 28 (1967) 395-420.

The infancy narrative closes with the paradox of the transcendent yet lowly Son. He who is acknowledged by God as his own Son flees for his life while other infants are massacred in his place. Even when the exiled Son returns home, the threat of further danger forces him into exile again, into Galilee of the Gentiles, which will be his place of exile for the whole of his public ministry. He will come home to Judea only to die. In the meantime, he who bears the exalted title of Son must simultaneously bear a title denoting his lowly, humble, obscure earthly status: "He shall be called a Nazorean" (2:23).[23] Jesus is the Nazirite from Nazareth. All that Matthew will later say about the Son who is the humble yet powerful servant (8:17; 12:18-21; 27:39-43) is already prefigured in his proleptic passion narrative. In what follows we will continue to see this "bending" of the title Son of God in the direction of obedient service and humble suffering—and thus in the direction of one of the meanings of Son of Man.

II.   BOOK I NARRATIVE (MATT 3-4): THE SON'S INITIAL PROCLAMATION OF THE KINGDOM

At the beginning of Book One of the public ministry, the baptism (3:13-17) and the temptation (4:1-11) confirm and carry forward this revelation of Jesus as Son of God. The scenes are charged with the theme of Old Testament fulfillment. In 3:15, Jesus rejects the Baptist's objection by pointing to their joint duty to fulfill God's will for them, marked out beforehand in

---

[23]For a discussion of this notoriously difficult "citation," cf. G. Soares Prabhu, *The Formula Quotations in the Infancy Narrative of Matthew* (Rome: Biblical Institute Press, 1976) 193-216; K. Stendahl, *The School of St. Matthew*[2] (Lund: Gleerup, 1968) 103-104, 198-199; R. Gundry, *The Use of the Old Testament in St. Matthew's Gospel* (Leiden: Brill, 1975) 97-104. Note that Matthew himself shows that he knows full well that he is making a global illusion which could not be verified in one precise text. For the only time in his introduction to the formula quotations, he uses the plural "prophets."

prophecy.[24] After the baptism (which is relegated to a participle), the theophany which is the main point of the pericope is described in terms taken from the inaugural vision of Ezekiel (Ezek 1) and the words of Deutero-Isaiah appealing for a theophany (Isa 63:19—cf. v. 11 in the Septuagint). The climax of the scene occurs, as it did in the infancy narrative, when God acknowledges his Son. Matthew changes Mark's "You are my Son" (Mark 1:11) to "This is my Son." Since Matthew has made clear that Jesus is God's Son from conception onward, it would make little sense for Matthew to portray the theophany as a private revelation to Jesus, as Mark does. Here, as elsewhere in Matthew, the secret revelation so beloved of Mark goes public. And there is no reason in the text to restrict the "public" revelation to the Baptist alone.[25]

Various Old Testament allusions behind the divine voice flesh out Matthew's conception of "Son of God." Among the texts alluded to is Psalm 2:7. Psalm 2 is a psalm of royal enthronement, in which God proclaims the King to be his Son as the King begins to rule over and therefore represent in his corporate personality the people Israel, which is also God's Son (Exod 4:22). As the King is installed, the foreign nations are warned to submit willingly to this powerful Anointed One. And so the dual theme which we saw in chapters 1-2, the royal Davidic Messiah who also sums up the experience of the whole people Israel, is continued. Perhaps there is even a hint that this Messianic King is also destined to rule the nations. Psalm 2, however, may not be Matthew's main focus. Since Matthew changes "You are" to "This is" in 3:17, he shifts the spotlight from Psalm 2 to Isaiah 42:1, where God presents his servant in the third person: "here is my servant . . . in whom I am pleased, upon whom I have put my

---

[24]The reasons for understanding the phrase "to fulfill all justice" (3:15) in terms of prophecy and salvation history are given in my book, *Law and History in Matthew's Gospel* (Rome: Biblical Institute Press, 1976) 76-80.

[25]There is a curious tension in the thought of Kingsbury at this point: the revelation is made "only in the presence of John and not before the crowds," and yet "it occurs openly" and is "public in nature" (*Matthew: Structure, Christology, Kingdom*, 49).

Spirit." Matthew's interest in this servant-aspect of Jesus' sonship is clear from the two passages from the servant songs of Isaiah which Matthew uses as formula quotations, 8:17 and 12:18-21. We should note immediately that nothing explicit is said in any of these passages about the servant's vicarious sacrifice unto death. Yet the theme may be present at the baptism, for there may also be an allusion in Matthew 3:17 to Genesis 22:2, 12, where God orders Abraham to sacrifice his only beloved son.[26] If it be true that the rabbinic theology of the vicarious and voluntary sacrifice of Isaac already existed in New Testament times,[27] then the idea of Jesus' sacrificial death for sinners may be present in Matthew 3:17, joined to a son-servant Christology by way of Jesus' iden-tification with the original "son of Abraham" (1:1), Isaac. It then becomes abundantly clear, even at this early stage, that Jesus' sonship and royal enthronement are intimately connected with servanthood, suffering, and vicarious sacrifice. The Son-concept is again "bent" in the direction of obedient, redemptive suffering, and thus in the direction of one aspect of the Son of Man concept.

This process of bending or reinterpretation reaches a high point in the temptation narrative. Caught up in an ecstatic vision portraying the apocalyptic, cosmic struggle between good and evil,[28] Jesus is tested, probed, "tempted" by the devil. At first glance, the Matthean emphasis on the full fast of forty days and forty nights points to a Moses typology (Exod 34:28).[29] But that is

---

[26]The Hebrew *yāḥîd* could carry the dual connotation of "beloved" and "unique, only one." The dual idea may well be present in the New Testament's application of *agapētos* to Jesus.

[27]This is the claim of R. Daly, "The Soteriological Significance of the Sacrifice of Isaac," *CBQ* 39 (1977) 45-75, especially 68-71.

[28]Along with W. Grundmann, *Das Evangelium nach Matthäus*[3] (Berlin: Evangelische Verlagsanstalt, 1972) 100, I think this is the probable sense of *anēchthē*, "he was driven up," "led up," "brought up."

[29]Note how Matthew adds the "forty nights" to Mark and/or Q and connects the time designation directly to the motif of fasting rather than tempting (contrast Luke 4:2). This highlights the reference to Exodus 34:28. Given the central use of Deuteronomy in this pericope, Matthew may also have in mind Deuteronomy 9:9 and 18, which are especially interesting because of the idea of intercession for the sins of others.

as far as the Moses typology goes.[30] The main theme of the narrative is that Jesus the true Son of God, the true Israel, triumphs in the desert over those very temptations to which the old Israel-and-Son-of-God succumbed during its desert sojourn.

That it is a question of Jesus' divine sonship is clear from the first words out of the devil's mouth in the first and second temptation: "If you are the Son of God. . . ."[31] The devil is taking up the public declaration made by God at the baptism and testing its truth and its exact meaning. In what sense is Jesus Son of God? That is the crucial question which will also be debated at Caesarea Philippi (16:13-28) and on Golgotha (27:40-43). This quasi-rabbinical debate, which stretches throughout the gospel, begins now, in the desert. The devil first interprets the title Son in terms of a miracle worker who is free to exploit his divine power for his own advantage—and perhaps that of his followers. When Jesus rejects that interpretation of divine sonship by pointing out that the true Israel and Son must draw life and nourishment from obedient trust in God's word, the devil takes him up on his claim to trust God in the midst of need. Very well, says the devil, if you define your sonship in terms of trust, then place yourself totally in God's hands by casting yourself down from the pinnacle of the temple. The crafty devil thus takes up the claim of Jesus and twists it to make a double temptation: Jesus is tempted to tempt God. Jesus replies by stressing the fact that filial trust is obedient trust. It waits upon God's plan and does not try to force God's hand. The status of sonship is not to be abused to make God's will dependent on ours.

Having failed with subtle disputation on the concept of son-

---

[30]In this we can see a certain parallel between the temptation narrative and the infancy narrative: an element of Moses-typology, but a predominant emphasis on Son and true Israel.

[31]The address makes sense the first two times, since the devil challenges this supposed Son to perform or to occasion a miracle. The third temptation is more of an enticing offer, demanding no miracle on Jesus' part, but rather an adoration of Satan which would merely imitate what many men do and what Israel did. The introduction, "if you are the Son of God," would be clearly out of place. Yet even here it is a question of a misapprehension of divine sonship as involving an easy way to glory. Thus, it is sonship, rather than messiahship, which is the precise focus of the temptations.

ship, the devil tries one last massive, frontal assault, where crass-ness replaces subtlety. The Son is promised cosmic rule the "easy" way, at the mere cost of worshiping the one who can give earthly kingdoms and their glory. The apocalyptic horror of the demonic assault on the divine has reached its climax. No further debate is possible. Just as Jesus has shown his authority to inter-pret Scripture correctly in the face of the devil's twisting of Scripture, now he shows the power his word has over Satan himself: "Begone, Satan."[32] The Son can use his power to defeat the demonic because he refuses to abuse that power to serve his own advantage. The Son is all-powerful because he remains obe-diently dependent on God. Thus he conquers where the old Israel failed. It is no accident that the Son rejects each of Satan's temp-tations by quoting from Deuteronomy. Deuteronomy reflects the sad history of Israel's repeated failures in the desert. Israel had failed to trust God's care, so concretely demonstrated in the manna (8:3); she had tried to put God to the test at Massah (6:16); she had fallen from her monotheistic commitment through idolatry (6:13). In obeying where Israel disobeyed, the Son proves himself to be the true Israel. He refuses the devil's offer of cosmic rule not because he is not destined for it, but because his path to the rule is the way of the cross. At the end of the gospel, the crucified and risen One will proclaim his cosmic power and command a universal mission (28:18-19). The Son will gain sway over all kingdoms precisely by refusing the offers and demands of Satan on the mount (4:8-10), of the Satan named Peter (16:21-23), and of the enemies at the cross (27:39-43). All of them are enemies of the cross because they think of sonship in terms of glory· without suffering. None of them can comprehend the innovative exegesis of Jesus, his bending of sonship in the direction of ser-vanthood and of the Son of Man who triumphs through suffering.

With the temptation narrative we reach the end of the first

---

[32]It is only in Matthew that Jesus dismisses Satan with his authorita-tive word. For Matthew, the devil can tempt Jesus only as long as Jesus allows it; compare Luke 4:13. The fact that Matthew alone has this blunt dismissal of Satan gives Jesus' rebuke to Peter in Matthew 16:23 (taken over from Mark 8:33) special sharpness: "Get behind me, *Satan*." Only twice in Matthew does Jesus address someone as Satan: in 4:10 and 16:23.

1st part of gospel vs... on a lot on titulos *clearly*

great section of Christological titles in Matthew's gospel. Amid the flurry of titles, notably in the infancy narrative, one title clearly stood out: Son of God. And yet Matthew has been very careful to bend this title in a particular direction: obedience, trust, humility, suffering, servanthood—the Son who is persecuted and tested and yet proves faithful. This bending of Son of God will bear interesting fruit when the title Son of Man comes on the scene.

But for the moment Matthew has exhausted his interest in titles and pursues his Christological interests in other ways. In fact, it is remarkable how much he says about Christ in the following pericopes without relying on titles—a healthy reminder that we should never restrict our study of Christology in the New Testament to titles. In the movement of his residence to Capernaum (Matt 4:12-17), Jesus shows himself to be the eschatological, messianic light prophesied by Isaiah, now rising on a religiously deprived and benighted Galilee of the Gentiles.[33] In 4:17, Jesus begins his public proclamation, and the authoritative, indeed all-powerful nature of the word he speaks will be abundantly illustrated in the following chapters.

A first example of this authoritative word is given in the call of the first disciples. Without any psychological preparations (contrast John 1), they are called and claimed by the word of Jesus, which puts an end to the past they knew and opens up a future they cannot comprehend. All they can do is obey Jesus' word and follow. At the end of chapter 4, in the summary of 4:23-25, the stage is set for chapters 5-7 (Jesus as teacher and herald of the Kingdom) and chapters 8-9 (Jesus as healer).

III.   THE SERMON ON THE MOUNT (MATT 5—7)

A treatment of the sermon on the mount (chaps. 5-7) really belongs with our consideration of Christian morality, but we should observe briefly the Christology that is presupposed in the sermon.

---

[33]In the designation "Galilee of the Gentiles," Matthew may see a pointer to the final commission (28:19), given by the Risen One in

1. Jesus as the *herald of the Kingdom* defines, proclaims, and promises true happiness to his disciples in the beatitudes (5:3-12). In both their passive aspect (the poor, the mourning, the meek, the hungry, the persecuted) and their active aspect (the merciful, the single-hearted, the peacemakers), the beatitudes mirror Jesus himself, the truly happy man, the embodiment of the joy the Kingdom brings.

2. Jesus as *teacher* defines his relation to the Law not in terms of destruction but rather in terms of prophetic fulfillment, indeed, eschatological consummation. Since in him all prophecy reaches fulfillment (5:18d), since for the Christian the center of religion has become not the Mosaic Law but Jesus the Fulfiller, the whole question of Law for Matthew has undergone a Copernican revolution. The burning question for Matthew is not the burning question which the contemporaries of Jesus were asking in A.D. 30: What is the relation of this man Jesus to the center of our religion, the Mosaic Law? Too much baptismal water has flowed under the bridge. For Matthew, the burning question is: What is the relation of the Mosaic Law to the center of our religion, the Lord Jesus, who is Son of God and Son of Man. And Matthew answers that question in 5:17-20 in terms of eschatological fulfillment of Law and prophecy, with the fulfillment of Law understood in analogy to the fulfillment of prophecy.[34]

3. Jesus as *Fulfiller* of the Law gives six examples of his eschatological fulfillment in the six antitheses (5:21-48). In six instances of Pentateuchal law, Jesus contrasts what God said to the wilderness-generation of Israel at Sinai with what Jesus himself says to his disciples now. As can be seen clearly in the fourth antithesis (vv. 31-32), the basic contrast is between two acts of saying ("it was said . . . but *I* say). The "it was said" is the reverent "divine passive," which has God as the understood

---

Galilee. But at the historical moment described in the narrative, Galilee of the Gentiles carries a pejorative note of humiliation: the chosen people to whom alone Jesus is sent during his public ministry are in a wretched religious state, surrounded and penetrated by pagan elements.

[34]What is said here in passing will be explained in detail when we treat the question of moral demand in Matthew.

agent.[35] That God is the understood speaker is confirmed by what immediately follows the "it was said": some law(s) of the Pentateuch, in either a word for word citation or a generalizing summary. We are not dealing here simply with the interpretations of Scripture by later rabbis.[36] In six instances of important socio-religious institutions permitted or commanded by the written Mosaic Law, Jesus dares to contrast his word with God's word. What is more startling still, in three cases (antitheses three, four, and five, on divorce, oaths and vows, and retaliation), Jesus revokes the letter of the Law and replaces it with his own diametrically opposed command. Despite the permissions and commands of the Law, there is to be no divorce, no oaths or vows, no legal retaliation. Given the highly Jewish coloration of all this material, the claim Jesus makes for the authority of his own word is astounding. No wonder the crowds, at the end of the sermon (7:28-29), are dumbstruck by his teaching authority. As regards the Law and authority over it, Jesus stands where God stands. In a Jewish or Jewish-Christian context, a higher status could not be imagined. And Matthew makes the claim, not by using any title, but by emphasizing the *exousia* (authority, power) of Jesus' word. In what follows, we must be attentive to this idea of *exousia* throughout the gospel, and must be on watch to see how Matthew links his *exousia*-concept to the explicit Christology of the titles, notably the title Son of Man.

In chapter 6, Jesus continues the role of teacher, but now turns to practical questions of "pious exercises." The Jewish

---

[35]Clear examples of this usage are supplied by the passive verbs in the beatitudes (shall be comforted, shall be satisfied, shall have mercy shown them, shall be called sons—each time with "by God" understood).

[36]Thus, the contention that the basic contrast is between saying and hearing should be abandoned. Such a contrast is not even present in verses 31–32. The rabbinic "parallels" brought forward by the scholars prove, on closer examination, to be wanting. For the opposite view, cf. D. Daube, " 'Ye Have Heard—But I Say unto You.' " in *The New Testament and Rabbinic Judaism* (London: Athlone Press, 1956) 55-62; W. Davies, *The Setting of the Sermon on the Mount* (Cambridge: Cambridge U.P., 1966) 101, especially n. 1; M. Smith, *Tannaitic Parallels to the Gospels* (Philadelphia: Society of Biblical Literature, 1951) 27–29.

practices of fasting (6:2-4), prayer (6:5-15), and almsgiving (6:16-18) are not rejected but rather corrected, in true prophet-like fashion, in the direction of a hidden, personal relationship with "your Father who sees in the secret place." Here the Son teaches his disciples how to live as true sons of this Father whom Jesus reveals. The trust, love, and God-centeredness of this filial relationship receives perfect expression in the Our Father (6:9-13), which Matthew insists on inserting into the traditional catechism of 6:1-18, even though it breaks the neat symmetry of the three sections.

After verse 18, Matthew's concern about architectonic structures in the sermon lessens. He collects various related admonitions of Jesus about trust in the Father, forbearance toward our brothers, perseverance in prayer and in moral action. The importance of fierce moral commitment and concrete moral action comes to the fore at the end of the sermon. The disciple must be among the few who successfully strive to enter the narrow gate (7:13-14). Disciples must prove that they are not false prophets by matching their claims with good deeds (7:15-20). For Jesus the eschatological judge will not be satisfied with the lip service of Lord, Lord,[37] or with flashy manifestations of special religious power, but only with the concrete *doing* of the Father's will. As is clear from such passages as 16:24-28; 24:37, 39; 24:42, 44; and 25:31-46, Jesus, the stringent eschatological judge who judges men according to their deeds, is precisely Jesus the Son of Man.[38]

The concluding double parable of the men who built on rock or sand reinforces this idea, and gives us the interesting equation of "doing the will of my Father" (7:21) with "hearing my words and doing them" (7:24, 26). The ultimate criterion of what *is* the will of the Father is the authoritative word of Jesus—Jesus who teaches his words now with authority, Jesus who, as Son of Man,

---

[37]Note how the invocation of Jesus as *kyrie* by the (false) disciples is explicitly branded as insufficient and in fact self-deluding.

[38]Kingsbury, *Matthew: Structure, Christology, Kingdom*, 107, remarks well: " . . . in reality Jesus stands behind the term *kyrios* as the Son of Man. . . . Jesus Son of Man is called *kyrios* because, as the eschatological Judge, he exercises dominion with authority derived from God himself."

will judge all men according to his authoritative words on the last day. Hence the importance for Matthew of the identity of the earthly Jesus, the risen Lord, and the judge of the last day. Hence the importance of the applicability of the title Son of Man to Jesus in each of these roles. Hence the importance of the final commission the risen Jesus gives his disciples in 28:19—"teaching them to observe all whatsoever I commanded you."[39] The commandments the earthly Jesus taught, the commandments the disciples are now commissioned to teach by the risen Jesus, will be the all-decisive norm when the Son of Man judges on the last day. We can see already the importance for Matthew of the authoritative word of Jesus the Son of Man. It ties together the various successive roles of Jesus, as well as the themes of church, discipleship, morality, and judgment.

---

[39]On all this, cf. G. Bornkamm, "End-Expectation and Church in Matthew," in G. Bornkamm-G. Barth-H. J. Held, *Tradition and Interpretation in Matthew* (Philadelphia: Westminster, 1963), as supplemented by his "The Risen Lord and the Earthly Jesus," in *The Future of Our Religious Past* (ed. J. Robinson; N.Y.: Harper & Row, 1971) 203-229.

CHAPTER FIVE

Commentary on Book II
(Matt 7:28—11:1):
The Full Bloom of the Mission in
Galilee

I. MATT 7—9: THE SON AND HIS DISCIPLES

The sermon on the mount gave Matthew an opportunity to write a Christology without too much dependence on titles. Likewise, the cycle of nine miracle stories in chapters 8 and 9 (the narrative part of Book Two) permits him to continue this title-less Christology, now illustrated by authoritative deeds rather than authoritative teaching.[40] This is not to say, however, that titles are totally lacking. When they do occur in this Christology-through-narrative, they are quite instructive.

(1) First, we see that the vocative use of *kyrie* to address Jesus by the believer is clearly exemplified (8:2, by the leper; 8:6, 8 by the centurion; 8:21 by a disciple; 8:25 by the disciples; 9:28, by the blind men). *Kyrie* obviously expresses the reverent attitude of the believer in the presence of a transcendent person whose word is all-powerful. What is implicit in all these examples is articulated perfectly by the centurion in 8:8: "Command (*eipe*,

---

[40]I think this admission that Matthew's Christology is not simply written by heaping up titles is important, if we are to avoid the temptation of reading titles into every pericope.

literally "say") with a word (*logō*)." Matthew's Christology of the authoritative word could not be clearer; and it is to this Christology that the title *kyrios* points. It is this Christology of the authoritative word which binds together discourse and narrative in the first gospel.

(2) The inadequate nature of the title teacher (*didaskalos*) is also exemplified. It occurs in the mouth of a would-be but unprepared follower (8:19) and in the mouths of the Pharisees (9:11). It is the sign of those who do not fully appreciate the authority of Jesus and his word, those who cannot accept the shattering demands he rightly makes on the complacently religious individual and on established religious traditions.

(3) But the most intriguing title in this section of Christology-by-narrative is Son of Man, which appears in the gospel for the first time at 8:20, to be followed relatively soon by 9:6. These occurrences are especially significant because, after 4:6, Son of God is almost absent from the gospel until 14:33. The one exception is 8:29, taken over from Mark 5:7. By contrast, Son of Man occurs nine times in chapters 7-14, in all three of its main meanings: lowly yet powerful servant on earth, dying and rising savior, eschatological judge who returns to save his own. Clearly, Son of Man is a Christological title to be reckoned with in Matthew, all the more so because it is Jesus' chosen self-designation.[41] For the moment, let us restrict ourselves to its function in the chain of miracle stories in chapters 8-9.

The first occurrence, 8:20, is found at the end of the first trio of miracle stories: cleansing of the leper, 8:1-4; healing of the centurion's servant, 8:5-13; healing of Peter's mother-in-law along with many others, 8:14-17. In 8:16, the summary statement, "he

---

[41]The fact that Son of Man is exclusively Jesus' chosen self-designation, always occurring in his mouth, never in anyone else's, and the fact that Jesus rarely refers to himself by some other title (e.g., the Son), are reasons why Son of Man should never be subsumed under any other title. Since no one else in the gospel ever uses the title when speaking of or to Jesus, I find Kingsbury's designation of Son of Man as a "public title" questionable. By contrast, Son of God is used by God the Father, Satan, Peter, the disciples, the demoniacs, the high priest, the passersby at the cross, the priests, scribes, and elders, and the two thieves; and yet Kingsbury designates it as a "confessional title."

healed all who were ill," leads into one of Matthew's formula quotations: "in order that what was spoken through the prophet Isaiah might be fulfilled, saying, 'He himself took our weaknesses and carried [our] sicknesses."[42] Matthew shows here a surprising originality in the New Testament tradition. The servant-figure of Isaiah, so often used in the New Testament in reference to Jesus' death, is here applied to his healing activity during the public ministry. Jesus' servanthood is not to be restricted to his death; it stretches throughout his public ministry.[43] Throughout that ministry he freely chooses to be a lowly servant among his people, associating with sinners, showing mercy to the outcast or mistreated (notice that the three miracles are performed for a leper, the servant of a Gentile, and a woman). In short, from his baptism onward, Jesus the servant embraces a sinful, suffering, sick humanity, in order to save his people from their sins (1:21) and bear their illnesses (8:17).

It is in this light that we must read the "buffer pericope" which separates the first trio of miracles from the second. A Jewish scribe offers, with great self-assurance, to follow the teacher (note the inadequate title) wherever he goes (8:19). Jesus replies that this member of the religious establishment does not know the cost of following the humble servant of God: "The foxes have lairs and the birds of heaven nests, but the Son of Man has nowhere to lay his head." What is especially fascinating here is

---

[42]The use of a formula quotation here is striking, because, in contrast to the infancy narratives, Matthew uses these special quotations sparingly during the public ministry proper. Between 4:14-16 (removal to Capernaum) and 21:4 (entry into Jerusalem) there are only three clear cases: 8:17; 12:17-21; 13:35. Two out of the three reflect servant Christology.

[43]This does not necessarily exclude Matthew's use of the servant figure in reference to Jesus' death. Indeed, the passion-predictions would argue for it, especially in the light of Matthew's retention of Mark 10:45 in Matthew 20:28 (contrast Luke's omission of the verse after Luke 18:34). Significant also is Matthew's addition of "unto the remission of sins" to the formula over the cup at the last supper. The tendency among some exegetes to exclude the idea of servanthood and sacrificial death in Matthew's Christology needs correction. Matthew's servant Christology should not be reduced to the one text in which *pais* appears (12:18); contrast Kingsbury, *Matthew: Structure, Christology, Kingdom*, 93-95.

that the first occurrence of Son of Man in Matthew refers neither to his death nor to his glorious coming as judge, but rather to his humble, deprived human existence during the public ministry. It follows perfectly upon the servant-citation from Isaiah[44] and is a healthy warning against reducing the importance of the Matthean Son of Man to a future role on the last day. Yet this humble, suffering servant is at the same time the powerful Lord who can command nature to be still and thus save his imperiled community of disciples (8:23-27).[45] Despite the majestic, somewhat glorified figure of the earthly Jesus in Matthew, he remains the lowly servant. He is the Son, God's Wisdom on earth, who nevertheless is meek and humble of heart (11:25-30), the triumphant King who yet rides into Jerusalem as the meek one, seated on the animal of peace (21:1-11).

The second trio of miracles consists of the stilling of the storm (8:23-27, with the invocation *kyrie* in v. 25), the healing of the two Gadarene demoniacs (8:28-34, with the invocation Son of God in v. 29), and the healing of a paralytic (9:1-8, with Jesus' self-designation, Son of Man, in v. 6). The invocation *kyrie* is, as we have seen already, merely the believer's formal address to the transcendent One who can speak the authoritative word. More interesting is the use of Son of God in a context of exorcism. The transcendent Son is even during his public ministry breaking the power of evil, a task he will complete by his death and resurrection. Although the title is simply taken over from the Markan parallel, it is a good reminder that, just as we should not absorb Son of Man into Son of God, so too the reverse absorption would be likewise illegitimate. The two titles are equally important.

Perhaps the most intriguing pericope in the second trio is the healing of the paralytic. Even more than Mark, Matthew is working on the double level or horizon of the sacred past of Jesus'

---

[44]As far as we can judge from the parallel in Luke 9:57-58, the whole context in Matthew 8 and, in particular, the sequence of formula quotation and pronouncement are Matthew's redactional work.

[45]The ecclesiological overtones of this and other miracle stories, as well as a great deal of the discourse material, hint at something we shall see more fully later: one of the specific traits of Matthew's Christology is its nexus with ecclesiology.

ministry and of the present ministry of Jesus' church. On the level of a narrative about the sacred past, Jesus the knowing and compassionate One immediately sees through appearances to the real faith of the helpers of the man and the real need of the man himself. Ignoring for the moment the physical evil oppressing the man, Jesus goes to the core of the problem, the spiritual evil which incapacitates the man even more: "Your sins are forgiven" (9:2). The Jewish scribes immediately see the claim to transcendent authority in this declaration. Jesus is blaspheming because he claims power that belongs to God alone. Without engaging in speculative debates over his precise relation to God, Jesus simply vindicates his transcendent authority to forgive sins by performing the more easily verifiable miracle of healing the paralytic's physical infirmity. In verse 6, Jesus explicitly states that he is performing the visible wonder "in order that you may know that the Son of Man has power on earth to forgive sins." Whether we read the phrase "on earth" as going with Son of Man or "forgive sins," the statement obviously refers, on the level of narration of past events, to the activity of Jesus during his public ministry. For all his humility and lowly status as servant, this healer nevertheless dares to designate himself, even during his public ministry, as the transcendent Son of Man who possesses God's own power to forgive sins. The judicial function of the Son of Man on the last day is anticipated in the now of the public ministry. Again, we are warned not to restrict the importance of Son of Man to the parousia.

Of course, this story is also meant by Matthew to be read on the level of his church's own faith-experience and ministry. The Son of Man continues, through his church, to exercise "on earth" this divine power to forgive sins (cf. Matt 16:19; 18:15-18). It is this second horizon of the church's present ministry which moves Matthew to change Mark's concluding phrase. In Mark 2:12, the onlookers glorify God, saying "we have never seen the like." In Matthew 9:8, the crowds "glorify God who gives such power [exousia] to men." The phrase "to men" makes no sense on the level of the past of Jesus; it makes great sense on the level of the present of the church. The powerful-yet-merciful Son of Man, who used his transcendent authority during his earthly life to forgive sins, continues to forgive sins in the life of his church. Thus, the same title refers to the activity of Jesus during his mortal life and his activity as risen Lord. Once again, we see that Son of Man is a concept which can span and tie together the various stages of salvation-history, precisely because of its many-sided meaning.

The picture of Jesus as forgiver of sins is continued in the "buffer pericope" of the call of Matthew (9:9-13), into which the evangelist inserts the citation from Hosea 6:6: "I desire mercy, not sacrifice" (so again at Matt 12:7). Indeed, the "lax" attitude of Jesus toward stringent religious observance marks a break with both the disciples of the Baptist and the Pharisees. It could not be otherwise, for the eschatological bridegroom has come to the marriage feast to claim his people as his bride. The new reality demands new treatment (9:14-17). Yet Matthew adds with typical concern for continuity-within-discontinuity: "But pour the new wine into new skins, and both are preserved" (Matt 9:17; contrast Mark 2:22). In all his astounding and revolutionary activity as humble servant, powerful healer, transcendent Son of Man, Jesus remains the fulfiller of the Law and the prophets, not their destroyer.

In the third trio of miracles (the ruler's daughter along with the hemorrhaging woman, 9:18-26; the healing of two blind men, 9:27-31; and the healing of a dumb man, 9:32-34), Matthew concludes his presentation of Jesus, the healer, whose authoritative word is able not only to heal illness and restore crippled faculties, but also to raise the dead. A telling reminder of the danger of Christology by titles alone is the fact that this exalted portrait of Jesus as life-giver and healer is presented without any Christological title of major importance. In fact, apart from the usual *kyrie* in 9:28, the only title that occurs is "Son of David" in 9:27. And that simply comes from Mark 10:48 by way of Matthew 20:31, of which Matthew 9:27 is a weak reduplication. Son of David is not a major title for Matthew; it is too limited by implicit reference to legal parentage and narrow nationalistic hopes (cf. 22:41-45). But as Kingsbury correctly observes, Matthew does use it positively to present Jesus as the humble King who goes out of his way to select "no-accounts" for healing.[46] With all that we have seen in chapters 8 and 9 concerning Jesus' humility, servanthood, mercy, and forgiveness, the use of Son of David at 9:27 is hardly surprising.[47]

At the end of chapter 9, Matthew repeats, by way of inclusion, the summary of Jesus' activity we found in 4:23 (= 9:35). Significantly, Matthew adds an explicit statement about Jesus' compassion for these troubled sheep without a shepherd. It is a fitting conclusion to the revelation of Jesus the merciful servant, the lowly yet transcendent Son of Man, which has been presented in chapters 8-9. It also provides a skillful transition to the missionary discourse in chapter 10.

II. MATT 10: THE MISSION DISCOURSE

The discourse which ends Book Two, the missionary discourse of chapter 10, reminds us of one of the most typical traits of Matthew's Christology: its nexus with ecclesiology. The summary of 9:35 had recapitulated the ministry of Jesus under three headings: teaching, proclaiming the gospel, and healing every kind of illness. What Jesus has been for a select group of Jews, the twelve disciples (10:1) or twelve apostles (10:2) are to be for a wider audience. They are to be Jesus to others (cf. 10:40). They receive the commission to continue Jesus' activities of proclaiming (10:7; cf. 4:17) and healing (10:1, 8, the latter verse giving a short summary of Jesus' deeds in chapters 8-9). Not only is the mission of the disciples the same as that of Jesus; their mission has the same serious eschatological consequences for others (10:14-15). And their destiny of persecution and martyrdom likewise mirrors that of Jesus (10:16-25, especially vv. 24-25). But they are not to fear, for they are given the consoling promise of

[46]Kingsbury, *Matthew: Structure, Christology, Kingdom*, 99-103.

[47]The connection of Son of David with healing may have already been present in Jewish tradition by the time of Jesus; cf. K. Berger, "Die königlichen Messiastraditionen des Neuen Testaments," *NTS* 20 (1973-74) 1-44—though one must be wary of Berger's use of sources.

the return of Jesus as the triumphant Son of Man (10:23).[48] When he comes again, there will be a strict judgment according to deeds. As the disciples confess or deny Jesus before men, so Jesus will confess or deny them before the Father on the last day (10:32-33). So every disciple must be willing to forsake everything and follow Jesus on the way of the cross. As goes the Master, so goes the disciple—on the paradoxical path of gain through loss (10:34-39). But there is no real loss; the smallest good deed will receive its due reward on the final day (10:40-42). Granted that many of these individual sayings apply equally well to all Christians, Matthew has carefully gathered them together under the rubric of the missionary discourse to the twelve apostles, the leaders of the church who, in a special way, mirror Jesus' mission and fate. Here, then, Matthew shows his particular interest in linking Christology and ecclesiology. And, in doing this, the only significant Christological title he refers to is Son of Man, the judge of the last day (10:23). Since this coming Son of Man is identical with the earthly Jesus who now speaks these missionary instructions, the Son of Man's judgment will correspond exactly to men's reaction to him when they encounter him through the mission of his disciples.

---

[48]Given the fact that the parousia has receded in Matthew's salvation-historical perspective, it is obvious that Matthew does not understand 10:23 as a promise of the return of Jesus before the disciples go through all the cities of Palestine on their initial mission. Possibly Matthew understands 10:23 as referring to the proleptic parousia at the end of the gospel.

CHAPTER SIX

Commentary on Book III (Matt 11:1—13:53): The Son and the Kingdom Meet Opposition

I. MATT 11—12: CONTROVERSY SAYINGS AND NARRATIVES

The intimate association of Jesus and his disciples, seen in chapter 10, spills over into the Third Book of the gospel, which chronicles the widening breach between Jesus and the Jews, especially their leaders. When, for instance, at the beginning of the narrative section, the wavering Baptist sends his disciples to Jesus to address the Christological question to him, it is because John has heard of *ta erga tou Christou*, "the works of the Christ," or better, "the Messianic works." Now it is no accident that this statement follows directly upon the missionary discourse. The "Messianic works" include both the acts of Jesus in chapters 8 and 9 and the similar works for which the twelve disciples are empowered in chapter 10. The joyful scene of physical and spiritual wholeness in 10:5, which borrows phrases from Isaiah 35:5-6; 42:18; 61:1, embraces the activity of both Jesus and the twelve. Together, by performing these "works of the Messiah," they are inaugurating the eschatological age, the age of healing proclaimed by Isaiah.

No wonder the Baptist, that fiery herald of the fearful "Coming One" who would cut down the tree and burn the chaff (3:7-

12)—no wonder the Baptist is confused by this humble, healing servant and his followers! After Jesus explains the true understanding of his mission to John's disciples, he turns to the crowds to give them a true understanding of John. More than a mere prophet, John was the messenger whom God had promised to send ahead of the Messiah, to prepare his way (11:10, quoting Exod 23:20 and Mal 3:1). Indeed, John is the greatest man in the world—but only in this human world, this present and passing age. Jesus' words suddenly turn around to make a negative comparison: "But the least in the Kingdom of heaven is greater than he." Given the whole context of the last few chapters, Jesus is indicating the superior, privileged role of the disciples who are closely associated with Jesus in proclaiming the Kingdom. In the mind of Matthew, unlike that of Mark, the true disciple *does* understand who Jesus is. This makes the disciple's position—and ministry—infinitely superior to that of the Baptist. The Baptist was indeed the eschatological preparer (v. 10), a kind of Elijah (v. 14). He is the greatest of all the Old Testament prophets and witnesses; in him all the prophesying activity of the prophets and the Law reaches its final expression.[49] But, obviously, the fulfiller of all prophecy is superior even to the super-prophet John. And, consequently, the disciples who understand Jesus and his fulfilling activity are superior to the herald who was operating with antiquated conceptions.

The idea of comparing John and Jesus leads to the next unit (11:16-19), in which Jesus himself, for the first time, expressly takes notice of the growing rejection of his mission by his own people. What was alluded to indirectly and by way of anticipation in chapter 10 (vv. 24-25, 32-33, 38) is now articulated fully. This fickle and moody generation, as inconstant as willful children at play, find John too ascetical and Jesus too worldly for their religious tastes (11:16-19).[50] Most important here is the designation

---

[49]Note in 11:13 Matthew's daring inversion of the almost invariable order of "Law and prophets." For Matthew, even the Law is subsumed under prophecy and is to be understood in analogy with prophecy. We will return to this verse in Part III.

[50]The precise meaning of the parable of the children at play is disputed; for one view, see O. Linton, "The Parables of the Children's Game," *NTS* 22 (1976) 159-179.

the earthly Jesus uses of himself in 11:19. Because this man Jesus seeks out sinners, tax collectors, and other no-accounts at parties and banquets, Jesus "the Son of Man" is reviled as a glutton and a drunkard. A more startling use of Son of Man could hardly be imagined. The title which in Jewish tradition was proper to some glorious eschatological champion or judge has already been used of the lowly, earthly servant, who nevertheless has transcendent power to forgive sins. But here, precisely in his search for sinners, it designates Jesus in all his vulnerability, his exposure to insult and humiliation.[51] Even the passion predictions cannot add all that much to the depths of insult expressed here. Son of Man is indeed a mysterious and multifaceted title.

The final phrase in verse 17 is also a mystery: "And wisdom is [literally, "was"] justified by her works."[52] The meaning in context must be that Jesus is justified not by the opinion of his audience, which is fickle and self-centered, but rather by the works of his ministry (the *erga* of v. 17 harks back to the *erga tou Christou* in v. 2). What is especially noteworthy here is that Matthew in verse 17 moves without a break from the designation of Jesus as Son of Man to the designation of Jesus as Wisdom. Grundmann suggests that Matthew, like Q before him, is preserving an old idea of the Son of Man as the appearance of Wisdom on earth.[53] The point of contact between the two concepts here is clear. The Son of Man, a transcendent or heavenly being in tradition, is, in the context of chapter 11, suffering rejection on earth. Likewise, the traditional Wisdom-myth represented Wisdom as coming down from heaven to seek a dwelling among men, only to suffer rejection by many, though she is accepted by those who recognize their own need. Despite his rejection by "this generation," Jesus, Son of Man and Wisdom, stands justified by his

---

[51] Of course, both title and context (e.g., the verb "came") indicate that Son of Man is not simply a variant of the personal pronoun. Even here there is a tone of solemnity and dignity; cf. H. Schürmann, *Das Lukasevangelium I* (Freiburg: Herder, 1969) 426 n. 134.

[52] The aorist may be a Semitic or a gnomic aorist; but, given the context, Matthew may be saying that the basic vindication has already taken place. "Works" rather than "children" seems to be the correct reading of the Matthean text ("children" being the correct Lukan reading).

[53] Grundmann, *Evangelium nach Matthäus*, 312.

messianic works—and by those of his believing disciples.[54]

In this context of the rejection of the Son of Man alias Wisdom, Jesus upbraids the cities which have refused to repent of their folly when divine Wisdom preached conversion and worked miracles (11:20-24; note the idea of miracles as a call to repentance). But, even at this critical juncture, the picture is not all dark.[55] Even if many of the Jews, in particular the Galilean cities (11:20) and the Pharisees (10:34), have rejected God's Wisdom because of their own supposed wisdom,[56] Jesus can still praise the Father for opening the eyes of Jesus' simple disciples to the eschatological revelation which Jesus the Son brings and is. The whole passage 11:25-30, which is made up of a prayer of praise to the Father (vv. 25-26), a word of revelation (v. 27), and an invitation to the believer (vv. 28-30), is suffused with the terminology of apocalyptic revelation and wisdom theology. Indeed, Matthew gives us here a fine example of that fusion of apocalyptic and sapiential themes which is characteristic not only of his gospel but also of a large part of the New Testament.[57]

In the first part of the pericope, the prayer of praise (vv.

---

[54]On this Wisdom-myth and Wisdom-Christology, cf. R. Brown, *The Gospel according to John I* (Garden City: Doubleday, 1966) cxxii-cxxv.

[55]Grundmann, *Evangelium nach Matthäus*, 316, suggests that the phrase, "at that time" in verse 25 means "at that critical, decisive turning point," when many Jews were rejecting Jesus.

[56]Contrast this dark background with the joyful context of praise and revelation which the pericope has in Luke 10:21-22; in Luke, the seventy-two disciples have just returned in joy from their successful mission (10:17, 20-21).

[57]I readily admit that the place of Wisdom-Christology in Matthew can at times be exaggerated. While M. Suggs, *Wisdom, Christology and Law in Matthew's Gospel* (Cambridge: Harvard U.P., 1970) tries to remain balanced in his judgment, F. Christ is perhaps too strong in his emphasis on Wisdom-Christology in the gospel tradition (cf. his *Jesus Sophia* [Zurich: Zwingli-Verlag, 1970]). M. Johnson has criticized Suggs' position in "Reflections on a Wisdom Approach to Matthew's Christology." *CBQ* 36 (1974) 44-64. Some of Johnson's points are well taken, but I do not think he does justice to Matthew 11:25-30. For criticism of Johnson's position, see E. Schweizer, "Christus und Gemeinde im Matthäusevangelium," in *Matthäus und seine Gemeinde* (Stuttgart: KBW, 1974) 54 n. 206.

25-26), Jesus thanks the Father, the Lord of the cosmos and of all salvation-history, for guiding his mysterious yet gracious plan to completion. The apocalyptic secrets of salvation (v. 25, *tauta*, "these things"), which were hidden from all eternity in heaven, have now, at the proper moment in the end-time, been revealed, not to all, but to the chosen ones. And, as usual, this end-time means the reversal of man's values and expectations. The elect of the end-time are not the religious establishment which could pride itself on its technical knowledge of the Mosaic Law ("the wise and the intelligent"). The chosen recipients of God's eschatological wisdom, his apocalyptic secrets, are rather the "no-accounts," the *'am ha'aretz*, the religious outcasts who do not observe punctiliously the Pharisees' traditions. These are the *nēpioi*, the mere children, the poor and meek of the beatitudes, who must rely totally on God's saving action because they know they have no religious claim or merit of their own. Yes, this is the gracious yet paradoxical plan of salvation willed by the Father (*eudokia*, v. 26).

In verse 27 the prayer of praise becomes a word of revelation, which speaks forth the fundamental apocalyptic secret now revealed to the elect. "All things" (*panta*) have been handed over by the Father to the Son. "All things" takes up the *tauta* ("these things") of verse 25 and so refers to the totality of apocalyptic secrets to be revealed. But these apocalyptic secrets do not involve esoteric road-maps for mystic journeys through the heavenly spheres or explanations of symbolic visions dealing with the various epochs of history, as is so often the case in Jewish apocalyptic. No, all the apocalyptic secrets of the end-time are reducible to one basic mystery: the mutual knowledge and relationship between the Father and the Son. Perhaps only in the Trinitarian baptismal formula at the end of the gospel (28:19) is the Son again put so clearly on a level of equality with the Father. In 11:27, each person is a mystery knowable directly only by the other. The knowledge and relationship form a unique, privileged, and exclusive mystery. The emphatic and exclusive formulation ("no one knows . . . nor does anyone know . . . except the one to whom. . . .") stresses that no one else can claim this mutual relationship as a right. The Son, and only the Son, is free to decide whom he shall admit to the apocalyptic mystery of Father and Son. The sons of the Kingdom, the sons of the Father, are such only by the free gift communicated by the Son, the unique revealer.[58] In almost Johannine fashion, the Son becomes not only revealer of the apocalyptic secret but also its content. He is not only the preacher of God's Wisdom; he is that Wisdom, revealed to the elect. The fusion of apocalyptic and sapiential themes in the service of a high Christology could not be clearer.[59]

The sapiential element comes to the fore most notably in the call or invitation of verses 28-30. The Son who is Wisdom speaks in the style of the personified Wisdom of the Old Testament, inviting all to enter into the apocalyptic mystery he brings and is (v. 28).[60] The restrictive phrase of verse 27, "no one knows . . . except the one to whom the Son wishes to reveal [him]," is now

[58]One can therefore understand why this logion has been called a meteor from the Johannine heavens. The mutual relation of knowledge between the Father and the Son, the unique status of the Son as revealer, and his sovereign freedom in choosing the recipients of the gift are all reminiscent of the Fourth Gospel. Yet we must remember that we are dealing with an early Q-formulation. We find Matthew 11:25-27 (but *not* verses 28-30) reduplicated almost word for word in Luke 10:21-22. In fact, this passage (indeed, the whole of Matthew 11) is one of the strongest arguments in favor of a written Q-document. Another reason for not giving Matthew 11:25-27 the label "Johannine" is that this theology of special revelation tied to Christology is not unique to this passage in Matthew. In Matthew 16:17, Christ pronounces a beatitude on Simon Peter because he is the archetypal recipient of apocalyptic revelation from the Father about the Son. On this point, see C. Kähler, "Zur Form- und Traditionsgeschichte von Matth. xvi. 17-19," *NTS* 23 (1976-77) 36-58.

[59]This is certainly the case in Matthew's theology; compare Luke 11:49 ("Therefore also the Wisdom of God said: 'I send to them prophets and apostles' ") with Matthew 23:34 ("Therefore *I* send to you prophets and wise men and scribes").

[60]For the call of Wisdom, see Proverbs, chapters 1, 8, and 9, especially 9:3, 5; Sir 51:23, 26, 27 (note in the Septuagint the connection of labor, yoke, and finding rest); Sir 6:24-28 (again, the connection of seeking wisdom, submitting to her yoke, and finding rest). Cf. also Jeremiah 6:16 ("You shall find rest for your souls") and Jeremiah 31:25 (just before the promise of the new covenant). On 11:28-30, cf. M. Maher, " 'Take my yoke upon you' (Matt. xi. 29)," *NTS* 22 (1975) 97-103, though the author does not distinguish clearly enough between the level of the historical Jesus and the level of the evangelist.

interpreted in a broad sense. "All" those who suffer under the yoke of the Law as interpreted by the Pharisees, with its 613 commandments and endless oral traditions attached, are invited to come not to another abstract doctrine or legal system, but "to me," to divine Wisdom in person. Jesus the Son, the apocalyptic revealer, the Wisdom of God, will give these poor the eschatological rest promised to God's people by his prophets, promised to those in need of instruction by the wisdom-teachers of Israel. Instead of the yoke of the Mosaic Law as interpreted by the overbearing Pharisees, the poor are to accept the yoke of Wisdom's apocalyptic revelation, which, as we have seen, is reducible to the relation of the Father and the Son. That is why Jesus can say, "Learn from me," without bothering to state any direct object of the learning. He is both teacher and content taught, the very basis and embodiment of the morality he demands. This yoke of apocalyptic Wisdom will, despite the designation "yoke," mean liberation and relief after the legalistic yoke of the Pharisees. For Wisdom in the person of Jesus is not a harsh taskmaster and a casuistic hair-splitter. Rather, he is the archetypal poor man of the beatitudes, meek and humble of heart, patient and kind toward sinners, totally dedicated and obedient to God. We find in this motif of Jesus as Wisdom the same paradox of divine transcendence united with human lowliness which we have already seen in the Son of Man-servant motif (recall 8:17, 20; 9:6; 10:23; 11:19). Now we can understand the strange conjunction in the same verse (11:19) of Jesus as earthly, despised Son of Man and Jesus as Wisdom vindicated by her works despite her rejection. One can only marvel at the breadth and varied resonance Matthew gives to his Son of Man Christology.

Two final points should be made concerning 11:25-30. (1) We have seen that "these things" (v. 25) and "all things" (v. 27) refer to the apocalyptic mysteries handed on by the Father to the Son and by the Son to the disciples. These apocalyptic mysteries are reducible to the secret of the relation of Father and Son, as revealed by divine Wisdom (the Son) in human form. The whole context is apocalyptic and sapiential, referring to the act of revelation. Consequently, despite the many contacts with Matthew 28:16-20, "all things have been given to me by my Father" is not to be completely equated with the declaration of the risen Jesus in

28:18, "all power in heaven and on earth has been given to me." While the context in 11:27 is the apocalyptic revelation of Wisdom, the context in 28:18 is the cosmic power bestowed on Jesus the Son of Man in virtue of his resurrection-exaltation. In 11:27 Jesus is seen as Son of Man and revealer even during his humble earthly life. In 28:18 he is seen as Son of Man and cosmocrator after the resurrection. Certainly, for Matthew, Jesus is not Son of Man and cosmocrator before his resurrection. The Son of Man ruling the cosmos in the explanation of the parable of the wheat and the tares is obviously the risen Jesus (cf. 13:37-38). It is not by chance, then, that, while Matthew uses the adjective "all" (*pas*) and the noun "authority" (*exousia*) frequently in the gospel, the phrase "all power" (*pasa exousia*) occurs in reference to Jesus' *exousia* only in 28:18, after the resurrection, after he is exalted as Son of Man to the status and function of cosmocrator. We shall return to this point when we treat 28:16-20.

(2) I have spoken of 11:25-30 as containing a Wisdom-Christology which is connected to the humble, rejected Son of Man in 11:19, where Wisdom is also mentioned. But some would no doubt object that 11:27 speaks of *the* Son, alongside of *the* or *my* Father, and that therefore the verse contains a Son of God Christology. But this is to suppose a vital point which must be proven: namely, that the absolute use of "*the* Son" is completely equivalent to and convertible with the title Son of God.[61] I would suggest that this simple equation is questionable. I do not deny that the titles *the* Son and Son of God are related, but the background and overtones of *the* Son are more complex than a simple equation. In his treatment of the Trinitarian formula in 28:19, E. Lohmeyer sees a connection between this triad and the Jewish apocalyptic "Trinity" of the Lord of the spirits (God), the Son of Man (or the Elect One), and the angels[62]—a pattern which one

---

[61]This seems to be a presupposition of Kingsbury's *Matthew: Structure, Christology, Kingdom* which is never fully examined; cf. pp. 63-65.

[62]E. Lohmeyer, *Das Evangelium des Matthäus* (ed. W. Schmauch; Göttingen: Vandenhoeck & Ruprecht, 1967) 413. Care must be taken, however, with those passages cited from the so-called Parables or Similitudes of Enoch. J. Milik claims that this section of the Enoch literature is Christian in origin, though Fitzmyer shows some reserve on the question; cf. J. Fitzmyer, "Implications of the New Enoch Literature from Qumran," *TS* 38 (1977) 332-345.

could also see reflected in Mark 8:38, with "Son of Man" (parallels in Matt 16:27; Luke 9:26), and in Mark 13:32, with *the* Son (parallels in Matt 24:36). One can also see the same pattern reflected outside the gospel tradition, in 1 Thessalonians 3:13 and 2 Thessalonians 1:7-8. Such examples should caution us about lumping together *the* Son with Son of God. As F. Hahn stresses: "The absolute *ho huios* [*the* Son] has to be examined separately. . . . In all the tradition about Jesus as the 'Son of God' the fatherhood of God and his union with the Father do not play any recognizable role; a distinction has therefore to be drawn between 'Son of God' and 'Son-Father.' "[63]

Hahn mentions the frequently suggested derivation of *the* Son from Son of Man (among others, Percy and Sjöberg have held this opinion). Hahn himself prefers a derivation from Jesus' characteristic use of *Abba*.[64] Yet the main point, I think, remains valid: *the* Son is not automatically to be equated with Son of God, and a number of exegetes have rather connected it with Son of Man. I would prefer to see *the* Son as having connections with both of the fuller Son-titles. By the time of Matthew, a cross-fertilization (or mutual contamination?) of titles has set in. While, therefore, I would not want to exclude all overtones of Son of God in 11:25-30, I definitely think that the larger context (especially 11:19) and the dominant motif of apocalyptic revelation suggest a connection with Son of Man as well. Chapter 11 as a whole thus confirms and broadens the important theological role Son of Man plays in the gospel.

The growing breach between Jesus and the Jews which Matthew conveyed mostly by sayings-material in chapter 11 is now documented by narrative as well as sayings in chapter 12. The motif of conflict was already struck in 9:3, with the scribes, and 9:34, with the Pharisees. In chapter 12, the mere rejection of Jesus turns into mortal hatred and a firm resolution on the part of the Pharisees (and also in 12:38 on the part of the scribes) to kill Jesus. It is not by accident that the first use of Son of Man in connection with death and resurrection occurs in this chapter. Although some of the sayings-material is loosely strung together,

---

[63]F. Hahn, *The Titles of Jesus in Christology* (London: Lutterworth, 1969) 307, 313.

[64]*Idem*, 309, 313.

the chapter can be conveniently divided into six sections.

1. The first Sabbath conflict arises from plucking the grain (12:1-8). Matthew edits Mark to highlight his theme of the transcendent, authoritative Son of Man who is nevertheless the merciful defender of those despised by the Pharisees. To Mark's *a fortiori* argument about David and the showbread (which is not terribly clear), Matthew adds a clearer *a fortiori* argument about the priests working in the Temple (here at least the Sabbath is explicitly mentioned). While the *a fortiori* argument from the showbread is not spelled out to its conclusion, the argument from the Temple is: "But I say to you that something greater than the Temple is here" (12:5-6).[65] When we remember that, at the cross, Matthew expands upon the apocalyptic signs which begin with the rending of the Temple veil (27:51), we can recognize the Christological thrust of Matthew's addition. In his very person, and finally by his sacrificial death, Jesus replaces the Temple and all the sacrifices prescribed by the Law. The mercy which prompts Christ to save his people is brought out at the end of verse 6, with the same citation of Hosea 6:6 which we saw in Matthew 9:13. The will of God in Scripture which Jesus, not the Pharisees, is safeguarding and fulfilling has been made clear by the prophets: not sacrificial cult but forgiving love is what God seeks from man. The Law Jesus fulfills was never meant to become a blunt weapon which the self-righteous could use to condemn the untutored in the Law, people who are nevertheless the truly innocent ones, the poor and the meek. Matthew then brings this Christological emphasis to a climax by omitting Mark's humanitarian consideration (Mark 2:27: "The Sabbath was made for man, not man for the Sabbath"). Matthew's additions thus flow immediately into the Christological conclusion: "For the Son of Man is Lord of the Sabbath" (Matt 12:8). The transcendent Son of Man, who is superior to such sacred institutions of the Law as the Temple and the Sabbath, is nevertheless the one

---

[65]The statement about something greater than the Temple may have been patterned by Matthew on the Q-logia about something greater than Jonah and Solomon. Certainly, in Matthew's composition, 12:6 points forward to and links up with 12:41-42.

who concerns himself about obtaining mercy for the despised, the one who defends the poor and innocent against the casuists. Once again we have the paradox of the authoritative Son of Man who humbles himself to play the role of merciful servant.[66]

2. The second Sabbath conflict revolves around a man with a withered hand in "*their* synagogue." Matthew again inserts an *a fortiori* argument: how much more important is a man than a sheep (cf. the similar argument in Luke 14:5; 13:15). Jesus uses the institutions of the Law like the Sabbath as occasions for doing good, i.e., God's will. But the Pharisees, plunging further and further into the spiritual blindness of their malice, take a decisive and terrible step. For the first time in the gospel, they specifically plot to kill Jesus (12:14). Now, while Matthew does not repeat verse 8 ("The Son of Man is Lord of the Sabbath") at the end of the second story of Sabbath conflict, no doubt it is the rubric over both stories. Because Jesus as Son of Man has claimed transcendent authority over the sacred institution of the Sabbath, and has even claimed to be superior to the Temple, he must be put to death.

3. Quite fittingly, the first mention of the death-plot occasions a citation from another passage of Isaiah's servant songs. Despite his transcendent authority as Son of Man, Jesus meekly withdraws in the face of the Pharisees' deadly machinations; the time is not yet ripe for the final clash. But this withdrawal does not mean a cessation of his ministry. The all-powerful servant continues to heal, though now in secrecy.[67] Matthew cites the servant song of Isaiah 42:1-4, perhaps with a glance at Isaiah 41:18 and 44:2. The reference to "my beloved" (v. 18) gives a neat cross-reference to the Son of God epiphanies at the baptism and the transfiguration (3:17; 17:5). Just as those supernatural manifestations revealed him to be Son of God, so too his humility

---

[66]Admittedly, the servant-theme becomes clear only in the light of what follows (12:14, 15-21).

[67]Although taken over from Mark 3:12, Matthew 12:16 is not a programmatic expression of a Messianic-secret theory. It is a practical measure taken in response to the Pharisees' threat, and exemplifies what the prophet says in verse 19.

and healing ministry reveal him to be the servant.[68] His mission is not one of strife, punishment, and destruction (vv. 19-20) but rather one of forgiveness and healing. And this will hold true even of the most despised of mankind, the Gentiles. Even they will obey the servant's teaching (v. 18) and place their hope in him (v. 21, "name" equaling "person"). Proleptically, this is realized during the public ministry by the centurion and the Canaanite woman; the full realization comes in the final commission (28:19).

4. In 12:22-37, Jesus rejects the Jewish charge of being in league with Beelzebul.[69] The healing activity which Matthew reports in 12:15 occasions a split among the Jews: the vacillating crowds ask half in amazement, half in disbelief: "Is this perhaps the Son of David?" "Could this possibly be the Son of David?"[70] As we have seen already, Son of David refers to Jesus especially in his healing ministry to the "no-accounts" of Israel. The "somebodies" in Israel, the Pharisees, intervene to try to prevent the crowds from reaching the obvious conclusion. They attempt to explain away Jesus' healing power by the malicious suggestion that he is in league with the prince of devils. Thus they try to reduce him to the status of a magician and implicitly make him liable to death. In rejecting this charge, Jesus stresses his es-

---

[68]There is an interesting parallel between 12:18-21 and the other formula quotation taken from a servant song, 8:17. In both cases, at least part of the context which triggers the citation is the healing ministry of Jesus, and in both cases the title Son of Man occurs in the wider context (8:20; 12:9).

[69]Matthew had anticipated the theme of division and hostility in his pale copy of this pericope in 9:32-34.

[70]Kingsbury, *Matthew: Structure, Christology, Kingdom*, 101, points out that the crowds frame the question negatively, for Israel does not recognize Jesus to be the Son of David. But *mēti*, the negative particle introducing a question, can also be used in questions where the answer is in doubt. W. Bauer, *A Greek-English Lexicon of the New Testament* (Chicago: Chicago U.P., 1957) 522, counts 12:23 as a case where the particle indicates doubt, not negation; cf. the question of the Samaritan woman in John 4:29. The pale mirror-reflection in 9:32-34, probably a creation of Matthew, argues for a positive meaning of the crowds' question in 12:23. In 9:34 the marveling crowds say: "Never has any such thing appeared in Israel." Rather than rejecting Jesus during the public ministry, the crowds play a vacillating role.

chatological nature. He possesses the spirit of God, the power of the Kingdom of God, and therefore Jesus is the eschatological figure who alone is stronger than the "strong one," Satan, who holds this present evil age under his control. Jesus is the eschatological conqueror who smashes the rule of Satan over the world. The meek servant is nevertheless the powerful destroyer of the anti-Kingdom, as is made clear by the action of the spirit in and through him. Since Jesus is Son of Man in mystery, in hiddenness, one might fail to recognize the transcendent one in his lowliness. The Son of Man, who has power to forgive sins, will forgive that sin. But to be confronted by a startling demonstration of the eschatological spirit and to sin against the light by attributing the work of the spirit to a diabolical origin—that is a willful closing of the eyes for which there can be no forgiveness. Again, Son of Man appears to signify the paradox of the heavenly one in humble earthly form.

5. In 12:38-45, Jesus rejects the Jewish request for a legitimating sign which would prove that Jesus' miracles come from God, not Satan. The Jews who refuse to believe in Jesus are a faithless generation which breaks the covenant with God ("adulterous" in v. 39). The only sign which will be given will be the mysterious sign of Jonah. While Luke 11:29-30 interprets "sign of Jonah" to mean the sign which Jonah was to the Ninevites by his call to repentance, Matthew allegorizes the story of Jonah in the fish and applies it to the death and resurrection of the Son of Man. Matthew thus creates a passion prediction concerning the Son of Man before the three traditional Markan passion predictions (Mark 8:31; 9:31; 10:33 = Matt 16:21; 17:22-23; 20:18-19), just as he adds another passion prediction with Son of Man after the Markan series (at the beginning of the passion narrative itself, 26:2). Thus, by his composition in 12:39-40, Matthew has again emphasized and enriched his theology of Son of Man. The Son of Man will be the suffering yet vindicated servant, who is also the culmination of the whole prophetic line including Jonah. Moreover, this suffering servant knows all beforehand. If he goes to his death, it is with full prophetic knowledge of what will happen. He is not suddenly overtaken by tragic events; he willingly marches toward them with the authority the Son of Man pos-

sesses even on earth.[71] Of course, Jesus as the fulfiller of all the prophets is not to be made into just another prophet. Something greater than Jonah, indeed something greater than all the prophets who preached conversion, is here (12:41). The Son of Man who preaches conversion and offers forgiveness to this generation during his earthly life, and who offers up his life unto the remission of sins to make a new world possible for the penitent, is the same Son of Man who will condemn this impenitent generation "on the day of judgment" (vv. 41-42). Matthew's theology of Son of Man even receives its characteristic sapiential overtones by the mention of the "wisdom of Solomon" in verse 42. The Son of Man is indeed something greater than Solomon, the archetypal teacher of wisdom, for the Son of Man *is* the Wisdom of God. Hence the fearful destiny which awaits this generation if it will not repent. The stronger one has come and given it a certain initial liberation from the evil one. If this generation simply relaxes in the freedom given it and does not heed the prophetic call to repentance contained in the exorcisms, then its last state will be worse than the first, then the sin against the Holy Spirit will be complete.

The final narrative of the Third Book (12:46-50) turns the readers' eyes from the generation which rejects Jesus to those who accept him: the disciples who are forming around Jesus a new community.[72] With regard to the relatives of Jesus, Matthew

---

[71]That Jesus is cast very much in a prophetic light by Matthew is one of the major theses of the monograph by A. Sand, *Das Gesetz und die Propheten* (Regensburg: Pustet, 1974).

[72]Thus Matthew anticipates a major theme of the Fourth Book. In fact, at the end of the narrative of each book, Matthew looks across the discourse immediately following to the theme of the narratives of the next book. In Book One, 4:23-24, he mentions the healings narrated in chapters 8-9 of Book Two. In Book Two, 9:33-34, he mentions the puzzled amazement of the crowds and the blasphemy of the Pharisees, who attribute an exorcism to the prince of devils. Thus Matthew anticipates not only the exorcism-dispute in 12:22ff. but also the whole theme of the widening breach between Jesus and Judaism. In Book Three, 12:46-50 points ahead to the ecclesiological concerns of Book Four. In Book Four, the second prediction of the passion (17:22-23) and the appearance of the Jewish officials collecting the *Temple* tax point forward to the fateful journey to Jerusalem and the final clash with the Jewish authorities in the Temple in Book Five.

softens the harshness of the Markan material,[73] though the relatives are still left standing outside. Matthew's main concern, however, is not polemics against relatives. They are used only as a foil to highlight the true family of Jesus, namely "his disciples" (Matt 12:49, a notable change from Mark 3:34: "those sitting around him"). The disciples are "those who do the will of my Father in heaven" (Matt 12:50, while Mark 3:35 has "the will of God"). Matthew's changes again reflect perfectly his weaving together of Christology and ecclesiology. Jesus the Son, who alone knows the Father directly (11:27), communicates a share in this divine relationship by communicating his teaching to the true disciples, who are willing to do the will of the Father (cf. the whole of 11:25-30). By following perfectly the teaching of Jesus, especially his way of love and mercy, they "become sons of *your* Father in heaven" (5:45). The Son, by his very teaching, is mediator of sonship to his disciples, his church. They are the group which stands at the end of the narrative of Book Three in stark contrast to a Judaism which shows ever increasing hostility to its Messiah.

II. MATT 13: THE PARABLE DISCOURSE

The discourse which concludes the Third Book of the ministry is the parable discourse (13:1-51).[74] In keeping with the narratives of Book Three, the parables portray the breach between

---

[73]Especially by omitting Mark 3:20-21.

[74]Obviously, both space and the scope of our investigation do not permit a detailed exegesis of the parables. Our goal in Part II restricts us to one main question: What Christology appears in the discourse? For the parables in general, cf. J. Jeremias, *The Parables of Jesus*[2] (N.Y.: Scribner's 1972); C. H. Dodd, *The Parables of the Kingdom* (London: Collins, 1965); D. Via, *The Parables* (Philadelphia: Fortress, 1967); N. Perrin, *Jesus and the Language of the Kingdom* (Philadelphia: Fortress, 1976); M. Boucher, *The Mysterious Parable* (Washington: CBA, 1977); and the *Semeia* volumes on parables and structuralism, published by the SBL. For Matthean redaction of the parables, see J. Kingsbury, *The Parables of Jesus in Matthew 13* (Richmond: John Knox, 1969); and C. Carlston, *The Parables of the Triple Tradition* (Philadelphia: Fortress, 1975) especially pp. 3-51.

Jesus and Israel widening to the breaking point. The very fact that Jesus now withdraws into a parabolic form of teaching is a sign of judgment upon Israel. Mark places his parable chapter near the beginning of the ministry (chap. 4). In Mark, Jesus has not first tried to present his teaching clearly, only to withdraw into parables when he is rejected. In Mark, Jesus speaks in parables from the beginning "in order that" the crowd, the outsiders, may not see or understand (Mark 4:12). All this is connected with Mark's "messianic secret" and his particular treatment of the hardening of Israel. In contrast, Matthew 13:13 has Jesus speaking in parables to the crowds "because" they do not see or understand. The Jewish crowds have had their chance from the fourth chapter of Matthew's gospel onward. But, especially in the case of the Galilean cities and the Pharisees, they have rejected Jesus with hostility; even at best, they have remained vacillating. So now, in an act of judgment, Jesus draws the veil of the parables over his teaching. For the outsiders, who for Matthew and his church equal the Jews, everything is now taught in unintelligible riddles.[75] Only the disciples, who possess faith and understanding, are given explanations. This division is even acted out within chapter 13. At verse 36 we are told: "Then leaving the crowds, he entered the house." The Jews become physically the outsiders, while only his disciples may enter into the house (the church?) and receive the explanation of the parable of the wheat and the tares. The separation of Jesus (and his church) from Israel could not be clearer. The Jews, like the relatives of Jesus, are left standing outside.

Putting aside the great parabolic themes of Kingdom (growth and contrast), of church (separation from Israel, mixture of good and bad), and discipleship (total commitment because of total joy), we must seek out the Christology implied in the parables. As so often in Matthean discourses, Christological titles are not prominent. What Jesus does and says spells out the Christology. Preeminently, then, Jesus appears in chapter 13 as a teacher,

---

[75]When Matthew 13:34-35 takes over Mark 4:33-34 (on Jesus' use of parables), Matthew drops Mark's statement that Jesus spoke parables to the crowds "as they were able to hear" (Mark 4:33).

specifically a teacher of wisdom, since the *meshalîm* (parables) were a privileged form of Old Testament and Jewish teaching on matters of wisdom.

Jesus' magisterial role is emphasized by the twofold use of "sit" (the ancient posture of teachers) in 13:1-2. In the separation between blinded Jews and seeing disciples which follows, Jesus is once again acting as the fulfiller of Law and prophets (this time, of Isa 6:9-10). Indeed, he relives and fulfills the bitter experience of Isaiah himself. Many prophets and just men of the Old Testament longed to look upon the eschatological fulfillment the disciples see (v. 17). And so in true sapiential fashion, Jesus pronounces a beatitude on the disciples. Of course, beatitudes had also passed over into the rhetoric of apocalyptic; here again we see the two streams of wisdom and apocalyptic coming together in Matthew's Jesus. The same combination can be seen in the short statement on the use of parables in 13:34-35. For the only time in Matthew, the evangelist cites a psalm-verse in a formula quotation. It is a sapiential psalm (Ps 78:2), which Matthew nevertheless ascribes to "the prophet," a perfect example of how Matthew subsumes all Scripture under prophecy. The idea of uttering in the end-time things hidden from the foundation (of the world) also has a touch of apocalyptic.

It is fitting that this statement should be followed by an apocalyptic scenario, the explanation of the wheat and the tares. Since the explanation (almost a catalogue giving a point by point, allegorical interpretation of the parable) is probably Matthew's own creation, we have a prime example of his own Christological thought. Most interestingly, the one who places good disciples in this present world is the Son of Man. The field is to be interpreted universally. It refers to the world, and not simply to the church,[76] though the situation and problems of the church are no doubt in Matthew's mind. But Son of Man and world go perfectly together, for both have a cosmic dimension. By his resurrection, Jesus has been exalted to all power over heaven and earth (28:19). The

---

[76]This is brought out well by J. Dupont, "Le point de vue de Matthieu dans le chapitre des paraboles," in *L'Evangile selon Matthieu: Rédaction et théologie* (ed. M. Didier; Gembloux: Duculot, 1972) 229.

resurrection has made him cosmocrator, something he was not before. And the proper title for this cosmocrator *presently* reigning over the world is not Lord (*kyrios*) but Son of Man. This is important to remember, because we automatically tend to equate the exalted Christ presently reigning over the cosmos with the title *kyrios*. Yet Matthew, both in 13:34-38 and by allusion in 28:19, ties the concept of cosmocrator to Son of Man. Once again, we see that Son of Man cannot be restricted, in its Matthean specificity, to the parousia. The exalted Jesus is now the Son of Man reigning over the world. The present world, for all its mixture of good and evil, is even now the Kingdom of the Son of Man (v. 41). Especially intriguing is the reference to the seed planted by the *Son* of Man: they are the *sons* of the Kingdom, who at the consummation will shine in the Kingdom of *their* Father. Do we have here a suggestion that the Son of Man, by sowing the good seed, communicates to the believer a share in sonship (cf. 11:25-30; 12:46-50)?

At any rate, at the consummation we again meet an apocalyptic "Trinity": Son of Man, angels, and the Father (vv. 41-43). What is noteworthy here is that the same person, the Son of Man, who is the main agent in this present age, is also the main agent (through *his* angels) at the end of the age. The union in the same Jesus of present cosmic rule and future judgment is perfectly expressed by Son of Man.[77] It is most fitting that "the end of the age" (*tē synteleia tou aiōnos*), a phrase unique to Matthew among the four gospels, should occur outside of 13:39-40, 49, and 24:3 (the apocalyptic discourse) only at 28:20.[78] There, too, the Son of Man who has just entered upon his cosmic reign by his

---

[77]This is seen by Kingsbury in *The Parables of Jesus*, 133; on p. 99 he rightly disputes Tödt's attempt to refer 13:37 to the earthly Jesus. However, in his *Matthew: Structure, Christology, Kingdom*, Kingsbury plays down the present activity of the Son of Man in favor of Son of God (pp. 113-122).

[78]At 24:3 it occurs in conjunction with "your coming" (parousia). Matthew obviously understands *parousia* and *synteleia* in verse 3 in reference to the coming of the Son of Man, as is made clear by the phrase "the coming of the Son of Man" in 24:27, 37, 39, and by the description of the parousia in 24:30-31. Note, by the way, how 24:31 echoes 13:41.

resurrection gives the mandate to sow good seed throughout the field of the world until he comes in glory as Son of Man at the consummation. The explanation of the parable of the wheat and the tares is also an excellent explanation of 28:16-20. And in both passages, Son of Man is the central Christological concept. When we remember that Son of Man is the only explicit Christological title used by Matthew in chapter 13, and that he himself has introduced it in a double present-future reference, we can only conclude that the title gives Matthew's own Christological interpretation of the various parables of growth and consummation (sower, wheat and tares, mustard seed, leaven).[79] The only explicit Christology of the parable chapter is a Son of Man Christology. The Christology of the discourse ending Book Three thus matches the Christology of the narrative.

---

[79]No doubt it is also presupposed at the end of the parable of the net, 13:49-50, which portrays the "consummation of the age" in terms similar to 13:41-42.

CHAPTER SEVEN

Commentary on Book IV
(Matt 13:53—19:1):
The Son and His Church

I. MATT 13:53—16:12: CHRIST WITHDRAWS HIS
CHURCH FROM JUDAISM

With 13:53 we begin Book Four, the formation of the disciples into the embryonic church. It is in this Book that the nexus between Christology and ecclesiology receives its sharpest expression. Certain ecclesiological references or overtones were already present in the Markan material (Mark 6-9) which Matthew takes over in large part for the stories of Book Four.[80] Mark

---

[80]In taking over Mark 6-9, Matthew does alter the structure of the Markan material at one important point. Mark 6:6b-8:33 is the culmination of the first part of the gospel, the Mystery of the Messiah. Mark 6:6b-8:33 is known as the bread section, not only because it is structured in two cycles around the two multiplications of loaves, but also because many of the other pericopes contain "bread" as a catchword. The bread section and the whole first part of the gospel reach their climax in Peter's confession, 8:27-33. With 8:31, the second part of the gospel, the mystery of the Son of Man begins. For a number of reasons, Matthew does not follow this structure. First of all, the two-part structure of the gospel does not serve his intention, since he does not develop a theory of the messianic secret. Second, he does not reserve sayings about the humiliation, suffering, death, and resurrection of the Son of Man to the second half of his gospel. Here he differs notably from Mark. In the first half of his gospel, Mark never uses Son of Man in reference to suffering or

already presented Jesus concentrating on the formation of his disciples as he travels about, inside and outside Galilee. The eucharistic nuances in the two accounts of the miraculous feeding, the abrogation of certain Jewish laws (even those contained in the Old Testament), the mercy shown to a Gentile woman, the warning against Jewish leaders, Peter's confession, the call to the disciples to follow the Master on the way of the cross, the power of the disciples to cast out unclean spirits, the disputes about who is greatest, the problem of scandal: all these Markan elements lay waiting for Matthew to use in his fusion of Christology and ecclesiology. As we shall see, Matthew adds as well as exploits. In particular, his expansion of the story of Peter's confession (16:13-28) and his addition of the discourse on the church in chapter 18 give the Fourth Book a clearer ecclesiological tone, while at the same time (especially in 16:13-28; 18:20) heightening its Christology.

In the first narrative of Book Four (13:53-58), Matthew indicates one reason why Jesus turns toward his small group of followers to form them as his future community: even his own home town rejects his teaching and refuses to believe.[81] His fel-

---

death; Mark 2:10 and 2:28 refer to Jesus' transcendent power to forgive sins and overrule Sabbath regulations. Only after Peter's profession at Caesarea Philippi does Mark use Son of Man in the context of suffering (8:31). In contrast, as we have seen, the first half of Matthew's gospel contains a number of sayings referring to the humble, suffering, even dying Son of Man (Matt 8:20; 11:19; 12:32 (?); 12:40). Especially in the light of 12:40 (death and resurrection of the Son of Man), the first passion prediction (Matt 16:21) cannot mark the same démarche in Matthew as it does in Mark (especially since Son of Man does not even occur in Matthew's first passion prediction). Third, Matthew clearly marks off Book Four by the discourse on church-life, which neatly rounds off the ecclesiological interests of 13:53-17:27. For these reasons, I would not agree with Kingsbury, who sees a major division of the gospel at 16:21 (*Matthew: Structure*, 7-25). Such a view simply takes over the main division of Mark with too little consideration of the restructuring activity of Matthew. Moreover, it asks the "fixed formula" ("from that time on Jesus began. . . .") to bear too much weight, especially since the supposed "fixed formula" occurs only one other time in the gospel (4:17).

[81]*Apistia*, unbelief, occurs here for the only time in Matthew's gospel. That this is a fiercely negative judgment on a group which Matthew

low townspeople, typifying Israel as a whole, are scandalized at the Wisdom of God coming in the form of a son of an artisan. He is too much like them to be the transcendent One. Again Jesus suffers rejection at the hands of the chosen people, as did the prophets of old (13:57). Yet even in rejection Jesus cannot be portrayed as suffering any real loss of majesty or power. Mark's embarrassing "he could not perform any miracle there . . . and he marveled at their unbelief" is changed by Matthew to the more reverent "he did not perform many miracles there because of their unbelief." This absence of miracles must be traced to Christ's free choice and his reaction to his rejection.

A second reason why Jesus urgently turns toward his fledgling community of disciples is that the dark clouds of martyrdom are already on the horizon. "At that time" (14:1), the time of his rejection by his own townspeople, Herod is also taking an unhealthy interest in Jesus.[82] Herod has martyred the Baptist, and now he thinks Jesus is the Baptist raised from the dead. Thus, unwittingly, Herod makes the Baptist prefigure the paschal mystery Jesus is to fulfill in Jerusalem. Matthew, as is his wont, condenses Mark's narrative to the bare minimum. One almost gets the impression that Matthew would have gladly omitted it except for the precious themes of increasing rejection and danger, now made brutally plain by the prophetic death of the Baptist. Indeed, Matthew changes Mark's description of the Baptist (Mark 6:20, "a just and holy man") to "prophet" (Matt 14:5). The Baptist prophesies even in his death the road which the Son of Man must travel (cf. Matt 17:10-13). Most significant is the connection of the end of the story of the Baptist's martyrdom with

___

sees as the type of the whole generation which rejected Jesus is suggested by the only occurrence of the related adjective *apistos* (unbelieving) in the gospel, Matthew 17:17: "O unbelieving and perverse generation!"

[82]Matthew does not use this small section of Mark 6:14-16 to create an inclusion with Peter's profession at Caesarea Philippi, as Mark does (Mark 8:27-28). By dropping the superstitious speculation about Elijah or one of the other prophets (Mark 6:15), Matthew shows he is interested only in the Baptist, the martyred prophet whose fate, like his person and preaching, foretells the way of Jesus the Son of Man. Matthew returns to this point and explains it toward the end of Book Four, in Matthew 17:10-13.

the next pericope in Matthew, the feeding of the five thousand (14:13-21). In Mark, there is no announcement of the Baptist's death to Jesus, and a pericope about the return of the apostles from their mission is narrated. The withdrawal into the desert is thus for the sake of the apostles, to give them some rest. In Matthew, on the contrary, the disciples of the Baptist announce his death to Jesus (Matt 14:12) and immediately upon hearing it Jesus withdraws into the desert (14:13). We are reminded of the withdrawal of Jesus in the face of the plot of the Pharisees to kill him (12:15). In 12:15 as in 14:13, the same verb for "withdraw" *(anechōrēsen)* is used; in fact, it has not been used since 12:15. Once again, we have the picture of the humble, suffering servant who must withdraw in the face of hostility. Yet immediately we are given a picture of Jesus as the merciful healer of his people (14:14), who miraculously feeds his followers with bread through the ministry of his disciples (14:19).

The references to church, ministry, and eucharist are clear. The foundation and nourishment of the church by Jesus is fittingly prefigured here, in the most ecclesiological of Matthew's five books. As always in these ecclesiological pericopes, Christ himself stands at the center. For Matthew, to have an ecclesiology that was not totally dependent on Christology would be unthinkable. It cannot be a question either of playing one off against the other or of absorbing one into the other. Both realities, and the vital connection between the two, are what interests Matthew. Yet not for a moment does he forget which is dependent on the other. High Christology is what makes high ecclesiology possible.

The dependence of ecclesiology on Christology is underscored in the pericope of the walking on the water (Matt 14:22-33). Even in Mark, there is an interweaving of ecclesiology with Christology. The disciples in the sinking boat, overwhelmed by the waters which in the Old Testament symbolize chaos, death, and sin, are a perfect symbol of the church battered by the tempests of this world. The wind is always against it. Toward the end of the night, when all seems lost, Jesus comes bestriding the waves of the storm. It is, of course, a manifestation of divine power over the forces of chaos, a theophany similar to those of

Yahweh in the Old Testament.[83] Matthew stresses the fear of the disciples in the presence of this theophany—another motif common to such Old Testament appearances of the divinity. Jesus calms their fear (and not first of all the storm)[84] with the stock words of the divinity in theophanies: "Fear not." He also speaks the triumphant and consoling formula of self-revelation: *egō eimi*, literally, "I am." One should not read into this the full Johannine theology contained in the "I am" statements of the fourth gospel. And yet the solemn proclamation should not be reduced in Matthew to a mere "it is I." Like the divinity appearing to console, help, or save his troubled worshipers, Jesus proclaims to his imperiled community: See, I am present to save you. We are reminded of the various prophetic oracles in the Old Testament which read: "Fear not, for I am with you, to save you, says the Lord."

Thus far, Matthew has been following Mark closely. Starting with verse 28, Matthew stresses his own ecclesial and Petrine concerns. So encouraging is this theophany and word of self-revelation that Peter, the leader of the disciples,[85] is emboldened to ask the Lord for the power to walk on the water to meet Jesus.[86] Jesus gives the disciple a share in his own power, and Peter is able to act on that grant of power until his fear in the face of such great peril weakens his faith. As he begins to sink, he repeats the prayer for aid spoken by all the disciples in 8:25: "Lord, save." Continuing the role of Yahweh in the Old Testament, Jesus stretches forth his hand to save his devotee from the

---

[83]Cf. Ps 77:20 (MT): "Through the sea was your path and your way through the deep waters, though your footsteps were not seen." Cf. Isa 43:16; Job 38:11, 16; Sir 24:5-6 (said of Wisdom!).

[84]In this emphasis on the spiritual problem of the disciples as opposed to the physical problem of the storm, and indeed in many other details, there is a close connection with Matthew's presentation of the stilling of the storm in 8:23-27.

[85]Matthew makes this point as early as 10:2, the formal list of the twelve apostles: "*First*, Simon who is Rock. . . ."

[86]In 14:28, the address *kyrie* (Lord) expresses the most solemn form of reverence. "If it is you" expresses not doubt but rather confidence that Jesus has the power to make such a thing possible, simply by his presence and his command.

waters of death.[87] Jesus rebukes Peter neither for his rashness in stepping out of the boat nor for his total lack of faith. Rather, in 14:31, Jesus asks a rhetorical question made up of Matthean motifs: "O thou of little faith, why didst thou doubt?" Jesus first taxes Peter with being *oligopiste*, a man of little faith.

For Matthew, the disciples do have faith and understanding, something that is not the case in Mark. In Matthew, the problem of the disciples is that, when a crisis comes, when danger looms and everything appears to be about to collapse, the disciples panic and act as though they had no faith. This is *oligopistia*, littleness of faith, which expresses itself in wavering, oscillating, doubting (*distazō*).[88] It is this littleness of faith expressed in wavering which causes the disciple in the church, or even the church leader, to lose his share in the power of Jesus. Jesus hears the suppliant prayer spoken out of this imperfect faith, and saves the leader from the waters of death. He does the same for the whole community by entering the boat; at his presence, the tempest dies down (14:32). At this manifestation of divine saving presence, the whole church (14:33, "those in the boat") bow down in worship (*prosekynēsan*)[89] and make a formal profession of faith, the faith of the post-Easter church: "Truly you are the Son of God."[90] The

[87]Cf. Ps 144:7 (MT): "Reach forth your hand from on high; save me and rescue me from many waters." Cf. also Ps 18:17-18 (MT).

[88]"Doubt" refers here not so much to speculative questions, and certainly not to a formal denial of faith. *Distazō* in Matthew refers rather to that personal, existential vacillation in the presence of danger or confusion which can seize even the believing disciple; so in the final commission (28:17: some of the eleven disciples doubted when confronted with the risen Jesus). On all this, cf. I. Ellis, "But Some Doubted," *NTS* 14 (1967-68) 574-580.

[89]In Matthew, the action of *proskyneō* (bowing down in reverence) is legitimately rendered only to God (4:10) or to Jesus (the majority of the other passages). Satan demands it and is refused (4:9-10). Once, in a thinly veiled parable (18:26), the servant in debt (sinful disciple) falls down before the King (God).

[90]The profession which the Gentile church, symbolized by the centurions and those with him keeping guard over Jesus, will make at the cross after Jesus dies and the cosmic signs are unleashed (27:54) is uttered here.—The absence of the definite article before "Son" in the Greek is of no significance; it is to be expected with the predicate nominative preceding the verb "to be."

believing community now professes what God has revealed (2:15; 3:17), what Satan has tested (4:3,6), what the demons proclaimed (8:29). As is typical with Matthew as opposed to Mark, revelation goes public. Instead of the Messianic secret,[91] we have a profession of faith in Jesus as Son of God, uttered by his disciples halfway through the gospel, even before Peter's confession at Caesarea Philippi. Granted the context of theophany, Son of God must be understood in its transcendent sense. The disciples are not simply talking about a Davidic king adopted by God on the day of enthronement. At the same time, the profession of Peter in 16:16 is not rendered superfluous by this acclamation in 14:33. As we shall see, Peter's statement of Christology will be fuller and more solemn; and the ecclesiological ramifications are made more specific and far-reaching. But Matthew 14:22-33 has at least made perfectly clear the specificity of Matthew's view of Christ: the transcendent Jesus, the Son of God, whose divine majesty could not be more graphically portrayed, is the guardian and savior of his imperiled church, especially its weak leaders.[92] As so often happens in Matthean redaction, what was already present in Mark becomes underscored and amplified, but also transformed. This is especially true of the welding together of a high Christology with a high ecclesiology.

In 15:1-20, the dispute about ritual rules, Jesus begins to remove his community from the teaching authority (magisterium) of the Pharisees. This is a process which will continue through the rest of Book Four; it is within the total context of Book Four that the pivotal ecclesiological declaration of Matthew 16:17-19 must be read. Matthew 15:1-20 abbreviates, inverts, and even adds to Mark 7:1-23. Matthew's modifications on the whole have the effect of sharpening the contrast and clash between the teaching of Jesus and the ritual laws taught by the Pharisees. In verse 3

---

[91]Contrast the profession of faith in Matthew 14:33 with the typical Markan conclusion in Mark 6:51-52 (astonishment, lack of understanding).

[92]And yet the saving and healing activity of Jesus is extended to "all" (v. 35) in Matthew's editing of the condensed Markan pericope which follows (Matt 14:34-36). Matthew never wishes the Lord of the church to become too "churchy" in the particularistic sense.

Matthew has the Pharisees attack Jesus' disciples (note the ecclesial dimension) with the charge that they *trespass* the (unwritten) traditions of the elders by not washing their hands before eating. Jesus takes up the battle-cry of "trespass" and counterattacks with the more serious question (v. 3): why do you Pharisees *trespass* the written commandment of God found in the Torah in favor of your unwritten traditions? Jesus' basic argument is that the Pharisees allow their tradition about dedicating one's goods to the Temple (*korban*) to annul in practice God's commandment concerning support of one's parents.[93] Far from being binding, such *human* traditions, as opposed to God's command, reflect the casuistry of hypocrites (15:7-9).

Up to this point, Jesus has been addressing a restricted audience (Pharisees) on a restricted topic (oral traditions as exemplified by hand-washing). In verses 10-11, both audience and topic are broadened. Jesus no longer follows a rabbinic line of argumentation but lays down an apodictic rule: true defilement comes not from anything entering the mouth but from the sin which comes out of the mouth, the sin which expresses the true state of man in his innermost being (cf. the explanation in vv. 17-20). What Jesus says in verse 11 rejects not only Pharisaic tradition, but many written laws of the Pentateuch (especially in Leviticus), laws which carefully distinguish between clean and unclean and forbid the latter. Not just oral tradition, not just the written Torah of Moses, but really one of the indispensable pillars of Judaism and many other world religions is smashed to pieces by this one sentence in verse 11. Sacred and profane, holy and unholy, are no longer questions of external objects and forces impinging on man from the outside. No, the holy and unholy proceed from within man, who can thus affect and even defile the world outside. With this programmatic statement, Jesus tears down in principle the barriers between Jew and Gentile, between

---

[93]In the fourth commandment, the original sense of "honor" is "support." The commandment was primarily concerned not with small children but with adult sons and the problem of aging parents. Notice that Matthew speaks of *God's* commandment (15:4), while Mark 7:10 refers the command to Moses. In Matthew, the contradiction becomes sharper and more serious.

the Pharisee and the *'am ha' aretz*, and (for Matthew) between the more stringent Jewish Christianity of the past and the Matthean church reaching out to the Gentiles. Jesus has given mankind the freedom to eat together, at tables both sacred and profane. But the freedom comes at a fearful price for Judaism, and with an unheard-of claim to doctrinal authority on Jesus' part. Without any argumentation, with an apodictic statement reminiscent of the antitheses in Matthew 5:21-48, Jesus revokes major commands and prohibitions in the written Mosaic Law. Implicitly, Jesus claims to know directly, intuitively, and without tortuous argumentation, what the will of God is. And when there is a conflict between Jesus' pronouncement and the Mosaic Law, the latter must give way. Without using any title, Jesus, by his sovereign action, claims for himself the kind of transcendent authority over Law and morality which, to the mind of any Jew, rightly belongs to God alone.

It is no wonder that the Pharisees take offense (v. 12). Judaism, and some Jewish Christians, likewise took offense when certain Christians admitted Gentiles to table-fellowship. Jesus' answer to such Pharisaic scandal is peremptory and harsh. The disciples are to "leave" the Pharisees (v. 14). In the story, of course, this could simply mean: "Leave them alone." In the context of the break between Matthew's church and the synagogue, the command has a much deeper sense. Despite their claims to an unbroken chain of authority reaching back to Moses, the Pharisees and the Judaism they represent are not the true community founded by God ("plant" in v. 13). The Pharisees are blind guides (= teachers) who will only drag their disciples to destruction with them (v. 14).

When we consider that Matthew has added verses 12-14 to Mark, we can appreciate how deep had become the gulf which separated Matthew's church from Pharisaic Judaism, a gulf which once did not exist. "Leave them": the magisterium of the Pharisees is rejected. It is quite fitting that the very next verse (v. 15) introduces Peter, the leader of the true planting of God; he seeks from Jesus the meaning of the mysterious axiom of verse 11. It is unusual in Matthew that the disciples should prove so lacking in understanding and that Jesus should rebuke them harshly in the Markan manner (cf. Mark 7:18). The reason for their obtuseness and the need for rebuke stem from the fact that, on the point of food laws, Jesus has gone beyond reinterpreting the Mosaic Law; he has simply abolished it. The disciples are like the early Jewish Christians who took some time getting used to this radical idea. But Jesus insists on the point, even with a certain earthiness (v. 17). *All* food entering the body is destined to be cast out of the body as excrement. All food equally ends up as the clearest form of physical uncleanness. Thus, to distinguish among clean and unclean foods is ridiculous, and physical uncleanness is anyway irrelevant. The only real uncleanness with which God is concerned is the spiritual uncleanness which does not enter into man but proceeds from him.[94] To round off the pericope with a graceful inclusion, Matthew returns in verse 20 to where he started, the question of washing hands. But this inclusion must not lull us into thinking that Matthew does not mean what he says in verses 11, 17-19.[95] As in three out of the six antitheses, so too here Jesus shows himself to be a teacher who possesses divine

---

[94]There seems to be a play on the different meanings of *koinoō* in verses 18-20: physical uncleanness of dirt and the spiritual defilement of sin; cf. J. McKenzie, "The Gospel according to Matthew," *Jerome Biblical Commentary* (eds. R. Brown, J. Fitzmyer, and R. Murphy; Englewood Cliffs: Prentice-Hall, 1968), II, 90 (section 107).—Note, by the way, how Matthew revises Mark's list of vices to make it reflect the basic code of the decalogue. Matthew is intent on saying that not ritual observance but fundamental ethical norms belong to the genuine expression of God's will.

[95]That Matthew keeps the Markan revocation of the food laws, with the tremendous consequences that involves, is not fully appreciated by G. Barth, "Matthew's Understanding of the Law," in *Tradition and Interpretation*, 90, and by C. Carlston, "The Things That Defile (Mark VII.14) and the Law in Matthew and Mark," *NTS* 15 (1968-69) 75-96, especially 88; see also Carlston's remarks in *The Parables of the Triple Tradition* (Philadelphia: Fortress, 1975) 28-35. Barth appeals to the fact that Matthew drops the phrase in Mark 7:19, "cleansing all foods." But, when one considers that Matthew in general streamlines Mark's material and that furthermore the phrase is awkward and grammatically ambiguous (does it modify Jesus or the latrine?), it is no wonder that he omits it. Nothing substantial is altered by the omission. Cf. also H. Hübner, "Mark VII.1–23 und das 'Jüdisch-Hellenistische' Gesetzesverständnis," *NTS* 22 (1976) 319–345.

authority over what Jews considered the perfect and unalterable expression of God's will: the written Law of Moses. To follow this authoritative teacher will necessarily entail withdrawing from the Jewish magisterium and adhering to the sovereign magisterium Jesus exercises and shares with his church.

The break with the restrictions of Judaism is also hinted at in the pericope of the Canaanite woman (15:21-28). The Canaanite woman and the centurion of 8:5-13 are the only two Gentiles Matthew allows to come into contact with Jesus during the public ministry.[96] In keeping with his outline of salvation-history, Jesus, like his disciples (cf. 10:5-6), is sent by God during the unique period of the public ministry only to the Israelites, who are globally designated as lost sheep (15:24).[97] Matthew allows the Canaanite woman[98] to approach Jesus by way of exception, to point forward to the dramatic change, to a universal mission which the death-resurrection of Jesus will make possible (28:16-20). Matthew has just declared that ritual laws separating people have been irrelevant for the disciples of Jesus. Now he declares what is the decisive criterion for discipleship: a faith which expresses itself in trustful prayer, despite apparent rebuffs (vv. 24, 26). Such a decisive criterion knows no barriers of race or nation. Faith will give even the despised Gentiles a share in the blessings

---

[96]The two stories have a number of similarities: a Gentile individual; a rank or status despised by Jews (pagan soldier who is part of an oppressive foreign rule and a pagan woman); illness or possession which affects not oneself but a loved one; the consequent prayer of intercession for the sake of another; an extraordinary expression of trust made by the person in answer to a statement of Jesus; the approval of the person's attitude by Jesus; the healing at a distance in response to the faith shown. In both cases, the center of attention is neither the power of Jesus nor the person who is cured, but the faith of the petitioner.

[97]Matthew probably intends to emphasize this restriction by restricting the ministry geographically to the land of Israel. One should probably read 15:21-22 as saying that Jesus withdrew to northernmost Galilee, on the border of the region of Tyre and Sidon and that out of that region the woman came to see Jesus in Galilee.

[98]Matthew may have changed Mark's "Syrophoenician" woman to a Canaanite to suggest the Old Testament opposition between Israel, the people of God, and the sinful Canaanites who were to be exterminated. The opposition is now transcended in Christ.

bestowed by the "Son of David," the paradoxical Messiah who is rejected by his own people while he heals the outcasts.[99]

But for the moment the Gentile who receives healing from the Son of David must remain an exception. The Messiah must return to his own people, to reveal himself[100] by healing every type of illness and to evoke from Israel the praise due its God (15:31). To this crowd which shows the repentance the merciful Messiah seeks, Jesus now extends the blessings of sharing in a foretaste of the Messianic banquet (15:32-39). Jesus does indeed give the bread to the children (cf. 15:26). The same eucharistic and ecclesial overtones we saw in 14:13-21 (the feeding of the five thousand) are present here in the feeding of the four thousand. Perhaps there is also the idea that those Jews who are willing to be called to praise Israel's God through his Messiah are still invited to share the Messiah's meal.[101]

Although the invitation to the Messianic banquet (present already in the church's life through the eucharist) may still be open to individual Jews, this by no means indicates any possibility of rapprochement with the Pharisees' magisterium. In 16:1-12, Jesus again rejects the authority of the Jewish leaders, in a pronouncement more explicit and programmatic than 15:1-20. The Pharisees and Sadducees,[102] representing the united front of Judaism, especially its authoritative teachers, begin the clash by

---

[99]Matthew adds the idea of faith in Jesus' reply (Matt 15:28; contrast Mark 7:29). Matthew likewise adds Son of David in 15:22, in keeping with the meaning we have already seen in 9:27 and 12:23; see also 20:30-31; 21:9, 15; 22:45.

[100]Note the mountain, the place of revelation, which Matthew introduces in 15:29 (contrast Mark 7:31).

[101]This continued invitation to the rightly disposed among the Jews would fit my contention that the missionary charge in 28:19 does not exclude the Jews: it is to "all the nations," not "all the Gentiles."

[102]Whether we consider the time of Jesus or the time of Matthew, the yoking together of the Pharisees and Sadducees, especially under the rubric of common doctrine (v. 12), is unhistorical. At the time of Jesus, the Sadducees were opposed on a number of key doctrinal points to the Pharisees, and at the time of Matthew's composition, the Sadducees had ceased to exist as a potent force within Judaism. I suggest that this is one of the mistakes Matthew makes in treating Jewish matters, mistakes which may indicate that Matthew himself is a Gentile; cf. pp. 17-25.

demanding a legitimating sign from Jesus (16:1; cf. 12:38-39). Jesus replies that their request only shows their malice and infidelity to the covenant. The only sign to be given the Jews will be the sign of Jonah, which Jesus in 12:40 interpreted as the death and resurrection of the Son of Man. Jesus then discourses to his disciples on the danger of the Jewish magisterium: beware of the leaven of the Pharisees and Sadducees (16:6). The disciples are confused about what Jesus can mean, since they have forgotten to bring bread with them on their journey. Jesus' reply is twofold.

(1) The disciples are again revealing that they are men of little faith (*oligopistoi*, v. 8). They fail to trust God's action in Jesus in the face of physical deprivation and danger. And yet they have the assurance of the two multiplications of loaves that the Father through Jesus will provide for the needs of the community.

(2) More importantly, they have not understood that he was not talking about material bread but about the leaven (= corruptive influence) of the Pharisees and Sadducees. Then Matthew characteristically adds that the disciples did come to understand that Jesus was commanding avoidance of the teaching of the Pharisees and Sadducees.[103] To sum up: immediately after an allusion to his death and resurrection, Jesus formally tells his disciples to reject the magisterium of the Jewish authorities. Then, in the next pericope (16:13-20), Jesus proceeds to replace the Jewish magisterium with a new Christian one.

II. MATT 16:13–28: CHRIST'S TEACHING AUTHORITY IN HIS CHURCH

In many ways, Peter's confession near Caesarea Philippi (16:13-20) is the high point of Book Four. The whole Book has been weaving together Christology and ecclesiology, and now this balance of Matthew's two key themes receives perfect expression through Matthew's own careful redaction. Matthew inherited a pericope from Mark that was definitely Christological in

---

[103]Just as characteristically, Mark has Jesus rebuke his disciples in the harshest terms for not understanding; they are really no better than the Jewish crowds (Mark 8:17-18; cf. 6:52).

focus: Mark 8:27-30 represents the hinge of the gospel, the turn-ing point between the Mystery of the Messiah (chaps. 1-8) and the Mystery of the Son of Man (chaps. 8-16). To Jesus' question, "But who do *you* say that I am?", Peter, as spokesman for the disciples, replies simply: "You are the Messiah." As usual in Mark, Jesus responds with a command to be silent. Clearly, Mat-thew has balanced this Christological emphasis with an eccle-siological emphasis by inserting a separate saying (or group of sayings) of Jesus to Peter.[104] What in Mark was a one-way decla-ration to Jesus becomes in Matthew a two-way declaration, a mutual conferral of titles. Peter first confers the title Messiah and Son of God on Jesus, and Jesus reciprocates by conferring the title Rock on Peter.[105] All Matthew's attempts to tie together and

---

[104]The original setting of 16:17-19 is disputed. Some (notably O. Cullman) suggest the last supper; more favor a post-resurrection appear-ance. An originally post-resurrection setting is also suggested for the special Petrine material in Matthew's version of the walking on the water (14:28-33). The possibility that both Petrine traditions go back to the first appearance of the risen Jesus to Peter might explain the occurrence of "Son of God" in Matthew's rewriting of both Mark 6:45-52 and Mark 8:27-30. The vocabulary in Matthew 16:17 is reminiscent of Paul's de-scription of the appearance of the risen Son of God (Gal 1:16). In favor of a post-resurrection appearance is C. Kähler, "Zur Form- und Tradi-tionsgeschichte von Matth. XVI.17-19," *NTS* 23 (1976-77) 36-58. Cf. also A. Vögtle, "Zum Problem der Herkunft von Mt 16, 17-19," in *Orien-tierung an Jesus* (ed. P. Hoffmann; Freiburg: Herder, 1973) 372-393; R. Hummel, *Die Auseinandersetzung zwischen Kirche und Judentum im Matthäusevangelium*[2] (Munich: Kaiser, 1966) 59-64; R. Brown *et al.*, *Peter in the New Testament* (N.Y.: Paulist, 1973) 83-101; F. Mussner, *Petrus und Paulus — Pole der Einheit* (Freiburg: Herder, 1976) 11-22; G. Bornkamm, "The Authority to 'Bind' and 'Loose' in the Church in Mat-thew's Gospel," in *Jesus and Man's Hope, I* (eds. D. Hadidian *et al.*; Pittsburgh: Pittsburgh Theological Seminary, 1970) 37-50; P. Hoffmann, "Der Petrus-Primat im Matthäusevangelium," in *Neues Testament und Kirche* (ed. J. Gnilka; Freiburg: Herder, 1974) 94-114. Many of these articles are concerned with the history of the sayings in Matthew 16:17-19 before Matthew wrote his gospel; we cannot enter into this difficult (and highly speculative) question here.

[105]It cannot be stressed strongly enough that, in the first century A.D., *Petros* was not used as a proper name. Jesus is not giving Simon a second proper name, which also incidentally carries a symbolic meaning. The Aramaic *Kêfā'* and the Greek *Petros* meant "rock," and only rock.

mutually interpret Jesus and his church now reach their climax. What 14:22–33 presented by way of dramatic narrative now receives its full explicitation in the words of Peter and Jesus.

Matthew's first alteration in the Markan tradition is in the initial question of Jesus. While Mark 8:27 reads: "Who do men say that I am?", Matthew 16:13 has: "Who do men say that the *Son of Man* is?" Matthew may have made the change for reasons of style and rhetoric: the change creates a play on words with "men" and "Son of Man." It also provides an inclusion with the final logion of the whole section, 16:28, where Matthew again inserts "Son of Man": ". . . until they see the Son of Man coming in his Kingdom." The entire section 16:13-28 spans two sayings of Jesus containing Son of Man. In 16:13, Son of Man is a question mark, a mysterious figure who has been combining glorious power and lowly service throughout the public ministry. In 16:28, "some" of those in Jesus' audience are promised that they will not die until they see the triumphant Son of Man coming to exercise his rule. Everything in 16:13-28 takes place under this Son-of-Man arch that Matthew has constructed.

In 16:14, the disciples show how much of a question mark the Son of Man remains. Interestingly, though, popular opinion identifies Jesus with some revered prophetic figures of the past, especially the figure of the suffering, martyred prophet. Matthew pointedly adds the name of Jeremiah, the great suffering servant among the prophets; later Judaism revered him as an intercessor for the people Israel (2 Macc 15:12-16). When we remember that Elijah was expected to return as prophet of the end-time, to prepare Israel for the judgment, we see that the various popular guesses did hit upon various aspects of the title Son of Man. But these piecemeal suggestions all fall short of the truth. So Jesus addresses a direct challenge to his disciples; surely they, the ones with understanding, must be able to do better than this. Simon Peter, as spokesman and leader, replies: "You are the Messiah, the Son of the living God" (16:16).

Obviously, Matthew has changed the import of Peter's con-

They did not first signify a proper name (our "Peter") which also meant rock. Consequently, the designation Jesus gives to Simon is just as much a title of office as the titles Simon addresses to Jesus.

fession in Mark, but we must broaden our vision to realize how much has been changed. In Mark, Jesus had asked basically: "Who am I?" Peter identifies the "I" with the Messiah. The identification in Matthew is much more complicated. Peter identifies the Son of Man mentioned in Jesus' question with both the Messiah and the Son of the living God. It is not a question here of Peter's using a title which has not been used previously in the gospel by some speaker in the narrative.[106] Rather, what is so important Christologically is that these separate titles are being brought together for mutual interpretation. In the case of Son of Man, there was no question that Jesus in some sense identified himself with the Son of Man (8:20; 11:19; and the very question in 16:13). The question was: What is the precise sense and range of this title as applied to Jesus? Peter's reply delineates some aspects of Son of Man by explaining it with two other titles, now drawn together for the first time in the gospel. This Son of Man is the royal Anointed One, the fulfillment of Old Testament prophecy, the scion of David who was destined to sit upon the throne of Israel in the last days. But further, this Son of Man is not just a bigger and better David, a more powerful earthly king, a man who is adopted as a son of God at his enthronement. With a full, solemn, almost liturgical formula, Jesus is designated the Son of the living God. "Living" is applied to God in the Old Testament and Judaism to stress that God has life in and of himself, and he alone gives it to others. The transcendent Son, who stands on the side of God vis-à-vis man, shares this quality of "living" so completely that he can promise his community that the powers of death will not prevail against it (16:18).

We can see therefore that Peter's confession, his definition of what Son of Man means, has a Christological depth and richness to it which far surpasses the previous occurrences of either Messiah or Son of God in the gospel. And we should not forget that, just as Messiah and Son of God explain Son of Man, the opposite is also true. Read in the light of everything Matthew has said about Son of Man up until now, the Messiah and Son of God

---

[106]Messiah appears in 2:4; Son of God in 8:29; 14:33; Son of Man in 8:20 and 11:19 (where Jesus, speaking to someone else, clearly identifies himself in his present state with the Son of Man).

become associated (1) with the mystery of the powerful transcendent One hidden in the deprivation and service of the public ministry, (2) with the mystery of the dying and rising servant, and (3) with the mystery of the judge who will come in glory. No other two verses in Matthew's gospel contain such a dense concentration of Christological thought as do 16:13 and 16. In Mark, Caesarea Philippi means a Christological turning point; in Matthew, it means a Christological synthesis. It is quite fitting, then, that this affirmation of "high" Christology on Peter's part calls forth in Matthew's gospel an affirmation of "high" ecclesiology on Jesus' part (16:17-19). Whatever the sources of verses 17-19, Matthew has edited them to form three stanzas (vv. 17, 18, and 19), each with three lines:[107]

[1] v. 17 (a) Happy are you, Simon, Son of Jonah,
　　　　　 (b) for flesh and blood did not reveal [this] to you,
　　　　　 (c) but my Father who [is] in heaven.
[2] v. 18 (a) And I say to you that you are [the] Rock,
　　　　　 (b) and upon this rock I will build my church,
　　　　　 (c) and the gates of Hades shall not prevail against it.
[3] v. 19 (a) I shall give you the keys of the Kingdom of heaven,
　　　　　 (b) and whatever you bind on earth shall be bound in heaven,
　　　　　 (c) and whatever you loose on earth shall be loosed in heaven.

The first line ("a") of each stanza makes some basic statement about or promise to Peter. Then the next two lines ("b-c") develop the basic statement by giving some reason, explanation, or consequence. In each stanza, lines b-c contain some sort of opposition or antithesis (v. 17, flesh and blood versus my Father; v. 18, the firmness Jesus gives his church on the rock versus the futile attempts of death to overturn the church; v. 19, binding versus loosing).

---

[107]On all this, cf. W. Grundmann, *Das Evangelium nach Matthäus*, 384. If Matthew drew verses 17, 18, and 19 from different sources, he must have edited them heavily to make them fit a common pattern. *Pace* C. Kähler, "Zur Form- und Traditionsgeschichte," 38–39, there is a Semitic flavor throughout the three verses. Taken in conjunction with the common pattern, this evenness of language would argue for a common source.

In verse 17, Jesus responds to Peter with a beatitude or macarism. He declares Peter especially fortunate, because this deep Christolological insight Peter has just enunciated has not come from his own resources or those of any other weak human being ("flesh and blood"). Peter's faith is totally a gift from God. The heavenly Father, who alone knows the Son, has revealed this Son to a chosen one. Matthew 11:25-27 is thus acted out. The apocalyptic mystery, which has remained hidden to the wise, i.e., to the Jewish magisterium, has been revealed by the Father's good pleasure to a mere untutored child like Peter.[108] Peter, the leader of the twelve, is the specially chosen recipient of revelation from the Father (v. 17bc) and of blessing and promises from Jesus (vv. 17a, 18-19).

And so, on the basis of the grace of faith the Father has given Peter, Jesus in turn gives the further grace of leadership, symbolized by a stream of images in verses 18-19. In verse 18a, Simon receives the title Rock (Peter), and Jesus immediately explains the meaning of the title: Simon is to be the firm, unshakable rock[109] upon which Jesus builds his eschatological community, the assembly of God, the faithful remnant of Israel in the last days, his church. Matthew makes clear the function of the rock in the parable of the house built on rock or sand (Matt 7:24-27).[110] The house built on rock does not fall, no matter how much it is battered, "because it is firmly founded on the rock." Parallel im-

---

[108]Interestingly, in Jewish apocalyptic literature, it is the Son of Man who, formerly hidden, is now revealed by the Most High to the elect; so *l Enoch* 62:7; 46:1ff; 48:1-7.

[109]The continuity of thought is slightly obscured in the Greek, where "rock" as a title for the man Simon is naturally used in the masculine form (*petros*, 18a), while the usual feminine form of the common noun "rock" (*petra*) is used in 18b. Probably in the original Aramaic the common noun *kêfā'* stood in both 18a and 18b. "This rock" in 18b clearly refers to the person called Rock in 18a; to refer "this rock" to Peter's faith or to Jesus is to abandon the obvious meaning for a contrived one.

[110]Indeed, in 7:24, Matthew uses the same word for "to build" and "rock" which we find in 16:18. In fact, the only two verses in the whole of the New Testament where "build" (*oikodomeō*) and "rock" (*petra*) are used in direct combination are Matthew 7:24 and 16:18. Luke 6:47, the parallel to Matthew 7:24, does not use "build" and "upon the rock" in the same precise phrase.

ages can also be found further afield. Abraham, the first patriarch
of God's people Israel, is called a rock in Isaiah 51:1-2: "Look to
the rock from which you were hewn. . . . Look to Abraham, your
father. . . . When he was but one I called him, I blessed him and
made him many." Peter has been called and blessed to be the first
patriarch of the new people of God, the church of Christ, which
replaces the "house of Israel" (Matt 10:6; 15:24). Peter, like Abraham, becomes a corporate personality.

That Jesus speaks here openly of his church is no surprise, at
least on the level of Matthew's theology. Already in 1:21 we were
told that "he would save his people from their sins." The negative
results of Book Three showed us that most of the Jewish people
refused to be "his people." The faithful remnant he is forming in
Book Four is destined to play that role. Moreover, the idea of
such a community is inherent in the titles Son of Man and Messiah. The Son of Man necessarily brings with him a group called
"the saints [or holy people] of the Most High" (Dan 7:27). And a
Messianic King without any people in his Kingdom would look
rather foolish. We should notice that verse 18b is put in the form
of a promise: "I *shall* build." Only after the death and resurrection does Jesus truly and fully "found" the church and send it on
mission. For only then will the Son of the "living" God have
defeated the powers of death (cf. 27:51-54; 28:2-4), have given life
to the dead, and have created a community of the new age capable of resisting the onslaught of death forever (v. 18c). In the Old
Testament, God is praised as the Mighty One, who alone can lead
a person down to the gate of Hades (death) and bring him back
again (e.g., Isa 38:10, 17-18; Wis 16:13).[111] In other words, in the
Old Testament, Yahweh alone has power over death. Once again,
then, we see how Jesus stands in the place of Yahweh. By his
death-resurrection, Jesus the Son has definitively broken death's

[111]Hades could mean the realm of punishment for sinners, and so the
kingdom of Satan, which shall never be successful in its attack on the
church. However, the canonical Greek Scriptures in both the Old and the
New Testaments regularly use Hades as a symbol of death or the abode
of the dead rather than as a symbol of "hell" in the sense of the abode of
the damned. Gates are a metaphor for might, especially military might on
the attack.

grip both on himself and on his community. Firmly founded on Peter, his church will never be shaken by the assaults of the nether world. It shall remain steadfast in its mission "unto the end of the age" (28:20).

In verse 19, the image changes. Jesus *will* give (again, the future) the keys of the Kingdom of heaven to Peter. Coming from verse 18c, we might think first of the keys to the gates of Hades,[112] but 19bc indicate a different application. The basic idea seems to be one of delegated authority. The closest parallel in the Old Testament is found in Isaiah 22:15-25, where Shebna is dismissed from his post as majordomo of King Hezekiah's palace, and Eliakim is appointed in his place. In Isaiah 22:22, God says of Eliakim: "I shall place the key of the House of David on his shoulder; when he opens, no one shall shut, when he shuts, no one shall open." Peter is thus the vice-gerent or prime minister of Jesus the Messiah in the royal household of the church. What this delegated power of the keys entails is indicated by Jesus in his condemnation of the Jewish magisterium in 23:13: "Woe to you, scribes and Pharisees, hypocrites, for you close the Kingdom of heaven in the face of men; for you yourselves do not enter, and you do not allow those who try to enter to do so." The power of the keys is therefore the power to teach the right way to enter the Kingdom, the authority to teach correctly the way "to do the will of God," to "do justice"—a burning concern of Matthew. Only those who practice the abundant eschatological justice Jesus teaches shall enter the Kingdom (5:20). It is Peter's task as vice-gerent to facilitate the entrance of the disciples by correctly passing on and interpreting the teaching of Jesus on the will of the Father.

That this interpretation of the keys is correct is confirmed by verse 19bc, with the dual image of binding and loosing. These are technical rabbinic terms. Applied to 16:19, they seem to refer to a rabbi's power to declare particular acts permissible or forbidden. Connected with this power of authoritative magisterium was the

---

[112]Cf. Rev 1:18, where the risen Jesus, appearing as the Son of Man, says: "I hold the keys of death and Hades," which is explained in the context as his triumph over death by his resurrection.

power to exclude someone from the community or to readmit him to the community. Authoritative teaching addressed to the community and disciplinary power over the community to enforce the teaching: these are the two ideas in "bind and loose." Jesus tells Peter that as the Rock and vice-gerent he must assure the stability and permanence of the church by correctly applying the *halakoth*, the moral teachings of Jesus, to new situations in the life of the church. Peter is to be the supreme rabbi for the new people of God, and his teaching will have the authority the Jewish magisterium lacked. Whatever Peter declares lawful in the church on earth, God will declare lawful in heaven; the same will hold true for what Peter declares unlawful. While Matthew still keeps the concepts of church and Kingdom separate, they come very close together in verse 19. The church is the visible, earthly assembly of the people of Jesus the Messiah, and therefore the place where the final, future, eschatological Kingdom of heaven is already present and active by anticipation.[113]

Looking back on 16:13-19, we can see how Matthew, vis-à-vis Mark, has both created a Christological synthesis and inserted a major ecclesiological pronouncement. The resulting union of Christology and ecclesiology is the high point of Book Four, and one of the most important passages in the whole gospel. Because Peter has accepted the revelation the Jewish teachers have refused, because he can see that the Son of Man is the Messiah and the Son of God, he will be invested with what is now removed from the Jewish scribes: the authentic magisterium. Thus, Peter is certainly for Matthew more than just a model for every disciple and a spokesman for the whole group of disciples. He also plays a unique role as firm basis of and authoritative teacher in the church.[114]

---

[113]But the Kingdom is not to be restricted to the church, either in time or in space. The Kingdom of God was present in Israel in the Old Testament (Matt 21:43), and after the resurrection the Kingdom of the Son embraces the whole world, not just the church (13:37-38). The church is that part of the world which recognizes its true ruler in faith and obeys his will voluntarily.

[114]In the last verse of the pericope, Matthew 16:20, Matthew rejoins the Markan narrative at the point where Jesus prohibits his disciples

With 16:21 ("from that time on Jesus began. . . ."), Matthew obviously begins a new pericope (16:21-28), which nevertheless continues the scene of Jesus and the disciples near Caesarea Philippi.[115] A change in place was signaled by 16:13, and no new change in place occurs until 17:1. The basic theme of 16:21-28 is the cross, and it can be conveniently subdivided into the cross of Jesus (vv. 21-23) and the cross of the disciple (vv. 24-28). In verses 21-23, Jesus solemnly begins to reveal[116] to his disciples the mystery of the dying and rising Son of Man. Although Matthew drops the title Son of Man from the first passion prediction he takes over from Mark, he clearly understands the prediction as referring to himself in his office as Son of Man. Matthew makes this clear by what precedes and follows. In 12:40, he had already inserted a veiled reference to the death and resurrection of the Son of Man, and the second and third passion predictions (17:22-23; 20:17-19) both use the Son of Man title. Moreover, he keeps the Markan reference to the vicarious sacrifice of the Son of Man (20:28) and even adds a fourth passion prediction with Son of Man

from making known his Messiahship (Mark 8:30). While Matthew does not take over from Mark any thoroughgoing messianic secret, he can keep the prohibition here. Matthew's "that he was the Messiah" refers to the whole relation of Son of Man-Messiah-Son of God in Matthew 16:13-20, and Matthew 11:25-27 had already made clear that this revelation was to be given only to the mere children. By the Father's decree, it is to be hidden from the wise and intelligent (11:25), i.e., the Jewish magisterium and the Jews who follow it.

[115]The need for a break and fresh beginning (contrast Mark and even more Luke) is necessitated by the fuller Christological confession and especially the expansive praise of and promise to Peter. Since Matthew not only retains but even adds to the rebuke to Peter, some caesura is necessary from a literary and psychological point of view. Matthew thus holds on to the bright and dark sides of Peter, without dissolving or blurring the tension.

[116]The verb "to show" is used by Matthew where Mark uses the verb we would expect, "to teach." "To show" may connote the revelation of some event which has been hidden in God's eschatological plan and which now is being realized; so in Rev 1:1. The apocalyptic sense of "show" would fit the context of the solemn unveiling of the details of the mystery of the dying and rising Son of Man. The verb *dei* "must, has to," indicating the necessity of the divine plan formerly foretold and now being realized, is also part of the apocalyptic vocabulary.

just as the passion begins (26:2). Undoubtedly, then, Matthew also understands the Son of Man to be the subject of the first passion prediction as well. The reason why he does not use the term here is that he has taken it from its place in Mark 8:31 and has thrown it back to the beginning of the whole pericope, Matthew 16:13. The entire section 16:13-28 thus falls between two occurrences of Son of Man, 16:13 referring to the earthly Jesus, 16:28 referring to the glorious judge. The first passion prediction provides the linchpin, the point of transition between the earthly and heavenly Son of Man. It is by the necessary corridor of suffering and death that Jesus will pass from his lowly earthly status to his eschatological glory. The theme of the martyred prophet, which Matthew had underlined in 16:14 by adding Jeremiah, is also stressed here by the insertion of "he must go to Jerusalem," the city which kills the prophets (23:37).

Jesus begins this apocalyptic revelation of the dying Son of Man because the revelation Peter received and enunciated (16:16), while accepted by Jesus as true, is incomplete without the further revelation of the Son of Man's death and resurrection. To see Jesus as the glorious Messiah and transcendent Son of God, yet to fail to realize what it means to identify this figure with the Son of Man, is to miss the most important revelation Jesus brings. And this is precisely Peter's problem. Verbally, formally, inasmuch as he answered Jesus' question about the Son of Man, Peter connected Son of Man with Messiah and Son of God. But he has failed to see the real point of the connection, what the title Son of Man is going to involve. That is why Peter immediately and officiously begins to rebuke[117] Jesus, and to insist that God, the merciful heavenly Father Jesus has talked so much about, would never allow such a tragedy. Peter's conception of a glorious Messiah and Son of God automatically excludes the idea of suffering and death. Precisely because he is so enamored of the revelation he has received, he has no room for the deeper mystery Jesus is now revealing. The latter only contradicts what he already knows. What Peter fails to realize is that by espousing the idea of a glorious Son of God exempt from suffering, he is repeating the

---

[117]Notice the strong verb *epitiman* in 16:22; it is used with Jesus as the subject in 16:20.

temptation of the devil in chapter 4: "If you are the Son of God
. . ." then use the power attendant on your divine status to avoid
suffering and to win an easy kingdom (4:1-11). Therefore, when
Matthew takes over the rebuke of Mark 8:33, "Get behind me,
Satan," it has a darker meaning than even Mark intended. In
Matthew 16:23, Jesus repeats his sovereign dismissal of the tempter (4:10), only now he speaks to the demonic disciple who would
tempt from the way of the cross by espousing an erroneous concept of Messiahship or Sonship.

Not content with this, Matthew adds another clever stab:
"You are a stone of stumbling to me." A *skandalon* is something
that trips someone up, a trap, a stumbling-stone, something which
causes a person to fall. In the Bible, it often means something
which leads a person into sin or separation from God. Coming as
it does after Matthew 16:18 ("You are the rock"), *skandalon*
probably means "stone of stumbling," an obstacle to Jesus on his
way of suffering. Satan, who is the cause of *skandala* in the world
(Matt 13:41), now confronts Jesus in this Rock who, by his rebellion against the cross, has turned into a stone of stumbling.[118]
Puffed up by the revelation he has received, he thinks the
thoughts of men, not of God. He conceives of the Messiah and
Son of God according to earthly dreams of easy glory, instead of
according to God's profound apocalyptic mystery of the cross. As
an adversary of God's hidden plan for the salvation of the cosmos,
he becomes the adversary *par excellence*, Satan. As long as he
persists in this role of enemy of the cross, he must be dismissed.[119]

Thus Peter is seen in his two contrasting aspects: he is the
Rock of the church when he professes faith in the true revelation
he has received; he is the stone of stumbling when he refuses to
believe the further revelation he receives. In 16:13-28, the role of
Rock is given him because of his positive reaction to the revelation of the Messiah and Son of God; the role of *skandalon* is

---

[118]On all this, cf. G. Stählin, "skandalon," *TDNT* VII, 348.

[119]"Hypage opisō mou," "get behind me" in Matthew 16:23, probably is the same sort of rough dismissal as the "hypage, Satan," "begone,
Satan," of 4:10. However, Grundmann, *Das Evangelium nach Matthäus*,
399, sees in the *opisō mou* a call to begin again to learn what following
Jesus really means.

assigned him because of his negative reaction to the revelation of the death of the Son of Man. One might diagram this as follows:

SIMON PETER IS THE:	BECAUSE HE RESPONDS:	TO JESUS AS:
1a blessed recipient of the Father's revelation b firm basis of the church c authoritative teacher in the church	POSITIVELY	Messiah and Son of the living God
2a Satan b stone of stumbling c follower of men's thoughts rather than God's	NEGATIVELY	suffering and dying (Son of Man)

The authoritative magisterium of Peter is thus put under a check and a proviso. Peter is the legitimate interpreter of Jesus' teaching in the church, as long as he passes on the teaching of Jesus, and not the thoughts of men, and as long as he teaches the whole of Jesus' revelation, and not just the part which is appealing to men. Peter, or any church leader who does not accept the whole message of Jesus, especially the message of the cross, becomes a demonic disciple, an adversary of Jesus and his church. The patriarch of the people of God can always become the betrayer of the people if he forgets that, for all his leadership, he is still a disciple following a crucified Christ.

And what is true of Peter as church leader is also true of Peter as model of every disciple.[120] Every disciple[121] must hear

---

[120]It must be emphasized that Peter functions in Matthew *both* as the unique head of God's people *and* as the universal type of any disciple who belongs to God's people. The danger of resisting the message of the cross threatens Peter in each of his two aspects. Unfortunately, G. Strecker, *Der Weg der Gerechtigkeit*[3] (Göttingen: Vandenhoeck & Ruprecht, 1971) 203-206, plays down Peter's special authority in favor of his role as a type of every Christian.

[121]Notice how Matthew 16:24 ("Jesus said to his disciples") narrows the audience of Mark 8:34 ("and summoning the crowd with his disciples, he said to them"). In Matthew's mind, the oscillating crowd, which

from the Messiah and Son of God the call to follow him on the way to the cross (v. 24). Discipleship is personal commitment to Jesus which can even lead to death. The great obstacle to this commitment is of course the clinging to the old security and the old self we have created. But the eschatological hour has turned everything upside down and reversed the normal rules of prudence. Trying to secure one's existence by the safety measures of this world will only result in the loss of oneself, the condemnation of oneself at the last judgment (the future tense is a true future, pointing to the last day). Only the apparently irrational sacrifice of self out of personal commitment to Jesus ("for my sake") will guarantee one's survival on the last day (v. 25). One must carefully weigh costs and results. On the last day, what profit will there be in having won control of men and their world if in the end one loses oneself to eternal perdition (v. 26)?

The last judgment, which has been hiding behind the future tenses in verses 25-26, is now formally depicted in verse 27. Again we have the Jewish apocalyptic "Trinity" of Son of Man, Father, and angels. The Son of Man who was identified with the earthly Jesus in verse 13 and implicitly with the suffering servant in verse 21 is now portrayed as the glorious judge of the last day. At the beginning, middle, and end of one large section, 16:13-28, Matthew has presented us with all three aspects of the title. What is especially noteworthy in verse 27 is that the Son of Man comes in the glory of *his* Father. We could receive no clearer reminder that passages dealing with *the* Son, *my* Son, *the* Father, *my* Father, should not automatically be put under the rubric of Son of God rather than Son of Man. For Matthew (as for Mark before him), it is possible to consider God as the Father of the Son of Man. The divine status of this eschatological judge is stressed by Matthew by changing Mark's phrase "the holy angels" (Mark 8:38) to read "*his* angels." The angels belong to the Son of Man as his own proper retinue. The ascent from earthly Jesus (16:13) through tragic death on the cross (16:21) to divine judge surrounded by his own angels (16:27) is staggering.

---

will finally cry out for Jesus' execution on the cross, is in no state to receive a message against which even Peter rebels.

And Matthew does not present this majestic sweep of his Christological vision simply for contemplative wonder. Matthew brings his entire Christological statement to bear upon the fierce moral endeavor demanded of the church and of individual disciples as they stand under the coming judgment. Matthew pointedly adds to Mark's depiction of the Son of Man: "And then he shall repay each man according to his concrete actions (*praxin*)." We are reminded of the insistent demands at the end of the sermon on the mount: test the fruits, not the appearances (7:15-20); do not call me Lord if you do not do the will of my Father (7:21-23); hear my words and do them (7:24-27). The cross the disciple carries may not be the physical cross of martyrdom. Every disciple is called to carry the cross of the Father's will, whatever form it may take. Christology for Matthew is never an exercise in abstract speculation. He joins Christology to ecclesiology under the blazing searchlight of the coming judgment to call the members of his church to strenuous, wholehearted doing of the Father's will. This is the "justice" the disciple must practice abundantly if he is to enter the Kingdom (5:20).

This call to stringent moral endeavor, this warning that church and disciple are not exempt from the searching scrutiny of the last day, is not meant to discourage or paralyze the audience of Matthew, but to call it to action. And so Matthew concludes this whole magnificent section with a solemn, consoling promise. With the assurance of the apocalyptic seer who knows the denouement of the eschatological drama,[122] Jesus comforts his own by promising that some of those witnessing his public ministry will not die "before they see the Son of Man coming in his Kingdom" (16:28). Matthew has purposefully changed Mark's "until they see the Kingdom of God coming in power." That phrase could easily mean the end of the world and the last judgment. Matthew, writing c. A.D. 90, is well aware that the original eyewitnesses to Jesus' ministry have died out. Nor does Matthew especially seem to think that his own generation will necessarily experience the consummation of the age (28:20). The parousia has

---

[122]This seems to be the sense of the solemn introductory *Amen* which is prefixed to certain sayings of Jesus; cf. K. Berger, *Die Amen-Worte Jesu* (Berlin: Walter de Gruyter, 1970).

receded in his vision of salvation-history. As we saw in Part I of this book, Matthew views the death-resurrection of Jesus as the turning point of the ages, the in-breaking of the new age into the old. The coming of the exalted Son of Man *to* his church in 28:16-20 is a "proleptic parousia." The victor is seen by the eleven disciples as he comes to them in his Kingdom, declaring that he now possesses all power in heaven and on earth. This all-powerful Son of Man, who has entered upon his reign, promises his sustaining presence to the disciples as they teach (and live) all he has commanded (28:19-20). It is with this consoling promise that Jesus concludes his portrayal of the strict judgment which the Son of Man will hold on the last day.

Reviewing the whole of Matthew 16:13-28, we can see that a number of points have crystallized. (1) Matthew has carefully joined a deep and varied Christology to a detailed ecclesiology, centered on Peter. (2) The Christology is framed by references in the beginning, middle, and end to the Son of Man. (3) Insight into Jesus as Messiah and Son of God comes only as a revelation from the Father and is to be praised. But the same revelation can be the cause of condemnation if one does not join it to the further revelation of Jesus as suffering and dying Son of Man. (4) What must be professed in Christology—the cross of the Son of Man—must also be lived out in one's life of discipleship. Despite all the eschatological blessings bestowed by the Son of God in 16:17-19, Peter and the whole church must still follow the Son of Man on the way of the cross, for this same Son of Man will scrutinize their concrete mode of discipleship most carefully on the last day. As is clear from this summary, Son of God is a key title in this whole section. But by no means can it overshadow or absorb the countervailing title Son of Man.

III. MATT 17:1–27: CHRIST CONTINUES THE FORMATION OF HIS CHURCH

The theme of the apocalyptic revelation of the Son is continued in the transfiguration narrative (Matt 17:1-13). Like the infancy narrative, the temptation narrative, and the two multiplications of loaves, there are overtones of Mosaic typology: Moses (the illuminated face), Exodus and Sinai (the ascent of the mount, the cloud, the divine voice giving a command), the feast of Tabernacles (the sojourn in tents in the desert). Typically, Matthew underlines in his story the transcendent majesty of Jesus the Son and the reverential fear of the disciples in his presence; at the same time, Matthew tones down the disciples' lack of understanding. Matthew also characteristically changes Mark's "Elijah with Moses" (Mark 9:4) to the coordinated phrase "Moses and Elijah" (Matt 17:3). The two men thus symbolize Matthew's beloved "Law and the prophets," the two witnesses to Jesus. Central to Matthew's conception, however, is his presentation of the transfiguration as an apocalyptic vision of the Son (Son of God or Son of Man?), given to a small group of the elect. Matthew alone explicitly refers to the event as a vision (*horoma*) which is not to be revealed to others until the resurrection of the Son of Man (17:9). As the event begins, the face and clothing of Jesus shine a brilliant white, thus taking on the appearance of a heavenly being (13:43; 28:3). Jesus is giving his disciples an anticipation of that vision of the glory of the Son of Man which is promised for the last day (cf. 16:27).

Matthew naturally keeps Mark's portrayal of Peter as spokesman, but he changes Peter's mode of address from "Rabbi" to "Lord." He also strikes out Mark's reference to the ignorance of Peter, who has so recently received a special revelation from the Father. Peter's suggestion about the tents is interrupted by the bright cloud, the symbol of God's presence which is revealed yet veiled. God's voice does not so much reveal anything new as it confirms Peter's own confession of the Son of God in 16:16. The divine voice repeats word for word what it had proclaimed at Jesus' baptism (Matt 13:17). However, since Matthew has quoted Isaiah 42:1-4 (the beloved servant) in 12:18-21, the Son-concept is once again given overtones of servanthood by the phrase, "the beloved, in whom I am well pleased." In God's beloved Son and servant, God himself is present and revealed to all who are willing to listen to the Son's teaching ("hear him!"). The only new element in this divine message is that this Son and servant is implicitly identified with the prophet promised by Moses in Deuteronomy 18:15: "A prophet like me will the Lord your God raise up for you . . . him you shall hear." The disciples react to this theophany in the way apocalyptic seers usually react to apocalyptic visions: they fall down, they are fearful, they are weak, they need someone to touch them and raise them up (cf. Dan 8:17; 10:9-10, 15-19; Rev 1:17). Jesus approaches them to touch and reassure them. Interestingly, while Matthew often uses the verb "to approach" to describe people coming to Jesus, only here and in 28:18 does he present Jesus (both times in a majestic context) approaching his prostrate disciples with a command.

Whatever be the relationship of the narratives in the oral tradition, Matthew definitely sees a theological connection between the apocalyptic events of transfiguration, resurrection, and parousia—and the Son of Man is involved in all three. Quite fittingly, then, as they descend the mountain, Jesus explicitly refers to the resurrection of the Son of Man (17:9).[123] The apocalyptic vision and Jesus' reference to the eschatological event of resurrection cause the disciples to raise the objection that, according to the Jewish scribes, Elijah, whom they have seen in the vision, should first return to earth before the Messiah (17:10). Jesus answers first of all by confirming the prophecy of Malachi, the last of the prophets in the Jewish ordering of the books of Scripture.[124] Matthew then rewrites Mark's somewhat confused version of Jesus' explanation of the Malachi text (Mark 9:12-13). Matthew stresses that, although Elijah has come (in the person of the Baptist), the Jewish scribes did not recognize him.[125] In contrast, the disciples, once they receive the teaching of Jesus, do understand (v. 13) what the Jewish scribes did not, namely that the Baptist played the role of Elijah come back. Implicitly, Matthew denigrates the Jewish magisterium vis-à-vis the enlightened disciples. Matthew also states more clearly than Mark that the martyrdom of the final prophet and precursor is itself a prophecy of the passion of the Son of Man. The Son of

---

[123]As Grundmann says in *Das Evangelium nach Matthäus*, 404, when he comments on Matthew 17:9: "The person transformed into divine glory and revealed as God's beloved Son is the Son of Man. In this also is 16:13-28 confirmed."

[124]Matthew 17:11, referring to Malachi 3:23: "Lo, I will send you Elijah, the prophet, before the day of Yahweh comes. . . ."

[125]In Matthew's redaction, the "they" of verse 12 has no other noun to refer to except "the scribes" of verse 10.

Man will likewise suffer at the hands of "them," i.e., the Jewish scribes.[126]

If the transfiguration confirms Jesus' status in the heavenly world, the healing of the lunatic boy (17:14-21) confirms Jesus' power over the demonic world. Matthew's editing of the Markan miracle story is typical. The narrative is streamlined, colorful or bizarre details (in this case, the details of the illness) are omitted, and attention is concentrated on the main actors (Jesus and the father, then Jesus and the disciples). The majesty of Jesus is emphasized. The long narrative of Jesus' confrontation with the demoniac (Mark 9:20-27), which could be taken to indicate a struggle between the two, is reduced to "Jesus rebuked him and the demon left him" (Matt 17:18). The faith of the father is heightened from the beginning. He immediately kneels before Jesus and addresses him as a believer: "Lord, have mercy" (17:15).[127] There is no confession of unbelief (*apistia*) on the father's part (contrast Mark 9:24). Over against the believing father stand the disciples, who, for all their understanding, still suffer from littleness of faith (*oligopistia*, Matt 17:20).[128] Faith means union with Jesus and a share in his power; lack of faith means lack of power. The lack of faith and power on the part of the disciples is what occasions Jesus' apparently strange outburst against the unbelieving (*apistos*) generation in 17:17. In this one story, Jesus faces all three possible reactions to himself: the faith of the father, the little faith of the disciples, and the unbelief of the Jewish generation which perversely opposes Jesus.

It is this opposition which comes to the fore in the next pericope, the second prediction of the passion (17:22-23). The

---

[126]Matthew thus creates an artful cross-reference between his first passion prediction ("he will suffer many things from . . . the scribes") and 17:12 ("so also the Son of Man is about to suffer at *their* hands"), which, in the context of verse 10 and verse 12, must refer to the scribes.

[127]Mark 9:17 has the father say, "Rabbi."

[128]Contrast Mark 9:28, where prayer is recommended. While Jesus' concluding statement in Mark sounds like an afterthought appended to the story, Matthew's shortened narrative, studded with words referring to faith and power, aims at 17:19-20 as its proper goal.

mystery of the Son of Man, which has been so insistently stressed since 16:13, is thus carried forward from 17:12. The prediction also serves the literary and dramatic function of implicitly reminding the reader of the imminent journey up to Jerusalem,[129] the beginning of which must be postponed in the narrative until 19:1, after Book Four can be concluded with the church order discourse (chap. 18). At the end of the prediction (17:23), Matthew characteristically strikes out Mark's mention of the disciples' lack of understanding. They are simply sad—which presupposes that they do understand what has been said.

The strange pericope of the Temple tax (17:24-27) continues a number of themes of Book Four: the Son who communicates his privileged position and authority to the church, the special position of Peter in the church, the relationship of the church to Judaism, and the opposition of Jewish officialdom. Besides summarizing a good deal of what has preceded, the Temple tax story also provides the transition to the church order discourse. The pericope itself touches upon a number of aspects of church life, and the final verse (17:27) uses the catchword "scandalize," which then appears as a verb or noun six times in the early verses of chapter 18 (vv. 6-9). The story begins with Jewish officials approaching Peter about the annual Temple tax of two drachmas. We should especially note that here Peter acts as spokesman, not for the disciples, but for Jesus! It is presumed that the first disciple will know his Master's mind on a particular question. The Jewish officials show they are not believers in Jesus by speaking of him as "your teacher." The officials seem unsure about Jesus' attitude, either because they know of his strange mixture of fidelity to yet independence of the Law, or because he qualifies as a Jewish teacher, and certain Jewish rabbis claimed exemption

---

[129]This may be the significance of the curious phrase at the beginning of 17:22: "When they [?] were being gathered together." The phrase may refer to the assembling of Jesus' disciples in preparation for the journey up to Jerusalem. If this be true, it would put the whole church-order discourse in a new light: the Son of Man gives instructions to his embryonic church as he leads it up to Jerusalem for his death-resurrection.

from the tax. Peter, without great reflection, answers that Jesus will pay the tax. When Peter enters the house,[130] Jesus, with his divine knowledge, already knows what has happened. He undertakes to instruct Peter by means of a parable formed as a question: Do the kings of this world collect taxes not from their sons, the princes,[131] but from others? Peter gives the obvious answer, and Jesus replies with the saying which is the main theological point of the whole story: the sons are free.

Book Four has emphasized the transcendent status of Jesus the Son, walking on the water, recognized by Peter, acknowledged by the Father. And Book Four has connected this divine Son with the church which is "his" (16:18), the church which he saves by joining it in peril (14:22-33), by guarding it from false Jewish teaching (16:5-12), by giving it a legitimate teacher who supplies stability (16:17-19). So closely associated with the Son are the members of the church that both he and they can be referred to collectively as the sons who are free from the special claims and obligations of Judaism. A greater than the Temple is here (12:6), and he has made all who follow his way of mercy sons of the merciful Father (5:45). Love, mercy, imitation of the perfect Father (5:43-48)—these, and not a Temple tax, are the obligations of the free sons. The Jews were supposed to be the sons of the Kingdom, but their unbelief caused them to be cast out (8:12). The true sons of the Kingdom come from the good seed planted by the Son of Man (13:38). The members of Matthew's church know that they are sons in the Son; they enjoy Jesus' freedom vis-à-vis the intricacies of legalistic religion.

---

[130]The tax was usually paid at one's place of residence, here Capernaum. Matthew made a great deal of Jesus' transfer of residence to Capernaum (4:12-16). It is possible that the house referred to is Peter's house, in which Jesus is thought to be staying. In this case, the ecclesiological sense of the story is deepened still further.

[131]It is more probable that "sons" is to be taken literally. It is possible, though, that "sons" refers to a king's subjects in his own kingdom while "the others," "the foreigners," would be resident aliens, vassal kingdoms, or conquered territories. But since the point of the argument is the freedom of Jesus the Son (communicated to his church), it seems best to take sons in the literal sense.

Yet freedom is not license. True liberty exists for service, and for love, even toward one's enemies, even toward the Jews. Liberty is no excuse for giving unnecessary scandal to others (cf. 5:9, 38-42, 43-48, 8:13; 12:7; 18-6-9). So Jesus confirms Peter's yes, but supplies a profound explanation for the external compliance. The final command about catching a fish and finding the necessary coins in its mouth may be a metaphorical affirmation of trust in the Father, who will supply his sons with what they need for their service of love. From the ecclesiological point of view, the final command is important because Jesus says the fish will yield a stater, worth four drachmas. Peter is thus given just enough money to pay the Temple tax[132] for Jesus and himself. The very last words of the pericope, "for me and for you," underscore this point. Peter is associated here not with his fellow disciples but with his Master.

IV. MATT 18:1—19:1: THE DISCOURSE ON CHURCH LIFE

Having set this scene of Jesus and Peter together, Matthew now introduces the other disciples,[133] who, seeing the leader of

---

[132]This pericope no doubt circulated in the oral tradition at a time when the Temple tax was still a burning question for the early Jewish Christians. The destruction of Jerusalem did away with the original problem, and the tax was transferred to the Temple of Jupiter Capitolinus. But, even when Matthew writes c. A.D. 90, for a church which is becoming increasingly Gentile, the pericope retains its important theological message about the freedom of sons, limited not by legalism but by a loving concern not to give scandal, even to enemies. Such advice would still have relevance for Matthew's church in its relations with individual Jews.

[133]Here, as is generally the case in Matthew, "the disciples" probably refers to the twelve. The other members of the "college" find their leader alone with Jesus. This acts as the narrative springboard to the question which opens the discourse. Matthew has suppressed the unedifying setting of the question in Mark 9:33-34: Jesus has to drag the question out of the disciples, who had been arguing on the road about who was the greatest.

the twelve alone with Jesus, are moved (by jealousy?) to raise the question of rank (18:1): "Who then is the greatest in the Kingdom of heaven?"[134] Jesus' answer ranges far beyond the initial topic and is usually entitled the discourse on church order or church life.[135] For the sake of convenience, I shall divide the discourse into five parts.

In part one (18:1-5), Jesus speaks of true greatness in the Kingdom. Beginning with a concrete parable, he calls a child into the circle of these would-be leaders lusting for first place. We must not view the child of 8:2 through the eyes of Christian ethics or modern romanticism. In the ancient world, the child was a piece of property, not a full person. He had no rights, no defense, no means of assuring his own security. In keeping with the eschatological reversal of all values which Jesus announces in his gospel, the true disciple must undergo a conversion and become such a child standing in the presence of God the Father.[136] By

---

[134]Commentators dispute the precise meaning of "Kingdom" in 18:1. Is it the future Kingdom after the last judgment, or the present stage of the Kingdom, the partial realization of the Kingdom made concrete in the church? The question is so difficult to answer precisely because Matthew's conception of Kingdom is a process-concept: the Kingdom was present with Israel in the Old Testament, breaks in, in a new way, with the Christ-event, is handed over to the church, and comes fully at the end of the age.

[135]The phrase "church order" is sometimes rejected because many aspects of church life, especially hierarchical order and formal worship, are not explicitly treated. The topic is rather how to maintain good order among brothers living in God's family, the church. On the other hand, we should not ignore those passages which do seem to have a special reference to leaders (the parable of the lost sheep, the question in verse 21, asked by Peter). Verse 17 describes a formal, juridical act of the church (ekklēsia), however democratic the procedure may have been. At the same time, Matthew has omitted the very tolerant saying in Mark 9:38-39 about the exorcist who is an "outsider"; Matthew apparently prefers a more tightly run community.

[136]Jeremias, The Parables, 191, points to Jesus' use of Abba. Of course, Jeremias is interested more in the historical Jesus. Matthew does not use the Aramaic word in his gospel, but he certainly does stress the message of the Father of Jesus, who becomes the loving Father of all disciples. I would combine Jeremias' use of Abba with the humility-concept Jeremias considers on pp. 190-191.

renouncing false security and self-esteem, the disciple waits in trust and looks for the loving protection and secure future which can come from God alone. The disciple freely becomes what the ancient child necessarily was: humble, low. He therefore meets the condition for entrance into the Kingdom.[137] The disciple who humbles himself (*tapeinōsei*) imitates what is for Matthew the essential attitude of Jesus, the meek and humble (*tapeinos*) of heart (cf. 11:29). The church is well ordered when it is filled with free sons of God (17:26) who freely humble themselves. It is this humility which constitutes true greatness, both in the church and in the final stage of the Kingdom (v. 4). Here on earth, Jesus the humble one is present especially in the humble members of the church. By caring for them, Christians care for Christ (cf. 10:40-42; 25:31-46). We can see that, for Matthew, the union of Christ and his church is a dogmatic truth which generates a moral imperative—for all Christians, but especially for the Christian leaders who are in the greatest danger of neglecting the lowly.

The second part of the discourse (18:6-9) turns from the question of greatness in the Kingdom to the question of scandal in the church. It also turns from the image of the child to the clear reality of the "little ones who believe in me," i.e., the simple and lowly members of the church (v. 6). Jesus and Peter had avoided scandalizing the Jews (17:27). All the more must the stronger members of the church, especially the leaders, avoid causing the simple to fall into sin. Matthew realizes that if Christian leaders take a haughty, Pharisaic approach to simple untutored Christians, the church will simply have latter-day Pharisees as its leaders and teachers. Matthew's constant polemic against the scribes and Pharisees is not only a polemic against outsiders, i.e., against the Jews. It is also a polemic within the church, a constant warning to Christian scribes and leaders not to reduplicate the pride and hypocrisy of the Pharisees. To do so would be to introduce into the church those scandals which are part of the apocalyptic

---

[137]It should be stressed here that this childlike humility is not a high stage of perfection for the few, an extra ideal to be attained if one seeks to be "great" in the Kingdom. It is the essential condition for entrance into the Kingdom. Thus does Jesus deflate ambition.

trials of the end-time (13:41; 24:10). Such scandals, caused by man's unbridled will to power, are, to be sure, the unavoidable destiny of a sinful world. It is especially disastrous, though, when the world's standards are introduced into the church. The disciple who causes such scandals will suffer the severest punishment imaginable (v. 7). When we realize that these words would apply particularly, though not exclusively, to church leaders, we can appreciate the seriousness and sharpness of Matthew's admonition. However, adds Matthew, scandal is not just a danger for church leaders or even for members of the church in their interpersonal relations. Each Christian can be the source of his own fall. Any of our faculties, any of our drives, can lead us into sin and so into eschatological loss. A true disciple will judge it preferable to suffer any temporal, physical loss here and now rather than risk the loss of oneself for all eternity. Matthew does not hesitate to threaten any Christian, however secure or exalted may be his position in the church, with the fires of hell.

The theme of "the little ones" helps to carry on the thread of the discourse and also to frame the third section: on seeking out the straying members of the church (18:10-14). The apparently insignificant members of the church are in reality the most significant, because they have the highest order of angels guarding them.[138] If God takes such direct notice of the supposedly unimportant members of the church, how much more should the church and its leaders be attentive to them? The point is driven home by the parable of the sheep which has strayed.[139] Unlike the Lukan parallel, the parable in Matthew exemplifies the conduct not of Jesus but of any church leader. The leader is to be the good shepherd in his community, taking pains to win back the straying Christian who might easily be overlooked because of his insignificant status. The heart of a genuine shepherd rejoices more in

---

[138]Matthew uses here two Jewish beliefs: (1) angels protect the faithful; (2) only the highest angels can see the face of God.

[139]In Luke 15:3-7, it is the parable of the *lost* sheep. In Luke, Jesus uses the astounding, risky action of the shepherd to portray and defend his own action toward the sinful. The parable reaches its conclusion in the proclamation of the joy in heaven over the salvation of one who was lost. Contrast all this with Matthew 18:12-14.

saving the one straying soul than in tending the stronger Christian who does not need so much care. Such a shepherd has indeed taken Jesus as his model: he does the will of the Father, the merciful Father who is particularly concerned about those who easily get lost in the shuffle.

The theme of sinful members of the church and the church's response to them is continued in part four: on church discipline and church prayer (18:15-20).[140] Verses 15-18, which describe a three-step process of fraternal correction and discipline, have an interesting parallel in the Qumran documents. Verses 15-17 supply one of the clearest examples of an analogy between the eschatological community at Qumran and the early church. Qumran is a healthy reminder that a radical eschatological community eagerly awaiting the end of this age did not necessarily think that it was free to dispense with leadership and order. Such is also the case in Matthew's church, but Matthew is at pains to point out that church order must be pursued within a context of Christlike mercy.

Accordingly, if any Christian sees a brother sinning, he should first try to correct the sinner privately, to save the latter's feelings and reputation. Winning over the brother means winning him back for the church. Even fraternal correction in secret is an ecclesial act. If this effort is not successful, reserve is still demanded. Not a rush to public judgment, but the support of a few other Christians is the next step. Let them "witness" to the truth (cf. Deut 19:15) in a private meeting which avoids a formal trial. But if the sinner proves stubborn, then the whole assembly of believers, the church (*ekklēsia*), is to be called together. If the sinner remains obdurate, then the holy people of God, as a group, is threatened with desecration. The only solution is excommunication. The sinner who has strayed and who repeatedly rejects pleas to return must be treated as someone who is not a member of God's people (*ethnikos*, a Gentile or pagan), someone who is a

---

[140]The various sayings in verses 15-20 probably come from different sources: verses 15-17 use the second person singular and narrate a process, while verse 18 uses the second person plural and enunciates a principle of sacred law. Verses 19-20 form a separate unit, and each of the two verses may originally have been independent.

public sinner (telōnēs, a tax collector).[141]

We should notice that, in this whole process of discipline, there is no intervention by a single authoritative leader. When the church acts authoritatively, it acts as a whole, though Matthew certainly knows the existence of church leaders (cf. 23:34; 13:52; and of course 16:17-19). For Matthew, church leadership does not swallow up the authority of the assembly of believers acting as one body. That is why Matthew can assign to the local church in 18:18 the power to bind and loose which is given to Peter in 16:19. Whenever the church leader acts, he activates and concretizes the authority which resides in the church as a whole.[142] This authority to make a weighty decision like excommunication resides in the local community because it is assured by Jesus that the Father hears the church's prayer (v. 19). The size of the community is of no consequence. Wherever Christians gather, Jesus is there. The mere fact that they are disciples of Jesus, praying in the name of Jesus, guarantees that their smallest prayer on earth is heard in heaven. For these two or three gathered together are free sons praying to their Father. And the Son who makes them sons is right in their midst as they pray (v. 20).[143] The purpose of Jesus' birth (1:23, "Emmanuel") and the promise of his final commission (28:20, "I am with you all days") find realization and are vividly experienced in the Christian community at prayer. For the praying church, Jesus is indeed God with

---

[141]The end of verse 17 has a harsh ring. Jesus openly associated with tax collectors and even performed miracles for Gentiles. The phrasing may come from the early, stringently Jewish stage of Matthew's church.

[142]On the other hand, the differences between 18:15-18 and 16:17-19 should not be overlooked. "Church" in 18:15-18 refers to the local church, and its power to bind and loose refers to excommunication. Matthew 16:17-19 is addressed to one person; "church" means the church universal; the function of Peter is described with a series of images (rock, build, gates of Hades, keys, bind and loose). The power to bind and loose for Peter seems to refer first of all to the power to teach authoritatively and to interpret the words of Jesus for the church. Thus, Matthew 16 and Matthew 18 should not be played off against each other; they are complementary.

[143]At this point it becomes obvious that it is the risen Jesus who speaks.

us. In the minds of pious Jews, the study of the Torah was what guaranteed God's presence (the *Shekînâ*).[144] For the praying church, it is Jesus instead who gives the assurance of God's presence. For the Matthean disciples who seek the Father's presence and the Father's will, the impersonal Law has given way to the personal Son.

Part five of the discourse (18:21-35) concludes the whole church order address by stressing that the last word on church discipline must be limitless mercy. Peter, the church leader, asks Jesus about the proper limits of forgiveness among members of the church. Seven being the perfect number, Peter suggests seven times as the outer limits of Christian forgiveness. In this, Peter is acting a bit too much like a rabbi. While acknowledging Jesus' "law" of forgiveness, he wants that law, like every human law, to have clearly delineated limits. That is precisely what Jesus refuses to indicate. By playing with the number seven and turning it into a symbolic number,[145] Jesus emphasizes that true Christian forgiveness knows no limits. The theme of mercy without measure is illustrated by the parable of the unmerciful servant. A high official ("slave" in Oriental court language) is brought before his king and is convicted of owing an unimaginably huge sum.[146] As punishment, the official and all he has and loves must suffer total ruin: the whole family is to be sold into slavery. The fact that the official prostrates himself and promises to pay the whole debt—

---

[144]So in the early tractate of the Mishnah (the first part of the Talmud), the Sayings (or Chapters) of the Fathers (*Pirqe Aboth*) 3, 2 (or, in some enumerations, 3, 3). The parallel yet contrast between this rabbinic saying and Matthew 18:20 says a great deal about the consciousness of Matthew's church.

[145]The Greek numeral in 18:22 could mean either seventy-seven or seventy times seven. Either way, Jesus answers that perfect forgiveness knows no limit. There is probably a paradoxical reference to the limitless desire for revenge in the song of Lamech in Genesis 4:23-24: "If Cain is avenged sevenfold, then Lamech will be avenged seventy-sevenfold." This is one passage of the Torah which Jesus definitely revokes; in fact, he revokes the whole concept of retaliation, however moderate, in 5:38-39.

[146]Ten thousand talents is typical of the hyperbole of parables; King Herod's yearly income amounted to only nine hundred talents.

an obviously impossible task—only shows his desperation. Precisely the hopelessness of his case, his complete helplessness, moves the master to show mercy. To limitless debt there can be no solution except limitless compassion. The master shows himself truly master by wiping out the entire debt with a sovereign act of grace.

Unfortunately, while the master's mercy changes the official's situation, it does not change the official. No sooner is he out of the royal presence than he comes upon a fellow servant who owes him a comparative pittance. The forgiven official shows no forgiveness: payment or punishment is his cry. The fellow servant repeats the plea so recently used by the official, indeed, in the exact same words. The one difference is that now the promise of payment is actually possible. But the forgiven official will not forgive, and by that very fact the pardoned servant becomes the wicked servant. He loses the mercy he received because he will not pass it on to another. The king replaces his decree of mercy with a condemnation to torture, a torture which must be endless because the debt is unpayable. In sum: a Christian cannot win God's forgiveness; but he can lose it, by refusing to extend it to a brother. It is this theme of "brother" which gives the parable its ecclesial interpretation in verse 35. A pure act of mercy has made us all free sons of the Father of Jesus, and therefore we are all brothers in the church in which Jesus dwells. To refuse a brother the forgiveness which has made us sons is to rupture the family bond and to break the lifeline of mercy binding us through Jesus to the Father. The church was created by the mercy of the Father made present to us in Jesus. The church can continue to exist only if the men who were made brothers by this mercy continue to exchange it—not with an external ritual gesture, but "from the heart." That is Matthew's last word on life and discipline in the church.

Once again, Matthew has written a Christology without titles, a Christology which at the same time is clearly an ecclesiology. It is Jesus the meek and humble of heart who commands childlike humility as the insignia for church leaders. It is the suffering servant, the one who will give his life as a ransom for the many, who warns church leaders against causing simple Christians to fall into sin. The good shepherd who spent his life seeking out the lost sheep of a recalcitrant Israel bids the shepherds of the church to search for the weak and straying. Every member of the church must share this gentle care for the sinful. At the same time, the powerful Son of Man, who shares with his church the authority to forgive sins, assures his lowly assembly that their final decisions carry eternal consequences, for better or for worse. For when they act decisively, Jesus-Emmanuel, the divine presence in human form, acts with them. Rather than puffing the community up with pride, this realization should move them to ever greater mercy. The mercy Jesus has shown them has made them the church. The survival of the church depends on their extending what they have received: mercy without measure. At this point, the nexus of Christology and ecclesiology is not just the dogmatic axis of Matthew's gospel; it is also the profoundest expression of his spirituality. So ends Book Four, the Book of the union of Christ and his church.

CHAPTER EIGHT

Commentary on Book V
(Matt 19:1—26:1):
The Son Confronts the Old People of
God for the Last Time

I.   MATT 19:1—20:16: VARIOUS STATES OF LIFE
UNDER THE CROSS

Once the embryonic church is formed and instructed, Jesus can proceed to lead it up to Jerusalem for the great turning of the ages, his death-resurrection. By that apocalyptic event (1) Jesus will be exalted as Son of Man with all power in heaven and on earth, and (2) the Kingdom of God will be definitively transferred from the Jewish people to the new people of God, the church. Since Matthew's focus throughout his gospel is a Christology united to ecclesiology, it is not surprising that the death-resurrection will have a twofold effect, in Christology (exaltation) and ecclesiology (transfer of the Kingdom). But all this still lies in the future. In Book Five (chaps. 19-25), the embryonic church is led up to Jerusalem by Jesus, and on the way it must learn more about its vocation as it goes its way on pilgrimage to the paschal mystery (chaps. 19-20). Once in Jerusalem, it will see Jesus clash with the leaders of Judaism for the last time (chaps. 21-22). After he pronounces his woes on them (chap. 23), he will leave them to instruct his church on the apocalyptic mysteries still to transpire (chaps. 24-25). Book Five contains a great deal of material per-

136

taining to individual problems of different forms of discipleship. Here we will simply note what is relevant to Matthew's Christology and ecclesiology.

Book Five opens with the announcement of the movement from Galilee into Transjordan (understood incorrectly as part of Judea, 19:1). As throughout the ministry, crowds follow and Jesus performs miracles of healing. Building on Mark, Matthew then presents a number of narratives culminating in pronouncements of Jesus on various forms of Christian discipleship. Matthew 19:3-12 deals with marriage and total continence. The Pharisees, who approach Jesus with the malicious intention of trapping him (*peirazontes*, testing, v. 3), ask his view on the grounds for divorce.

Jesus instead turns to the more fundamental question of the very nature of marriage. Sexuality, marriage, and monogamy all come from the Creator's will at the very beginning of history. Since the unique unity of marriage is the will of the Creator himself, no human power can undo what God accomplishes in joining man and wife together. Jesus gives his pronouncement in the form of an apodictic command: therefore, separation is simply not to be attempted (v. 6). The Pharisees object to Jesus' appeal to the original intent of the Creator by citing the contrary command of Moses, regulating the divorce document. Jesus replies that Moses only allowed divorce because the Israelites were so resistant to God's word of revelation ("hardness of heart," v. 8). But, says Jesus, returning to his main point, divorce does not belong in the original plan of the Creator. Jesus then concludes the argument with another authoritative pronouncement ("but I say to you"), this time cast in the form of casuistic law. Whoever divorces his wife, except when the union is illicit,[147] and marries another, commits adultery. Once again, Jesus shows himself capable of revoking a major institution of the Torah (understood by the Pharisees as a command) simply on his own authority. Jesus claims to know directly what the Creator's will is. When the Mosaic Law permits something contrary to God's will, the

---

[147]For the meaning of Matthew's "exception," see Part Three of this book, pp. 248-257.

Mosaic Law must give way, simply because Jesus says so. Here we have operative a common apocalyptic idea. The eschatological age Jesus brings restores the blessings and order of paradise, and so any intervening order meant for the age of sin must give way.

Nevertheless, Jesus' disciples express consternation, and understandably so. Jesus has just abrogated an institution sanctioned by the Law and the rabbis, an institution which made marriage palatable. Without divorce, it would be better not to marry. Jesus takes up this hardly serious exclamation and takes it seriously. Yes, replies Jesus, it is true for certain people that marriage is not the vocation to choose. Besides the obvious cases of physical castration, there is the case of the man who freely chooses total abstinence because his life has been totally overwhelmed by and enveloped in the Kingdom of God.[148] The gift and the demand of God's rule in his life are so complete that marriage no longer holds meaning for him. In any case, the Kingdom which is now breaking into one's life must change one's way of living. Marriage without divorce or celibacy chosen for the Kingdom: these are the signs of a community which lives by the powers of the age to come. And it is Jesus, the bringer of the new age, who alone can know these eschatological mysteries of marriage and continence and teach them to his church.

After the married and the celibate, little children receive a mention as also belonging to the church. They are not to be despised or kept from Jesus, for they are the type of all those little, simple believers to whom the Kingdom rightly belongs.[149] By his open-hearted treatment of the "nobodies" of the ancient world,

---

[148]Traditionally, this total continence has been understood in terms of unmarried persons, who freely choose to remain so (cf. 1 Cor 7:25-39). It is possible, though, that Matthew understands it to refer to an innocent husband in a broken marriage, who must now remain alone; cf. Q. Quesnell, " 'Made Themselves Eunuchs for the Kingdom of Heaven' (Mt 19, 12)," *CBQ* 30 (1968) 335-358.

[149]Note the "*of such* is the Kingdom" in verse 14. The children typify those who stand before the Father with no claim and yet with total confidence. It may be reading too much into 19:13-15 to see a reference to infant baptism. But Matthew definitely does want the children to be considered part of the church, whatever that may involve in his mind.

Jesus again shows himself to be the meek and humble of heart.

Another "state of life" in the church is considered in 19:16-30: the rich man who, in this particular story, is also young. How is he to realize his call to discipleship? While we are not told till the end of the story of his youth and wealth (v. 22), we know from the beginning that something is wrong, since the youth addresses Jesus in the style of non-believers: "Teacher" (v. 16). Matthew proceeds to change Mark's version of Jesus' question to the young man. Mark says that Jesus asks: "Why do you call me good? No one is good but God alone" (Mark 10:18). Matthew naturally finds such a statement offensive to his high Christology. Accordingly, Matthew rewrites the whole introduction. Instead of having the young man address Jesus as "*good* teacher" (Mark 10:17), Matthew has the man ask, "What *good* should I do to have eternal life?" (Matt 19:16). This permits the less explosive retort: "Why do you ask me about what is good?" This response of Jesus allows a fairly smooth transition to the commandments which Jesus then lists. To Mark's second table of the decalogue Matthew adds the command to love one's neighbor as oneself (Lev 19:18). Commentators have often emphasized this addition to show that Matthew sees the whole Law summarized in and interpreted by the command of love. This is true to an extent, but usually the commentators fail to follow our story through to its conclusion. After hearing the commandments, *including love of neighbor*, the young man can say, apparently truthfully, that he has kept them all.

Yet something still is lacking. What is it? Here we have a most important point. Matthew puts love of neighbor at the end of the recitation of the decalogue, seeing in it the summation of all that is best in Old Testament morality. But even love of neighbor is not sufficient. A Jew who is not a disciple—and who is not going to become one—can claim compliance. Love of neighbor, in itself, still stands on the side of the old dispensation. The one thing lacking is something which transcends all the commands of the Old Testament, even love. The one thing lacking is total commitment to the person of Jesus, a commitment which entails renunciation of everything that keeps us from discipleship. Jesus decides that, in order to be totally dedicated to God's will in all simplicity (v. 21: to be "perfect"),[150] the rich young man must do two things: (1) he must give over all his possessions to the poor and so express his love of neighbor in a new, radical way; and (2) he must then follow Jesus with no earthly security to fall back upon, if things go wrong at the end of this dangerous journey to Jerusalem. The radical doing of God's will proves too much for a man who is completely moral, yes, even completely loving, according to the Torah. For all his love of neighbor, he cannot accept the break and new beginning, the new wine, Jesus demands. "Follow me": the touchstone and criterion of morality in the new age is not any commandment, but the person of Jesus himself. All morality finds its center and criterion not in love of neighbor, but in the person of Jesus. That is the problem with riches: they so easily hinder the Copernican revolution by which we make Jesus the center of everything. That is why it is so difficult for the rich to enter the Kingdom.

Now wealth, like marriage and children, were considered by Jews to be signs of God's favor. And so, as in 19:10, so in 19:25, the disciples are thrown into a quandary. Jesus assures them that the salvation of the rich, which, humanly speaking, is impossible, remains a possibility for the omnipotent God, who can move even the rich to renunciation and discipleship. Peter, again the spokesman, wants to be assured that the disciples who have practiced the renunciation Jesus demands will receive their reward. Betraying his twofold interest in church leaders and in all disciples, Matthew has Jesus give a twofold answer. First, the twelve disciples will share the eschatological rule and judicial power of the Son of Man on the last day, at the "regeneration." They, the

---

[150]As can be seen from 5:48 and the whole context of Matthew 5, to be perfect (*teleios*) is not an ideal for monks and contemplatives. It is the basic obligation of every Christian, and involves total dedication to the will of the Father, having a one-track mind when it comes to the things of God. Matthew therefore is not teaching a two-tier morality here (the commandments for ordinary Christians, the evangelical counsels for the perfect). "If you wish to be perfect" in verse 21 answers the question in verse 20, "What is still lacking"—i.e., in order to enter into eternal life (cf. v. 17).

patriarchs of the new people of God, will judge the old Israel.[151] Second, all Christians who have answered Christ's challenge of renunciation and have left all *for his name's sake* will receive much more in return, yes, even eternal life. For the eschatological age is by definition the age of reversal (v. 30). Verse 30 acts as a transition to the parable of the laborers in the vineyard, at the end of which the words of verse 30 will reappear (20:16).

The parable of the laborers (20:1-16) is related to the question of Peter about reward in a two-edged way. On the one hand, Jesus reaffirms the reward to be given those who have been working as Christian ministers from the beginning (i.e., the twelve), who have borne the burden of the day's heat in the vineyard of God's people (v. 12). At the same time Jesus defends the sovereign liberty of God to call and reward others as he wills, with no obligation to give an accounting to anyone (vv. 14-15). The earlier disciples and leaders are warned not to grumble against God's mercy. Places of leadership in the church, and even long track-records of service, do not necessarily guarantee higher places and greater rewards on the last day (cf. 20:23).

II. MATT 20:17—21:22: THE MESSIAH COMES TO JERUSALEM

In 20:17, Jesus begins the last leg of the journey up to Jerusalem, and accordingly utters the third passion prediction (20:17-19). It is the fullest of the three Markan predictions, and mentions the Gentiles as the actual agents of the passion. Contrary to the Markan predictions and his own version of the first two predictions, Matthew here has Jesus speak openly of being

---

[151]This is certainly the original sense of the saying in Matthew 19:28. It is possible that Matthew reinterprets the idea in an ecclesial light: the twelve shall function as the rulers of the new people of God, the church. But this demands taking Israel in the sense of the Christian church, a usage not found elsewhere in Matthew. Moreover, regeneration *(paliggenesia)* is more naturally taken as the equivalent to Matthew's "consummation of the age" (28:20).

crucified instead of simply being put to death (so also 26:2, the fourth passion prediction, added by Matthew). Once again, the paradox of the Son of Man surfaces. The Son of Man will sit on his glorious throne at the "regeneration," sharing his rule with the twelve disciples (19:28); but first he must win that throne by becoming the crucified Son of Man. By implication, the same route is marked out for the twelve. If they are to share the throne, they must share the cross. The implication is lost, however, on the mother of the sons of Zebedee (20:20-28). Totally misunderstanding how one enters into the Messianic banquet, she wishes to use her influence to gain her sons the two best seats at the banquet, right next to their master. Jesus first asks whether they can endure the sufferings (the cup) which he must undergo in Jerusalem.[152] Even when they profess their willingness, a willingness belied by their flight after Jesus' arrest (26:56), Jesus makes a disconcerting reply. Suffer they will, but not even sharing Jesus' sufferings gives one a handle on God. Rank in the Kingdom hangs solely on the decision of Jesus' Father, who might well ask the pushy disciples: "Am I not free to do what I want with what is mine?" (20:15).

The jealous anger of the other members of the twelve only reveals how little they have assimilated Jesus' predictions of the passion and his instructions on true greatness in the Kingdom. He summons them all and makes a blunt comparison between the way the kingdoms of this world are run and the way his church must be ordered. All the power and force used by earthly despots to secure order in their realms are antithetical to a church that runs on love and mercy, healing and forgiveness. Jesus does not reject a "holy ambition" to be great or first among the disciples, provided the ambition recognizes the law of eschatological reversal. To be great in the church means to be a servant, one who is defined by his living for the advantage of others, not self. To be first in the church means to be a slave, a non-person with no rights, whose

---

[152]Matthew omits Mark's reference to baptism, i.e., to the waters of death engulfing an individual (Mark 10:38-39). Perhaps by the time Matthew writes, the idea of a baptism which Jesus bestows on his disciples could mean, in the mind of the evangelist, only the Christian sacrament.

whole existence consists in obeying others. That is the only sort of leadership possible in a church going up to Jerusalem for crucifixion. This law of slave-service in the church is firmly grounded in the slave-service of Jesus. While Mark introduces the next Son of Man saying (10:45) with a simple "and this is so because," Matthew makes the saying both the reason and the point of comparison for all that has preceded: "Just as the Son of Man. . . ."[153] The disciples are empowered to perform this service for the church, because Jesus the Son of Man has first performed it for them. He is the enabler and the exemplar for his disciples. This Son of Man, whom Peter has identified as Messiah and Son of God, this Son of Man, who will sit on his glorious throne as judge, this Son of Man first exercises his rule in the form of service unto death. And the death of the Son of Man is no ordinary death; it is sacrificial death, a giving of his life as a ransom on behalf of and in the place of the mass of mankind.[154] Now all the references to "being handed over" in the passion predictions become clear. The Son of Man is the suffering servant of Isaiah 53:10-12, who gives his life as an offering for sin, who surrenders himself to death and thereby takes away the sins of many.[155] This is the full service the Son of Man renders to his

---

[153]*Hōsper*, "just as," often carries both a causal and a comparative sense in the New Testament.

[154]"The many" refer to the totality which is saved vis-à-vis the one man who dies for the sake of the totality.

[155]The Septuagint version of Isaiah 53:10-12 first uses the simple form of the verb "to give," *didōmi*, as in Matthew 20:28, and then uses twice the compound form "to hand over," *paradidōmi*, which is found in a number of the passion predictions. The importance for Matthew of this interpretation of Jesus' death as sacrifice cannot be diminished by the observation that he is "merely" taking over the pericope from Mark. Time and time again Matthew has omitted, changed, and transposed Markan material to suit his theological purpose. If he takes over Mark 10:45, the presumption must be that the theology of vicarious sacrifice suits Matthew's redactional viewpoint. This consideration is especially weighty when we consider that Luke omits the saying. When we add to all this the fact that Matthew adds "unto the remission of sins" to the cup-word at the last supper (26:28), the conclusion seems unavoidable that Matthew gave an important place in his theology to the death of the Son of Man as life-giving sacrifice (cf. also 27:51-54).

disciples, a service they must share if they wish to share his future rule. Church order rests on nothing less than the sacrificial death of its leaders.

As though to emphasize this point that the triumphant journey up to Jerusalem is actually the culmination of loving service, Matthew makes the last act of Jesus before his entry into the holy city an act of healing. Two blind men show they have the faith of true disciples by crying out for help to him who is both Lord and Son of David. They recognize even in their blindness the Messiah who cares for those whom everyone else tells to be quiet. These little ones, neglected by others but healed by the servant who takes away our illnesses (8:17), prove their discipleship by "following" (20:34).

Without any break in the story, Matthew narrates the triumphal entry into Jerusalem (21:1-9). Matthew's dependence on Mark makes his modifications of the pericope all the more interesting. The major change is the introduction of the formula quotation from Zechariah 9:9, with an introductory line from Isaiah 62:11. So intent is Matthew on a literal fulfillment of Zechariah's prophecy that he has Jesus ride on two animals. Theological affirmation triumphs over historical probability, or even historical imagination.[156] The prophecy speaks to Zion, calling attention to the Messianic king who comes now, not to the nations in general, but to the holy city, to ratify and fulfill all God's promises to his chosen people. If, after some initial enthusiasm, Zion rejects her king, it will not be for want of notification. One reason for the rejection will be that this king is not the type Zion really wants. He rides the ass, the animal of peace, as opposed to the horse, the steed of war, in order to emphasize that he is peaceable and meek. Matthew is so intent on stressing Jesus' quality of meekness that he is willing to drop from the citation of Zechariah two other adjectives which he would certainly attribute to Jesus: "just and saving." Far from being the military conqueror and political ruler many Jews wanted, this king, the true Messiah, is meek and humble of heart (11:29), the bestower of happiness on the meek and the peacemakers (5:5, 9).

---

[156]For a more extended treatment, cf. Part One of this book, pp. 21-22.

Whether the crowds realize it or not, their acclamation of him as Son of David (Matt 21:9, in addition to Mark) is most fitting. He is in truth the Messiah who has regard for the lowly and the poor, the sick and the disenfranchised, as verse 14 makes clear.

Parallel to the pattern of prophecy and fulfillment, Matthew has inserted another typical pattern in 12:1-9, that of command and accomplishment (found a number of times in the infancy narrative). Jesus gives his disciples a precise command about finding the two animals, and the disciples fulfill his command in strict obedience. This obedience of the disciples to the command of Jesus takes precedence in Matthew's treatment over Jesus' supernatural knowledge, which is more prominent in Mark. Matthew shows us a peaceable Son of David, a meek Messiah, whose authoritative word nevertheless commands obedience from true disciples.

At this point in the narrative, Matthew changes Mark's order notably. After the triumphal entry, Mark has Jesus simply look around and then return to Bethany. The cleansing of the Temple takes place on the following day. Matthew not only places the cleansing (or rejection?) of the Temple on the same day, but also surrounds it with a number of verses to portray the varied responses to the Son of David among the people of Jerusalem (21:10-17). First, the city as a whole is "shaken"; the word for "shaken" (*eseisthē*) is used elsewhere for an earthquake. The eschatological King is shaking the foundations of the holy city, the city which years ago was frightened by the events surrounding his birth (2:3). Unfortunately, the city has not learned much in the meantime; it has to ask: "Who is this?" The failure of the holy city to listen to Zechariah and to recognize its King when he comes to it is perfectly summed up in that one question.

The crowds' response is intriguing: "This is the prophet Jesus, the one from Nazareth of Galilee." On the level of the story, the crowds' answer could be meant to portray their ignorance too, their choice of a woefully inadequate category.[157] But Matthew may have something more profound in mind. We saw that in

---

[157]This is the view of Kingsbury, *Matthew: Structure*, 88: "For Matthew, however, such a confession [prophet] has only negative value. . . . " I am not so sure that it has only negative value. Especially with the

his portrayal of Jesus' entry (riding on the animals of peace), in his citation of Zechariah (dropping "just and saving" to highlight "meek"), and in his choice of acclamation (Son of David, the healer of the lowly), Matthew stressed that this King is not a political or military leader, but a peaceable, humble healer, who nevertheless can speak an authoritative word. On a natural level, after the messianic procession, we might well expect the crowds to identify Jesus as King or Messiah. The fact that they respond that he is a prophet, indeed, *the* prophet, may be seen by Matthew as a positive bending of the royal-Messiah idea in the direction of a more spiritual conception. Especially when we remember how Matthew, throughout his gospel, has bent the titles Son of God and Messiah in the direction of servant-prophet-lowly Son of Man, the designation "prophet" may not be judged negatively by Matthew. The same may be true of "from Nazareth": it reminds one of the humble, unlikely origins of this Son of David (cf. 2:23).

The dual picture of the authoritative King who is also the humble Son of David is continued in verses 12-16. The authority of the one "greater than the Temple" (12:6) is shown by his casting out the buyers and sellers. For Matthew, this action may signify not so much a cleansing of the Temple as a judgment upon it. The Temple has failed to fulfill its mandate in Scripture to be a house of prayer; therefore it will be rejected and destroyed (cf. 22:7; 23:38; 27:51).[158] That is why Matthew leaves out of the quotation of Isaiah 56:7 the phrase included by Mark: "for all the nations." Writing after the destruction of Jerusalem in A.D. 70, Matthew knows the Temple was not destined to be a universal house of prayer. That vocation, which the Jewish Temple had lost, has now passed over into the Christian church (28:16-20). In verse 14, the King who comes with authority to judge even the Temple shows himself again the merciful Son of David by healing the blind and the lame, those sick who were excluded from Temple worship because of their illnesses. The old and the new cultic communities stand facing each other. The Messiah rejects the

---

definite article in 21:11 ("This is *the* prophet") there may be an allusion (on Matthew's part) to the prophet-like-Moses of Deuteronomy 18:15, 18; cf. Matt 17:5.

[158]Notice the interesting contrast of "my house" in 21:13 and "your house" in 23:38.

established but corrupt sanctuary of Judaism and gathers about himself the outcast and the maimed to form his eschatological community. Significantly, the very miracles Jesus performs in the Temple have a dual effect. One is almost transported into the dualism of John's gospel. The children, the lowly ones despised by others but received by Jesus (cf. 18:2-3; 19:13-15) recognize in this healer of the outcast the Son of David. But the guardians of cult and magisterium, the high priests and the scribes, take offense at the children's acclamation of the truth. Jesus indicates that the Jewish officials do not even know their own Scripture well. Otherwise they would see in this acclamation the fulfillment of Psalm 8:3. The children represent the mere babes (*nēpioi*: so here and in Matt 11:25) to whom the Father has revealed the Son. The praise they give is enough to silence the vengeful foes, who in this case are the "wise and intelligent" leaders of Judaism.

Instead of allowing a day to intervene between the cursing of the fig tree and the verification of the curse, as Mark does, Matthew presents the whole miraculous event early on the morning of the next day (Matt 21:18-22) as Jesus returns to Jerusalem after spending the night in Bethany. Probably Matthew sees in the fig tree producing leaves but no fruit a symbol of a Judaism which is rejected because its religion is all hypocritical show, paying lip-service to but not doing the will of God. Matthew, however, is more intent on a Christological and a parenetic point: the power of the word of Jesus to cause the tree to wither immediately, and the exemplary lesson on faith this miracle holds for the disciples. A faith which does not waver[159] but which confidently expresses petitions in prayer will receive what it requests. What Matthew has stressed throughout the miracle stories receives a perfect summation here.

III.   MATT 21:23—22:45: THE FINAL CONTROVERSIES WITH THE JEWISH LEADERS

Matthew has now concluded the major actions of Jesus in

---

[159]Here the word for waver is *diakrinomai*; Matthew uses *distazō* in 14:31 and 28:17.

Jerusalem before the passion (21:1-22). What follows is the teaching which fills the rest of his days before the passion (21:23-25:46). Matthew begins with the first controversy story (on Jesus' authority); then he passes over to three parables of judgment upon Israel (the two sons; the wicked tenant farmers; the wedding feast); he then returns to the controversy stories, numbers two to five (tribute to Caesar; marriage and the resurrection; the greatest commandment; Son of David and Lord). The controversy stories are concluded by the woes pronounced on the scribes and Pharisees (chap. 23), which in turn serves as the bridge to the final discourse in the gospel, the eschatological discourse (chaps. 24-25). These scenes of teaching and dispute begin with Jesus entering the Temple (21:23). The Temple will remain the place where Jesus teaches until he announces solemnly: "Behold, your house [i.e., the Temple] is left to you desolate" (23:38). Then he will leave the Temple, only to predict its destruction (24:1-2). Thus, for the last time, on one solemn day of teaching which stretches from 21:23 to 23:39, the legitimate teacher of God's will makes a final appeal to the Jewish leaders and people within their sacred precincts. But they will not listen. The teaching must end with the woes on the scribes and the Pharisees and then the apocalyptic discourse. There is nothing further to say. The discourse at the end of Book Five marks the close of the public ministry (26:1, "when Jesus had completed *all* these words"). The Passover and the passion begin (26:2).

The first controversy story (21:23-27) raises the basic question which lies beneath all the controversies between the Jewish authorities and Jesus: What precisely is the authority of Jesus, and where does it come from (21:23)?[160] In true rabbinic fashion, Jesus replies with a counter-question: First tell me your opinion about the Baptist's authority and its origin. Was it truly divine, or

---

[160]Matthew now speaks of high priests and elders. This follows the tradition he has received, and is historically correct. These priests and elders would not have had much occasion to clash with Jesus in the Galilean countryside. Their question "By what authority do you do *these things*?" refers primarily to the events surrounding the triumphal entry and the cleansing of the Temple. But it is Jesus' teaching which provides the precise occasion for the challenge, and it is the authority of his teaching which is especially vindicated by the exchange.

merely human? The leaders are caught on the horns of a dilemma. Either they admit the heavenly origin of a prophet who excoriated them for their lack of true repentance (cf. 3:7-12)—and so condemn themselves—or they deny the legitimacy of the most important and popular prophetic figure of the time before Jesus—and then risk the wrath of the people. Being unable to go either way, they are forced to plead ignorance (v. 27). But, since they have been asked about a well-known religious figure second only to Jesus in popularity and significance, their admission is a condemnation of their own failure as teachers and leaders of the people. If they confess ignorance on so pivotal a question, who should listen to their teaching on any point? And so Jesus triumphantly responds: "Then I, for my part, do not tell you on what authority I do these things." The leaders *cannot* say because of ignorance; Jesus *chooses* not to say, because his teaching authority is superior to these incompetents. Such a message was extremely important for Matthew's church, engaged as it was in a struggle with the Jewish magisterium of its day. This superior authority of Jesus has been transmitted by him to his church (Matt 16:17-19).

There follows the first of the three parables of judgment on Israel, the parable of the two sons (21:28-32). The parable contrasts doing the will of God after repenting of earlier rebellion and rendering God lip-service without doing his will.[161] The tax collectors and prostitutes, the religious outcasts of legalistic Judaism, had repented because of the Baptist's eschatological preaching and living. On the other hand, the self-satisfied leaders felt no need for repentance and therefore failed to do God's will ("justice"). Even when they saw the startling conversion of the outcasts they refused to reconsider. Consequently, the outcasts enter the Kingdom while the leaders are excluded.[162] In this contrast Matthew and his church would see the later contrast be-

---

[161]The almost insoluble problem of deciding which son was mentioned first in the original text need not detain us here.

[162]The Greek of verse 31b represents a Semitic idiom. *Proagousin hymas eis*, which might literally be translated, "they go in before you," but actually means, "they go in and you do not." In this I agree with Jeremias, *Parables*, 125 n. 48, against W. Kümmel, *Promise and Fulfillment* (London: SCM, 1969) 78 n. 198.

tween the Pharisees who rejected the Christian gospel and the sinful but repentant Gentiles who enter the church while the Pharisees exclude themselves. It may also be that Matthew in addition intends an admonition to Christians within the church: they likewise are exposed to the danger of being sayers instead of doers (cf. 7:21-23).

The second parable of judgment, the parable of the evil tenants of the vineyard (21:33–46), continues the image of the vineyard (cf. 21:28). But now the tone of judgment becomes more threatening, especially because the ones judged are no longer simply the leaders but also the whole people. Central to Matthew's understanding of the parable is his insertion at verse 43: "The Kingdom of God will be taken from you and will be given to a people bearing its fruits." In Mark 12:1-12, the vineyard symbolizes Israel, as is clear from Isaiah 5:1ff. The parable is aimed only at the leaders. In Matthew, the vineyard becomes the Kingdom, present even in the Old Testament in Israel. While the leaders are still indicted in a special way, it is the whole people Israel which suffers the loss of the Kingdom.[163] The Kingdom is handed over to another people, the new people of God, the church (compare the parallel between verse 41 and verse 43). Of course, this church contains Jews, but it is not Jewish by definition; it is not Israel. The church is a "third people," neither Jew nor Gentile, yet made up of both. The continuity between this church and Israel (if one may even speak of continuity) is not one of simple growth or smooth succession. There is a tragic break. The Kingdom is wrenched from the one and given to the other. If there is any connection at all between Israel and the church in salvation-history, it is because both had contact with Jesus, the bearer of the Kingdom.

Thus, Matthew's ecclesiology is clearly enunciated in verse 43, and the whole parable must be read in its light. In the parable,

---

[163]One can detect here a certain tension between the thrust of the parable in Mark and its Matthean application. For Matthew, however, the tension would not be great. In the passion narrative, Matthew himself portrays how the leaders of the people are the chief instigators of Jesus' rejection, though they finally convince and involve the crowds (27:15-26).

Matthew tends to streamline the narrative and to bring out clearly the parallels with stages of salvation-history. The owner of the vineyard is explicitly called "the master of the house" from the very beginning (v. 33), thereby making the reference to God more obvious from the start. Being God, he does not ask for only some of the fruits (as in Mark 12:2), but rather "for his fruits"—which naturally means the complete doing of God's will. Matthew groups the slaves of this householder into two sets, probably representing the prophets before and after the exile. Matthew stresses that even after the exile, Israel did not repent. The post-exilic prophets met the same suffering and martyrdom as the prophets before the exile (v. 36). Israel's whole history is one great rejection of the prophets, and so it is not surprising that Jesus fares no better. However, Matthew carefully distinguishes from the prophets of the Old Testament the son who is sent "later" or "last" (v. 37). The Markan designation of the last envoy as "son" fits Matthew's Christology perfectly. In verse 39, Matthew probably reflects the historical circumstances of the crucifixion in having the tenants first throw the son out of the vineyard (here, Jerusalem),[164] and then kill him.

With a fine dramatic and ironic touch, Matthew has Jesus ask his enemies what "the Lord of the vineyard" will do when he "comes" in judgment. Once again, the leaders are forced to condemn themselves (cf. 21:31). *They* are the evil tenants who will be destroyed while the vineyard, the Kingdom, is given to another people who will render God his fruit by doing his will (vv. 41, 43). Jesus replies in verse 42 that this is indeed the eschatological reversal prophesied in Psalm 118:22-23. The builders, the Jewish leaders, have rejected Jesus because he did not fit into their plans for building the people of God.[165] Their rejection is acted out in the passion and crucifixion of the Son. But, by the resurrection,

---

[164]Even when parables become detailed allegories, the symbols are not always univocal. From verses 41 and 42, Matthew obviously understands the vineyard to mean the Kingdom. But that cannot be the meaning in verse 39; in no sense can the Son be thrown out of the Kingdom. The vineyard in verse 39 must be Jerusalem.

[165]In verse 42 the imagery shifts for a moment from agriculture to architecture because of the metaphors employed in the psalm verse.

God has reversed that decision and has made Jesus the keystone of a new structure, the new people of God, the church (cf. the "building" motif in 16:18). This is a marvelous turnabout and new beginning, a miracle possible to God alone. The leaders[166] realize to their chagrin that Jesus is speaking about them, but they dare not precipitate the passion now, since the crowds' estimation of Jesus as a prophet still protects him (cf. 21:11, 26). But, as Matthew has intimated already, Jesus' prophetic role will ultimately involve the prophetic destiny of martyrdom. In short, Matthew has not taken over a Christological parable from Mark and obscured the Christology for the sake of ecclesiology. Rather, the Christology is kept and even heightened, while at the same time being united to an ecclesiology. The union spells judgment for Israel.

The third and final parable of judgment, the parable of the wedding feast (22:1-14), has a certain parallel in Luke's parable of the great supper (Luke 14:15-24). But the differences are so many, it is difficult to say whether Matthew is using Q.[167] Certainly he has rewritten his tradition with motifs borrowed from the parable of the wicked tenants. As in the parable of the wicked tenants, father and son appear vis-à-vis a hostile group, but now the father is a king, an obvious symbol for God. Once again, the chief agent sends forth two different groups of slaves with a request. Again murder is committed and the punishment is the destruction of the murderers. Again what the murderers lose is given over to others, who previously had no claim on it. Again the whole narrative is schematized to present a neat outline of salvation-history. If anything, the line of history is clearer here, except that there is no mention now of the death of the Son, who appears honored

---

[166] In verse 45, the Pharisees have replaced the elders; Matthew thus has the same united, though historically unlikely, front of Sadducees (chief priests) and Pharisees which he presents in 3:7; 16:1, 6, 11, 12.

[167] Luke speaks of a great supper (not a wedding banquet) offered by "a man" (not a king, and there is no son). In Luke, not some but all the guests make excuses concerning other preoccupations. Only one slave is sent; he is not murdered or maltreated. The supper is filled rather with the poor and maimed, and when that does not suffice, those from the highways and hedges are forced to come in.

(glorified) from the beginning. In an originally independent parable Matthew has attached to the conclusion (vv. 11–13), the son is not mentioned at all, although we can infer from the Matthean context that the king is participating in the wedding feast of his son. However, despite the mention of the son (which is an addition vis-à-vis Luke), the emphasis in Matthew 22:1–14 as a whole is more on salvation-history and ecclesiology than on Christology.

This third parable opens, for a change, on a note of joy, though it will close on a very somber chord. The wedding feast is the eschatological banquet which God prepares for his Son, to be celebrated at the end of time. Two sets of slaves (prophets) are sent out to invite the Jews to the feast. The first refusal is answered with divine patience and a renewed attempt to win over the recalcitrant guests who insanely refuse a free gift. The second time, while most of the invited guests go away to their private concerns (the mass of the Jewish people?), some (the leaders?) kill the slaves. The divine wrath is kindled, and the King destroys Jerusalem and its murderous leaders in A.D. 70.[168] Since those originally invited showed by their deeds that they were not ready and worthy, the invitation is now spread to the roads going out of the King's city, i.e., to the Gentiles. New slaves (the Christian missionaries) bring in everyone, bad and good alike (the universal mission), and the hall is filled (the church as a worldwide mixture of good and evil).

At this point (v. 11), Matthew ties on a second parable, to warn the church that it remains as subject to judgment as Jerusalem was. At the parousia, the King enters the wedding hall to inspect his guests. The boor without the clean wedding garment is the Christian who may have accepted the missionary call to Christianity but who has not earnestly prepared himself for the

---

[168]K. Rengstorf, "Die Stadt der Mörder (Mt 22, 7)," in *Judentum, Urchristentum, Kirche* (Berlin: Töpelmann, 1960) 106-129, tries to deny any necessary reference to A.D. 70. He points to the theme of military expeditions and the destruction of cities in the Old Testament. Be that as it may, he cannot really explain why Matthew should interrupt the natural flow of the story (from verse 5 to verse 8) with a theme that is totally out of place; cf. Part One, p. 13.

eschatological banquet by repentance and a life filled with the fruits of repentance. He has no excuse for his sordid state; he is as unworthy as were the Jews. Fittingly, then, he suffers the same fate as that predicted for the sons of the Kingdom (the Jews) in 8:12: excluded from the banquet, he is thrown into hell, the outer darkness, filled with lamentation and pain. Matthew then sums up not only 22:1-13 but all three parables of judgment with the sad truth of verse 14: "The called are many, the elect are few." This axiom bespeaks first of all the tragedy of the Jews, who early and late were called and refused. But the title, "the called" (klētoi), was also the eschatological designation which early Christians used of themselves. As we see in Paul, many early Christians made no distinction between call and election; God's call would naturally result in election or final glorification (Rom 8:28-30, 33; 1 Pet 1:1, 15). Standing at the end of the first century, Matthew has learned the wisdom of distinguishing between the two words. And verses 11-13 emphasize this is not simply a question of distinguishing between Jews and Gentiles, as verses 1-12 might intimate. The church as it now stands is under judgment, for it is a mixture of good and evil. Only the last judgment will manifest who has been really chosen for the eschatological banquet and who belongs with the rejected Jews outside.

After the third of the three parables of judgment, Matthew rejoins the Markan order of narrative. The controversy stories which began in 21:23-27 (the authority of Jesus) are now resumed and are followed down to the end of the public ministry: the coin of tribute (22:15-22); the resurrection of the dead (22:23-33); the greatest commandment (22:34-40); and the Son of David (22:41-46). Jesus' ministry thus ends on a note of bitter acrimony, as his enemies launch attack after attack only to be discomforted again and again by the wisdom of their opponent. When, in the final controversy story, Jesus switches to the attack and asks a question of his enemies, they are immediately unmasked as incompetent teachers unable to answer a question on the subject which they are supposed to know perfectly. The enemies of Jesus finally see there is no chance of defeating him by debate. The only way left is judicial murder. And so the ministry ends and the passion begins.

We can appreciate, therefore, the critical position these last four controversy stories have in Book Five. In Matthew's redaction, they follow upon Jesus' three parables of judgment and so appear as the Jewish leaders' counter-attack and their last attempt to overcome Jesus in a verbal duel. The various parties of Judaism take turns trying to trip Jesus up with some question especially dear to the given party's point of view. If one angle fails, surely another will succeed. None does.

The second controversy, on the coin of tribute (22:15-22), is precipitated by the two Jewish parties holding opposite views on the question: the Pharisees and the Herodians. The Pharisees, as stringent observers of both the written and the oral Law, were angered by the Roman poll tax, which forced them (1) to admit Israel's subjection to pagan foreigners and (2) to acknowledge Rome's sovereignty with a coin bearing the graven image of Caesar (the denarius). The Herodians, on the other hand, were the supporters of the puppet ruler Herod Antipas, who owed his power to Roman support. Naturally, the Herodians favored payment of the tax. The question the two parties pose is meant to force Jesus to side with one or the other party—and lose either way. Either he sides with the Pharisees and thereby makes himself vulnerable to charges of being a zealot revolutionary, or he sides with the Herodians and thereby loses the respect of observant Jews and popularity with the nationalistic crowds. The questioners show they are unbelievers by addressing Jesus as "teacher." Yet, with almost Johannine irony, they proclaim the true state of affairs: Jesus is truthful and does teach the way of God in truth, with no dilution or favoritism (22:16). Jesus knows full well the malice hiding behind the mask of these fair words, a mask he immediately rips away. This game of testing Jesus is just a sign of rank hypocrisy, the inner split between word and thought, between word and deed, so common in the professionally religious man.

But Jesus proceeds to show his adversaries that he does act exactly as they claimed in verse 16: without hesitation, he speaks the simple truth. At the same time, he shows up their hypocrisy by asking *them* for a coin of tribute. In other words, he does not carry such a coin; they do. Now, to carry and use the coins of a sovereign is implicitly to recognize his sovereignty. The questioners willingly use a coin bearing Caesar's image and inscription; to that extent, they accede to and cooperate in his rule. To be consistent, they should be willing to give to Caesar what belongs to Caesar, just as they must give to God what belongs to God. Jesus of course does not make of this pronouncement a detailed theory of church and state. His axiom is an open-ended principle which evades the trap while speaking the truth. By his trenchant yet almost witty rule, Jesus unmasks the malice of his opponents and shows himself a past master of the wisdom traditions of Israel, which delighted in a battle of wits and a brilliant riposte. Jesus' enemies can do nothing but marvel and then beat a hasty retreat.

The group which historically was the main opponent of the Pharisees, the Sadducees, now appears in the third controversy, a question about the resurrection (22:23-33).[169] They likewise begin with the telltale address, "teacher." Supposing correctly that Jesus held the doctrine of the resurrection of the dead, they create a ridiculous case which is meant to make a laughing-stock of both the doctrine of the resurrection and this teacher who holds it. The case involves seven brothers, each of whom successively marries the same woman, because of the so-called levirate law of marriage, based on Deuteronomy 25:5-6 and Genesis 38:8. The question they pose as to which brother will have the woman as wife at the resurrection is intended to show how ridiculous belief in the resurrection is. Jesus' reply is blunt and twofold: these supposed leaders know (1) neither the Scriptures (2) nor the power of God. Jesus then explains those two points in reverse order.

First, the power of God is so great that, when he raises the dead, he does not simply bring them back to their old earthly state, somewhat improved. The idea of a return to an old earthly life was indeed a vulgar view of the resurrection present in some

---

[169]As indicated in Part I, pp. 20-21, Matthew probably does not appreciate the precise nature of the Sadducees. The fact that they ask a question especially relevant to their theological position and that Jesus argues correctly according to their presuppositions is due to the Markan pericope Matthew takes over.

Jewish writings of the time. But Jesus does not share such an unsophisticated view of resurrection. At the resurrection, says Jesus, God's power will totally transform men, making them similar to the angels, who exist in God's presence.[170] Marriage, which belongs to the present world which is passing away, will no longer exist in the new world transformed by God's power. Jesus' second argument is drawn from that part of Scripture to which the Sadducees attributed unique value, the Pentateuch. The Sadducees denied the resurrection precisely because it was not taught in the five books of Moses. To reply to that objection, Jesus shows that God's words to Moses in Exodus 3:6 imply the resurrection. Centuries after the patriarchs had died, God can still say, using the present tense, "I *am* the God of Abraham, Isaac, and Jacob." The ever-living God is not to be defined or named by using dead men who have ceased to exist. God's choice of this designation shows that in some way these patriarchs continue to live in religious relationship with him. This time, Matthew notes that it is the crowd which is struck with amazement at Jesus' teaching. The Sadducees, to whose company belong the high priests who will conduct Jesus' trial, are ominously silent.

When the Pharisees see their colleagues silenced, they get together and select one of their number for the fourth controversy, on the greatest commandment (22:34-40). Once again, the "tempter" displays his lack of belief by the address, "teacher." The question, which of the 613 commandments in the Law was the greatest, was hotly debated. Some held in theory that the commandments were equally important, while other rabbis recognized that practical necessities demanded some sort of gradation. Jesus designates as the greatest commandment the love of God which is demanded in the opening words of the great Jewish prayer, the *Shema'* ("Hear, O Israel"; cf. Deut 6:4-5). Jesus clearly puts this duty first: this command is the greatest. Yet he immediately puts a second alongside of it. Similar to love of God is the love of neighbor commanded in Leviticus 19:18. Mat-

---

[170]The phrase "in heaven" in verse 30 may be a Semitic euphemism for "in God": the angels and mankind after the resurrection will exist and live "in God."

thew has stressed this second commandment already in 5:43 and 19:19. Here it is joined to love of God to form the double "peg" on which the whole of Jewish Scripture, the Law and the prophets, "hangs." In other words, this double command contains in essence all that written revelation in the Old Testament has to say. Everything else can, as it were, be deduced from and reduced to this basic principle.[171] Scripture and with it God's will are thus viewed as a whole and are not fragmented into endless individual prescriptions.

We should note, of course, the context in which Jesus makes this pronouncement, according to Matthew. Jesus is facing a hostile Jew in a controversy story, and the argument never rises above the horizon of the Old Testament. We saw that, in the case of the rich young man, who was at least better disposed than the questioner of 22:35, love of neighbor was placed with the commands of the decalogue. Having kept the commands of the decalogue, plus love of neighbor, the young man still lacked something needed for him to enter eternal life: total renunciation in order to follow Jesus as a disciple. One must keep that in mind when one is tempted to treat Matthew 22:34-40 as the summit and summary of Jesus' moral teaching. It is rather the summit and summary of Old Testament morality, in keeping with the question which was asked. Jesus indeed takes over this summary and affirms it in the face of a hostile question from a Jewish leader. But at the same time, we should remember that the gospel as a whole shows us that Jesus himself, not any Old Testament command, however lofty, is the center of Christian morality.

The fifth and final controversy, on the Son of David (22:41-46), is actually a controversy story in reverse. Since his adversaries have exhausted their theological arsenals, Jesus seizes the initiative and addresses a theological question to the Pharisees, who especially cherished the nationalistic hope of a future

---

[171]While the joining together of love of God and love of neighbor can also be found in Hellenistic-Jewish writings of the time, there is no real parallel to this concise expression of the double command as the presupposition, substance, and basis of all written revelation.

Davidic Messiah. Jesus asks whose son the Messiah is supposed to be. From whom is he descended?[172] The Pharisees promptly answer according to their beliefs: David. Jesus then poses the theological problem. David, under the inspiration of the Holy Spirit, addressed the Messiah as "Lord" when he wrote Psalm 110:1. If David uses such a title of respect and distance for this Messiah, how could he be simply David's son? The Pharisees cannot answer, and thus Jesus shows that the "experts" on the subject of the Messiah really do not know who the Messiah is. The point has both Christological and ecclesiological importance for Matthew. (1) It is no wonder that the Pharisees did not and do not recognize Jesus as the Messiah; they cannot even understand the messianic prophecies in the Old Testament. If they did, they would recognize in Jesus the paradox of the Son of David: the fulfiller of Jewish history and the humble healer of the outcast—who is at the same time the exalted Lord of David and of all men. (2) Jesus, who indeed teaches the way of God in truth, shows that the Jewish leaders are unreliable teachers who do not know what they are talking about. *Only* Jesus teaches God's way in truth, and he has communicated that truth to his church after rejecting the Jewish magisterium (cf. 16:1-19). In short, the last controversy story returns to the point of the first (21:23-27), a point confirmed by all the parables and stories in between: Jesus, not the Jewish leaders, has the authority and ability to teach God's will.

IV.   MATT 23:1-39: THE FINAL CONDEMNATION OF THE JEWISH LEADERS

The narrative of the Fifth Book is practically at an end. Acting as a bridge between the narratives and the final discourse is

---

[172] We can appreciate today that this would be no idle question, since certain streams of Judaism (e.g., Qumran) also expected a Messiah of the house of Aaron, i.e., a levitical Messiah, who would take precedence over the Messiah of Israel, i.e., the Davidic Messiah. The Pharisees represented mainstream belief in a Davidic Messiah.

chapter 23.[173] It is a collection of many different sources (Mark, Q, M) and represents many different strata of the tradition. The initial verses (23:2-3), enjoining obedience to the Pharisaic magisterium, must come from a time when Matthew's church was still trying to avoid a definitive break with the synagogue. And yet the injunction of verses 2-3 is contradicted by the critique of Pharisaic teaching on oaths in verses 16-22, to say nothing of 16:1-19. Consequently, 23:2-3 does not represent Matthew's own theology. At best he can understand it as an expression of Jesus' fidelity to the Law and Jewish customs for the duration of his public ministry, before the cosmic change brought about by the death-resurrection. One must carefully sift all this heterogeneous material to find Matthew's own mind. And Matthew's mind can at least be found in the three-part structure imposed on the various traditions. Part One (23:1-12) is addressed to the crowds and the disciples and speaks about following the Pharisees' teaching but not their actions. Part Two (23:13-29) contains the seven woes hurled at the scribes and Pharisees because of their hypocrisy. Part Three (23:28-38) is a short lament over Jerusalem. It points ahead to chapters 24-25.

Part One begins, as we have noted, with a stringent statement of adherence to the teaching authority (the chair of Moses) possessed by the scribes and the Pharisees (vv. 2-3).[174] Yet the possessors of the authority are immediately criticized for what will be referred to as their hypocrisy, a certain kind of religious schizophrenia. The religious split in them is seen in two basic forms: they say but they do not do (v. 3), and what they do they

---

[173]Grundmann, among others, wishes to put chapter 23 with chapters 24-25 as one great discourse. But there are a number of difficulties in this procedure. (1) Chapter 23, in the Temple, has a different setting from chapters 24-25, on the Mount of Olives; and 24:1-3 makes the break quite clear. (2) The other four great discourses are addressed to the disciples (with the crowds). While this is true of chapters 24-25, most of chapter 23 is actually addressed (in the second person plural) to the scribes and the Pharisees. (3) Precisely because it is a bridge to the apocalyptic discourse, chapter 23 raises the theme of final judgment, especially at the end (vv. 34-39). But most of chapter 23 has little to do, as far as the subject matter is concerned, with the apocalyptic discourse.

[174]This claim to a succession of legitimate teachers and tradition can be found in the Pirqe Aboth, 1,1.

do only for external show, not as an expression of interior reality (vv. 5ff; cf. 6:1-18). One is reminded very much of the problem of the false Christians in 7:21-23: they say "Lord" but do not do the will of the Father. What they do do is showy, flashy religious deeds (miracles) which lack interior substance. In both cases, we have the fundamental split in professionally religious man which is hypocrisy: saying but not doing, or exterior show with no interior substance. Interestingly, this split is also called by Matthew, in both cases, *anomia*, "lawlessness" (7:23; 23:28). *Anomia* has nothing to do with "antinomianism," which is a theoretical opposition to the Law. The Pharisees were hardly guilty of antinomianism, but they were guilty of *anomia*. In the Septuagint, *anomia* often is used, not for theoretical opposition to Law or particular commandments, but rather for that fundamental rebellion against God's will which marks the truly evil person.

The fascinating point here is that both the legalistic Pharisees and the free-wheeling charismatic Christians could be equally guilty of *anomia*. The "life-styles" may be different. But the rejection of God's will for the sake of one's own will is the same, and the resultant split is the same. In 23:4-11, Matthew is intent on not allowing such hypocrisy and lawlessness to invade the church order of his community. In a mocking tone, he portrays the Jewish leaders' concern for status symbols: higher visibility at prayer (v. 5), first place in banquet halls and synagogues (v. 6), obsequious greetings and titles in public (vv. 7-10). All this pomp and ostentation are diametrically opposed to the church order Matthew sketched in chapter 18. The pomp and circumstance transform an order of service into a hierarchy of oppression, such as Matthew sees in Judaism.

Matthew focuses upon one telltale symptom of the transformation from service to self-service: the apparently insignificant question of titles. The Jewish leaders wish to be known and greeted as rabbi, teacher, father, spiritual guide. Matthew sees the danger of introducing such practices into his church— perhaps they have already begun to creep in.[175] And so he strictly

---

[175]In any discussion of the "anti-Jewish" statements of Matthew's gospel, one must bear in mind that Matthew is not simply engaging in polemics against Jews. Often these statements are aimed at possible abuses within the church.

forbids titles of honor among Christians who are all equal. This equality results not from any theory of Jeffersonian democracy but rather from what God the Father has done for Christians in Jesus the Son. The saving act of the Father, made a reality in the Son and communicated to the disciples through the teaching of the Son, is what is to form church order. There is only one true Father, the Heavenly One; he alone gives us spiritual sonship (v. 9). There is only one true rabbi and teacher (v. 8), and Matthew's whole gospel has made clear who he is—the very one who is addressed as teacher and rabbi by the Jews who do not believe in him. Jesus the Messiah is the only spiritual guide any Christian really needs (v. 10). If Christians aid one another—as they must!—and if some in the community fill leadership roles, it is simply a matter of one brother acting as the servant of his other brothers. The principle remains: you are all brothers (v. 8). The only way we can receive exaltation from God at the last judgment is to lower ourselves to serve our brothers in the church. To grab at exalted positions in the church will result in a "put-down" from God on the last day (v. 12). Jesus is simply reminding the disciples of what he has already told them about life in the church in 18:1-5 and 20:23-28. His message is exemplified now by the negative, reverse-image of order in the Jewish community. What we have here is the now familiar Matthean theme: the break between church and synagogue, with Jesus as the norm of life for the recently liberated church.

The second part of chapter 23, verses 13-36, is the heart of Matthew's message in this chapter. Jesus now addresses not the crowds or disciples but his chief adversaries in matters of teaching: the scribes and Pharisees.[176] In the style of the Old Testament

---

[176]The phrase "scribes and Pharisees" is a set formula in Matthew, occurring nine times. Luke's order and wording of the phrase varies, and Mark never has Matthew's set formula. Unlike Mark and Luke in some passages, Matthew simply does not distinguish between the scribes and the Pharisees. Originally, "scribe" was the name of a profession (lawyer and theologian), and "Pharisee" referred to a member of a group of pious Jews devoted to strict observance of the Law, oral and written. For Matthew, the scribes and Pharisees equal the official representatives of Jewish theology and piety, the Jewish magisterium which regrouped and

prophets and later apocalyptic writers, he announces God's imminent judgment (the "woe") upon those who refuse to heed the call to repentance.[177] Nothing could be further from the strict Jewish-Christian tone of 23:2-3 than the seven woes which indict the Pharisees both for their practice and their theory. When, with the seven woes, the Pharisees are seen as the eschatological fulfillment of all the murderers of the prophets in the Old Testament, the breach is complete. Any "tactical" hope of maintaining union with the synagogue has been abandoned.

Matthew draws up a list of seven woes, each woe specifying how the scribes and Pharisees are hypocrites and blind guides. Significantly, the first woe (v. 13) speaks of their use of the key to the Kingdom.[178] "You shut (*kleiete*, the same root as *kleidas*, keys, in 16:19) the Kingdom of heaven." By their teaching, and especially by their rejection of Jesus, enforced by sanctions, the Jewish teachers have closed any entrance into the eschatological Kingdom either for themselves or for those Jews who would have liked to have entered. Here the concept of entering the Kingdom comes tantalizingly close to that of entering the church. Concretely, it is by preventing Jews from entering the church that the Jewish magisterium prevents them from entering the Kingdom. By using the word "shut" or "lock," Matthew neatly conjures up by association the opposition between the Jewish magisterium,

---

led Judaism after A.D. 70. There does remain in Matthew one slight distinction between scribes and Pharisees. While "scribe" always carries a negative tone when it is used with "Pharisee," Matthew does know of Christian scribes as well; therefore the word in itself need not signify an adversary of Jesus.

[177]Possibly there is an inclusion here with 5:3-12. Jesus began his ministry by pronouncing beatitudes over his disciples. He is forced to end his ministry by pronouncing woes against the Jewish leaders. The beatitudes were a prophetic proclamation of happiness to those who seemed miserable; heaven is promised them. The woes reveal the true, wretched state of those who appear honorable and just: heaven is declared closed to them. In the woes, the judgment of the last day is anticipated; that is why the seven woes form such a fitting bridge to the apocalyptic discourse.

[178]While Matthew uses the verb "to shut" (*kleite*), Luke 11:52 uses the noun: "You took away the key [*kleida*] of knowledge."

represented by the scribes and Pharisees, and the Christian magisterium, represented by Peter.

The opposition between the two magisteriums would have become fiercely visible in the Jewish and Christian missionary endeavors. The second woe (v. 15) reflects this sharp competition by stating that the full convert to Judaism, the circumcised proselyte, became twice as worthy of damnation ("a son of Gehenna") as was the Pharisaic missionary.

The third woe (vv. 16-21) attacks the hypocrisy, the inconsistency, of the Pharisees on the particular ground of their casuistic teaching on oaths. The Jewish teachers distinguished between which oaths were binding and which not, so that one could pronounce an oath-like formula without really being bound. Jesus points out the inconsistency of this hair-splitting in what is very much an *ad hominem* argument. In 5:33-37 (the fourth antithesis), the Matthean Jesus simply rejects all oaths and vows.

The fourth woe (vv. 23-24) speaks of the obligation of tithing, which zealous Pharisees had extended to all plants. Interestingly, Jesus does not reject the Pharisees' teaching outright in this instance. Rather, their error lies in ignoring the important obligations of the Law (justice, mercy, and fidelity toward one's fellow man) in favor of minutiae. Once again we hear an echo of Matthew's stress on love of neighbor as the cutting edge of proper interpretation of the Law.

The fifth woe (vv. 25-26) touches on another Pharisaic practice, the scrupulous washing of cups and dishes. But this time the Pharisaic practice immediately becomes a metaphor. The cup represents the Pharisaic man who is more concerned about external cleanness than internal purity. Jesus demands that the interiority of a man be cleansed first, so as to avoid the fatal split the Pharisees exemplify (cf. 15:1-20).

The sixth woe (vv. 27-28) continues the problem of the split between outer and inner. The Pharisees are like tombs which are pleasant to look at because of their whitewash; but the covering does not correspond to the nauseating corruption within, which a levitical mind would see as the essence of legal impurity. The Pharisees are a walking contradiction of visible justice (doing God's will) and hidden lawlessness (rebellion against God's will).

They are indeed *hypokritai*, play-actors faking a part on the stage of religion.

The seventh and longest woe (vv. 29-36) takes up the image of tombs and uses it in a terrible indictment of the Pharisees as the eschatological murderers of the prophets. Just as Jesus is the fulfiller of prophecy and the culmination of the whole line of prophets, so too the Pharisees, in a sort of demonic counterpart of prophecy and fulfillment, fulfill the eschatological role of the murderers of the prophets, foreshadowed in the evil kings of Israel's history. The set amount of prophetic blood to be shed has not yet reached the brim. In a grim command which is also a grim condemnation, Jesus tells the Pharisees to play their counter-prophetic role by martyring him and his disciples. Thus they will show themselves to be the "sons" of the murderers of the prophets in the double Semitic sense: the physical descendants and the exact imitators.[179] But the tragedy of this generation's sin lies in the fact that Jesus is not just another prophet or even the eschatological prophet. He *is* divine Wisdom, who now suffers definitive rejection by Israel's leaders, who in turn are rejected by God. As divine Wisdom, Jesus himself has sent prophets, wise men, and scribes to Israel, in both Old Testament times and in the days of the early church.[180] The sons of Zebedee will stand shoulder to shoulder with all the murdered just men of the Old Testament: from Abel, the first mentioned (Gen 4:1-16), to Zechariah in 2 Chronicles 24:20-22.[181] The price for this constant rejection of God's emissaries by Israel must now be paid by "this generation," which is in a sense the last generation of the people Israel. Because of their rejection of the Messiah, they will cease

---

[179]It is most fitting that just at this point Jesus should hurl at the Pharisees in verse 33 the very rebuke John the Baptist used in 3:7. Matthew can place the Baptist and Jesus in a certain parallel position because both are the martyrs and prophets of the end-time. With Matthew's emphasis on Jesus as the transcendent Son, there is no danger of the parallel becoming a rivalry or equality.

[180]Since Jesus speaks here as divine Wisdom (cf. Luke 11:49), there is no need to restrict the reference to the Christian mission. The whole history of Israel vis-à-vis the divine emissaries is of one piece.

[181]In the Hebrew order of the books of Scripture, Chronicles stands last.

to be Israel. Israel will be destroyed in the Jewish war, just as surely as will Jerusalem; only "Jews" will remain (28:15).

At this point, there is nothing left to say to the scribes and Pharisees. Their rejection could not be more complete or terrible. Verses 29-36 have brought us a long distance from verses 2-3. All Jesus can now do in the third part (vv. 37-39) is speak a lament over the beloved holy city, Jerusalem. Jerusalem typifies and sums up this unholy bloodlust of Israel. And yet despite its repeated rejection and murder of Gôd's messengers, Jesus has repeatedly spent himself in wooing this recalcitrant city and trying to extend it his protection against the coming judgment. The tragedy is that she has for the last time refused the free gift offered. Consequently, the Temple, *"your* house" *par excellence*, is left desolate—visibly so in A.D. 70, but even now, proleptically, as Jesus leaves the Temple for the last time, to pronounce the apocalyptic discourse (cf. 24:1-3; 27:51). From the time of the passion onward,[182] Jerusalem will not see its Messiah again until she sees him as the dread eschatological judge, coming in glory as the Son of Man. On that day, a day of a second triumphal entry, Jerusalem and the Jews will be forced to acknowledge and hail the coming one. But on that day he will come as judge, not as the meek king of Zechariah. On that day it will be too late.[183]

V.   MATT 24:1-44: THE ESCHATOLOGICAL DISCOURSE FROM MARK

Jesus has finished speaking at length to the people and their leaders. Turning away from the people Israel,[184] he now ad-

---

[182]The phrase "from now on," "henceforth" (*ap'arti*), occurs in reference to the great turning point of the death-resurrection also in 26:29, 64.

[183]I do not see in verse 39 any hope held out for the future conversion of the Jews *en masse* at the end of time. In this, Matthew's vision of the future differs notably from Paul's in Romans 11.

[184]The "going out" (*exelthōn*) from the Temple (24:1) may even reflect desertion of the Temple by the glory of Yahweh prior to the destruction of "the house": "and the glory of the Lord went out (*exēlthen*) from the house" (Ez LXX 10:18). Cf. Matt 23:38: "Behold your *house* is left to you desolate."

dresses only the new people of God, the church,[185] the group which follows him out of the Temple, away from Judaism. The apocalyptic or eschatological discourse Jesus now begins speaks of the troubled future of the church in history until the day when it—or rather the "elect" members of it—will join the triumph of the Son of Man (24:30-31). Once again, Matthew draws upon all his different sources, though he does not mesh them as much as in some of the other discourses. Matthew 24 largely follows Mark 13, with a few deletions and additions. On the other hand, the very end of Matthew 24 and the whole of chapter 25 are his additions to Mark, and are taken from Q and M. This difference in sources must be kept in mind when interpreting these two chapters. The Markan message is kept fairly intact in Matthew 24, with a few modifications. For the peculiarly Matthean view of eschatology, we must look rather to the Q and M material which Matthew has carefully appended to Mark.

Matthew 24 begins much like Mark 13. Jesus clearly prophesies the destruction of the Temple (v. 2). This causes the disciples to raise the larger eschatological question. While Mark 13:4 still reflects a perspective in which the destruction of Jerusalem and the end of all things are closely connected, Matthew 24:3 distinguishes more carefully: "When will these things [the destruction of the Temple] be, *and* what will be the sign of your coming [*parousia*] and of the consummation of the age [*synteleias tou aiōnos*]?" Matthew thus clearly distinguishes between two questions: (1) the destruction of Jerusalem ("these things"), and (2) a sign which announces the parousia of Jesus,[186] which introduces the end of the present world. Therefore, although

---

[185]Mark makes of the eschatological discourse an esoteric revelation, communicated only to Peter, James, John, and Andrew. Matthew turns it into a revelation to "the disciples" in general. Nevertheless, they still ask "privately" (Matt 24:3); it is a revelation meant only for the church.

[186]*Parousia*, a Greek word designating the official visit of a ruler to a city or the glorious manifestation of a savior-god, entered Christian terminology as early as Paul (1 Thess 2:19)—and no doubt before him. Yet Matthew alone among the four gospels employs the term; so here in 24:3, and then in verses 27, 37, 39. The use of the technical words *parousia* and *synteleia* witnesses to Matthew's careful reflection on the question of eschatology.

Matthew takes over a good deal of Mark 13 word for word, he is rereading Mark with a distinction that is not so clear in Mark himself. All this is quite natural, since the material of Mark 13 (and probably the whole gospel of Mark) was composed before A.D. 70, while Matthew is reading Mark anew from the vantage point of A.D. 90. Events subsequent to Mark demand distinctions: the destruction of the Temple has taken place, but the *parousia* and *synteleia* have not.

What enables Matthew to maintain Mark's presentation despite the changed perspective is the tendency of prophetic and apocalyptic writers, canonical and non-canonical alike, to take historical events and "blow them up" on the larger screen of the final cosmic events of history. Some cataclysmic event in history becomes the model for the greater, ultimate cataclysm which puts an end to history. Often the two events, past historical and future meta-historical, mesh in the symbolic presentation, so that the reader is not always sure which is referred to in a given passage. This intended fuzziness and the blurring of borders contribute perfectly to the air of mystery the apocalyptic writer wishes to create. It is this "compenetration" of two events standing in a certain proportion to each other which allows the rereading of Mark by Matthew in a new eschatological framework. In his rereading, Matthew is able to keep the basic Markan building-blocks in their original order. We can conveniently group them into five sections: confusion and upset in the church and the world (24:4-14); the Jewish war and the desolation of the Temple (24:15-22); the warning against false prophets (24:23-28); the coming of the Son of Man (24:29-31); the parable of the fig tree (24:32-35).

It was a commonplace in apocalyptic that the chaos preceding God's final saving act would loosen all natural bonds of affection and loyalty and plunge the world into terrible conflict. Verses 4-14 portray such increasing disorders both in the church and in the world at large. The watchword placed over all these prophecies is the exhortation: do not be led astray (v. 4). Reasons for being led astray include the appearance of false messiahs (v. 5), the outbreak of wars and various other disasters (vv. 6-7).

Worse still for the church will be the persecution and martyrdom it will face at the hands of all the nations of the earth. All this pressure from without will cause cracks within: mutual betrayal and hatred, false prophets, and a lack of morality which leads to a lack of love (vv. 9-12).[187] Yet the emphasis in both verse 8 and verse 14 is that the outbreak of these "messianic woes" is not to be automatically equated with the end of the world: the end is not yet. The good news of the Kingdom, as proclaimed by Jesus, as passed on to his disciples, and as recorded in Matthew's work, must first be proclaimed to all the nations throughout the whole inhabited world.[188] Only then will the end, the *synteleia*, come. What is needed in the present crisis is neither enthusiasm nor despair, neither prophecies of an immediate parousia nor a loss of hope in Christ's coming. What is needed is the person who will bear up courageously and endure (*hypomeinas*) until the incalculable end does come (*eis telos*, v. 13).

The messianic woes and the corresponding need for perseverance are exemplified in the archetypal event of the destruction of Jerusalem and the Temple (vv. 15-22).[189] For Matthew and his church, the destruction and the sufferings surrounding it may be

---

[187]Since Matthew adds verses 10-12 to the Markan tradition, he seems to reflect a state of great strain in his own church, one which is sadly affecting "many." On this, cf. W. Thompson, "An Historical Perspective in the Gospel of Matthew," *JBL* 93 (1974) 243-262. Of course, one must take the statements with a grain of salt. One is dealing with the stock apocalyptic theme of the dissolution of all natural ties of affection.

[188]Matthew abridges Mark's treatment of the mission to the world (Mark 13:9-13), since he has already used this material in his missionary discourse (Matt 10:17-22).

[189]What is most interesting in Mark 13, and especially in verse 15, is that there is, strictly speaking, no prophecy of the destruction of the Temple but rather a prediction of a desolating sacrilege in the Temple. It is described in terms of the setting up of the statue of Zeus Olympios in the Temple by Antiochus Epiphanes IV in 167 B.C. (cf. Dan 9:27; 11:31; 12:11; 1 Macc 1:54; 6:7). Indeed, Matthew makes the reference to Daniel the *prophet* clear (v. 15). Naturally, Matthew, writing c. A.D. 90, would reinterpret this description, as indeed most Christians have after him, to refer to the destruction of Jerusalem. *Erēmosis*, desolation, could refer to the devastation or depopulation of a city.

past events.[190] But they are viewed as the beginning of a fresh era of suffering and travail, in which the church is still held fast. Both then and now, avoidance of hesitation and decisive action are called for (vv. 17-18). In the face of the terrible crisis, which threatens to overwhelm everyone without distinction, the church should not lose heart. God will protect his elect and guide the end of history for their benefit (v. 22).

Verses 23-28 describe in detail the problems the church faces as it turns from A.D. 70 toward the indefinite future, to be terminated at some point by the return of the Son of Man. Since that return will appear to be delayed, the temptation will be to accept false messiahs and false prophets, who will try to lead astray even the faithful members of the church with their messianic uprisings in the desert or their esoteric revelations communicated in strict secrecy. By contrast with all these counterfeits, the true parousia of the Son of Man will be like lightning: on the one hand, sudden, unexpected, unpredictable, and on the other hand public and visible to all—no more able to be hidden than a corpse surrounded by vultures (vv. 27-28). And despite the grisly image in verse 28, the Son of Man is understood in this context first of all as savior, not as judge. He comes to put an end to the afflictions besetting his church.

The climactic scene of the parousia is portrayed in verses 29-31. It is introduced by a picture of the chaos in the church and society now extending to the whole of the universe. Using stock apocalyptic images from the Old Testament, Matthew paints the shaking of the physical props of the cosmos and of the spiritual powers behind them. Then—and only then—will the "sign of the

---

[190]The reference to the Sabbath in verse 20 is sometimes incorrectly taken to show that Matthew's church is still a strict Jewish-Christian community which rigorously observes the Sabbath. But Matthew's treatment of the Sabbath elsewhere does not make a legalistic rigorism likely (cf. Matt 12:1-8, 9-14). The parallel with "winter" in 24:20 shows that the Sabbath is understood as an external circumstance of the flight which could cause hardship. The Sabbath (like winter) would not prevent their flight altogether, but would make it more difficult—perhaps by exposing them all too publicly as Christians and non-sympathizers with the zealot cause.

Son of Man" appear.[191] For all those who have rejected him—certainly the Jews but not only them—his coming will mean judgment; and so "all the tribes of the earth" mourn (cf. Zech 12:10-14).[192] The depiction of the Son of Man in verses 30-31 goes beyond the usual Synoptic passages (cf. e.g., Matt 16:27) and likewise beyond Daniel 7:13-14. The Son of Man who is now teaching on the Mount of Olives, and who is about to suffer agony and death, will then be revealed with power and great glory. He will send out *his* angels[193] accompanied by the trumpet of judgment. But, for the elect, for those members of the church who have proven to be good seed in the mixed-up situation of the present age, this scene of judgment turns into one of salvation. They are gathered into the heavenly barns (cf. 13:36-43).

Verses 32-35 conclude the Markan material with the parable of the fig tree. The discourse up until now has depicted a series of apocalyptic events, but has provided no exact times. Both the parable of the fig tree and the parables Matthew appends to Mark drive home the double truth that the time is not to be calculated, yet the final events are most certain to come, suddenly and publicly. Uncertainty about the precise time and certainty about what will happen blend in the five parables of the fig tree, Noah, the evil servant, the ten virgins, and the talents. In verses 32-35, Jesus points out that the sprouting fig tree instills in everyone a certainty that full summer is near. And yet the exact moment is not known. So it is with the Son of Man. When the disciples see "all these things" come to pass, i.e., everything narrated in the previous delineation of events, then they can be sure that the Son

---

[191]The phrase probably means "the sign which is the Son of Man," though some cosmic phenomenon or blazing light cannot be excluded, given the context of verse 29.

[192]There is an intriguing connection here with the Johannine tradition. Matthew is combining the Son-of-Man image with a text from Zechariah dealing with the pierced one. Not only does the gospel of John play with the two concepts (John 3:14-15; 19:37), but the Book of Revelation explicitly brings the two together (Rev 1:7).

[193]Matthew adds the possessive "his" here to Mark as he did in 16:27 (cf. Mark 8:38). Matthew is intent on stressing the divine status of this Son of Man.

of Man is standing at the door.[194]

Verses 34-35 provide something of a problem. Obviously Matthew cannot mean that the end of the world will come before Jesus' generation dies out. By the time Matthew writes, it already has. Possibly Matthew might be applying the verses to his own generation. And yet both verse 36, which seems to forbid any such speculation, and the whole theological outlook of Matthew, in which the parousia recedes into an indefinite future, make that interpretation doubtful. Another possibility is that, for Matthew (as opposed to Mark), verse 34 refers to the proleptic realization of the end-events which Matthew portrays in the death-resurrection of Jesus. The language is very similar to 5:18, where a reference to the death-resurrection is probably present in the last part of the verse, "till all things come to pass." At any rate, the emphasis is on the abiding validity of the words of Jesus in the midst of all the cosmic disturbances. His teaching is the one sure point of stability in a world which is passing away amid upheavals, and so the disciples must hold firmly to this teaching. The words he spoke as Son of Man on earth will serve as the criterion by which the glorious Son of Man will pass judgment. Finally in verse 36, speculation about the exact time of all these events is excluded in the bluntest way imaginable. Knowledge of the exact date is restricted to the Father alone; neither the angels nor the Son of Man knows.[195]

Matthew continues the theme of certainty about the parousia yet uncertainty about the time with a group of parabolic sayings taken mostly from Q (24:37-44). The unit is dominated by the two parables of Noah (vv. 37-39) and the thief (vv. 43-44). Sandwiched between them are short parables about two workers

---

[194]The context seems to demand the Son of Man as subject of the verb "is near" in verse 33.

[195]The whole context argues in favor of taking the absolute use of "the Son" as equivalent to the Son of Man. Here again we have our apocalyptic "Jewish Trinity." Only in this way is the full force of the statement and its position at the end of the Markan discourse appreciated. The Son of Man who is the climax of the whole discourse, the Son of Man who will most certainly return at his glorious parousia, that Son of Man is himself ignorant of the exact date of his parousia.

in the field, two workers at a mill (vv. 40-41), and (apparently) a waiting servant (v. 42).[196] The basic message is clear: the approaching crisis is certain yet undatable; therefore the only possible response is watchfulness. Noah's generation is faulted not for gross sinfulness but for being unaware of the impending disaster. They failed to be watchful. Watchfulness entails not being lulled into false security by enjoyment of the present to the detriment of a future-oriented existence. The Christian living in the present must be radically directed to, open to, that future moment which defines his whole existence: the parousia of the Son of Man (vv. 37 and 39),[197] the hour of the Son of Man (v. 44).[198]

VI.   MATT 24:45—25:46: THE ESCHATOLOGICAL DISCOURSE ADDED TO MARK

This same theme of watchfulness runs through the three large parables which follow: the faithful and unfaithful servants (24:45-51), the ten virgins (25:1-13), and the talents (25:14-30). They provide excellent examples of how Matthew uses the parousia-motif to reinforce his moral exhortation to his church. The fact that some of the goods of the Kingdom have already been entrusted to the church must not instill a false sense of security and self-satisfaction. Watchfulness and diligent activity must guard and increase these goods until the Son of Man makes his certain yet undatable appearance. The goods given to the church confer upon it a perilous status; more than others, it is subject to the coming judgment.

---

[196]The thought of these parables seems to be that the sudden crisis will reveal the hidden differences among the men to be judged.

[197]Matthew is so intent upon the technical term *parousia* that he destroys the neat comparison between "days of Noah" and "day(s) of the Son of Man" found in Q (cf. Luke 17:26, 30-31).

[198]Sandwiched between the two major parables (Noah and the thief) stands a short reference to a servant awaiting his master (*kyrios*, v. 42). The use of *kyrios* in a context totally dominated by Son of Man indicates that *kyrios*-terminology can serve in Matthew's mind to designate Jesus as Son of Man.

The parable of the faithful and unfaithful servants (24:45-51) is aimed especially at the leaders in the church. They are the servants set over the Lord's household, commissioned to care for their fellow servants, and therefore in a position to mistreat them. The unexpected and sudden coming of the Lord marks the end of stewardship and the time of reckoning. The faithful servant is rewarded with greater authority and responsibilities (cf. 19:28; 25:28-29), while the evil servant suffers the eschatological rejection and damnation already promised to the Jewish leaders, "the hypocrites."[199] Alongside of Matthew's special interest in church leaders, what is perhaps most interesting is his stress on the long time which passes before the Lord's return (v. 48: "My Lord delays," *chronizei*). Matthew uses this theme, indeed the very words *chronizō* and *chronos*, as a link tying together the three parables of servants, virgins, and talents. In the parable of the virgins we read at verse 5: "Since the bridegroom was late," *chronizontos*. In the parable of the talents, we read at verse 19 that the Lord came back "after a long time," *meta de polyn chronon*.[200] Just as Matthew warns his church that the parousia could occur at any moment, he also warns the church to reckon with the possibility of a delay. In the face of such a delay, the church, and

---

[199]Luke's phrase, "with the unfaithful" (Luke 12:46) is probably original, since it forms an inclusion with the "faithful" servant at the beginning of the parable. "Hypocrite" is a favorite Matthean term, which is used elsewhere almost exclusively of Jews or Jewish leaders (one exception would be 7:5). The rebuke "you hypocrites!" occurs frequently in chapter 23, the woes pronounced against the scribes and Pharisees. The terrible indictment of church leaders in 24:51 is that they have proved as faithless as the Jewish leaders and therefore deserve the same eschatological punishment. We see again that Matthew's fierce denunciation of Jewish authorities has a parenetic purpose: what happened of old to the Pharisees can happen also to you, the church. The idea of the impartial and universal nature of judgment is also underlined by the Matthean "theme song" at the end of verse 51. It has been used of the Jews in 8:12; of all those to be judged in 13:42, 50; and of Christians in 22:13 and 25:30.

[200]Interestingly, Luke, who also uses the parable of the talents to deal with the delay of the parousia, does not have this phrase at the parallel to Matthew 25:19, namely Luke 19:15. The use of *chronizei/ chronos* as a keyword uniting these parables thus seems to be the work of Matthew himself.

especially its leaders, must not become lax in official oversight and in personal morals.

The parable of the ten virgins (25:1-13) shares with the parable of the faithful and faithless servants a number of common points: the delay of the key figure (here, the bridegroom), the ignorance of when exactly he will come, the right and wrong response to this situation of ignorance, and the judgment or separation brought about by the sudden arrival. We notice in both parables that the delay of the key figure plays an essential role; the time of delay, along with its sudden ending, is what brings to light the qualities of fidelity or infidelity, preparedness or negligence. A slight difference, though, is noticeable in the way the delay-motif is used. In the parable of the servants, the evil servant himself remarks upon the delay of his Lord; in fact, his reliance on the indefinite delay is what leads him into negligent and immoral behavior. The problem with the virgins is that the foolish ones had not reckoned with the possibility of delay. Matthew thus corrects two excesses which could creep into the attitude of a church faced with an indefinite future: laxity which feeds on the fact of postponement, and shortsighted piety which does not face the fact of postponement. To be "prudent" (*phronimos*) like the good servant (24:45) and the five wise virgins (25:2, 4) means to be prepared (25:10, *hetoimoi*) and watchful (25:13, *grēgoreite*).[201] The parousia will be sudden, but not necessarily soon. Ignorance should call forth vigilance, not negligence. For the division between good and bad on the final day will run through the church as well as through the whole world (cf. the separation-motif in 25:31-46).[202]

---

[201]The command to be watchful in 25:13 is obviously understood metaphorically, since none of the virgins literally stayed awake in the parable. The watchfulness-motif is so traditional (Mark 13:34, 35, 37; 1 Thess 5:6, 10; 1 Peter 5:8; Rev 3:2, 3; 16:15) that there is no need to detach 25:13 from the body of the parable as an addition which does not fit the imagery of the parable; for the contrary view, cf. Jeremias, *Parables*, 52.

[202]There is no need here to go into the questions of the details of marriage customs and how they affect interpretation of the parable of the ten virgins; for this, cf. Jeremias, *Parables*, 51-53, 171-175; Bornkamm, "Die Verzögerung der Parusie," *Geschichte und Glaube I* (Gesammelte Aufsätze III; Munich: Kaiser, 1968) 46-55; for Matthean redaction, cf. K.

The third of the three parousia-parables dealing with delay stresses how Christians, and especially Christian leaders, are to spend the time of watchfulness before the end. They must not only preserve but also work with and increase the eschatological goods with which they have been entrusted. This is the demanding message of the parable of the talents (25:14-30).[203] Not every Christian receives the same amount of blessings and ability. But one must work with what one has, according to his own ability (v. 15: *kata tēn idian dynamin*). Each will be judged according to the amount he received in trust and how much he worked (*ergasato*) with it to gain some further profit (*ekerdēsen*, v. 16). Those Christians who have worked wisely with the gift they received will receive as their reward still greater authority and responsibility in the world to come.[204] They will be declared on the last day to be good and faithful servants and will be invited to share the eschatological joy of their Lord (v. 21, with perhaps a reference to a banquet). Fear, pusillanimity, self-centeredness, an unwillingness to work and take risks for the sake of growth—all these are signs of evil and lazy servants, close equivalents of the disciples of little faith we met earlier in the gospel. Fear, if allowed to dominate a disciple's life, brings on a paralysis of good works; there is no growth. The problem is, the judge of the last day will prove a most exacting taskmaster, who will demand precisely that growth of which the cowardly are incapable. Of the three delay-parables, the parable of the talents is the one which depicts the judgment scene in greatest detail, and thus conveys the most somber warning. Sterile timidity is no light matter for a disciple, no secondary

---

Donfried, "The Allegory of the Ten Virgins (Matt 25:1-13) as a Summary of Matthean Theology," *JBL* 93 (1974) 415-428.

[203]"Talents" in the parable refers to a large sum of money. Because of the metaphorical use of the word in this parable, "talent" gained in modern languages the further meaning of "native ability," an idea which is expressed in verse 15 by *idian dynamin*.

[204]One should beware of misreading this parable as affirming the Pharisaic system of merit. The point of the parable is the need for total commitment, fidelity, and sacrifice in the face of delay and then stringent judgment.

fault; it brings about definitive exclusion from the Kingdom (v. 30). Quite pointedly, this parable is aimed at not the unbeliever, but rather the Christian servant, who is entrusted with the goods of the Kingdom and who is therefore judged most stringently.

The impartial final judgment passed upon all, the stringent and sometimes surprising criteria, the motif of separation, and the concluding dark note of eternal damnation—all these Matthean themes culminate in the great final scene of judgment, Matthew 25:31-46. Although the scene has parabolic elements (the comparison with a shepherd and his flock in verses 32-33), the body of the narrative is a straightforward depiction of what will take place on the last day. Instead of talk about "your Lord" or "the bridegroom," we are told directly who this Lord and bridegroom is: Jesus the Son of Man, enthroned as divine King and judge. The dominance of Son of Man Christology in the whole of the apocalyptic discourse is thus reconfirmed. If anything, the divine status of the Son of Man is emphasized even more here. In Matthew 16:27, the Son of Man was said to come in the glory of his Father. Here, in 25:31, the Son of Man comes in his own glory, attended by his angels, and sits on the throne of his glory. The Father is mentioned only indirectly, as the ultimate source and determiner of the eschatological blessings (v. 34). What should be especially noted here is that, as in 16:27, Matthew has the Son of Man speak of "*my* Father," another reminder that Son-Christology is not reducible to Son-of-God Christology. It is no accident that we meet again in this context the apocalyptic triad of Son of Man, angels, and the Father of the Son of Man.

Before this Son are gathered all mankind, "all the nations."[205] The cleavage between good and bad thus goes through the whole of humanity; it does not run neatly between the church and unbelievers. The criterion for the definitive separation is not constituted by church membership but by the deeds of love and

---

[205]I have tried to show that the proper translation of *panta ta ethnē* in verse 32 is not "all the Gentiles," but "all the nations," in my article, "Nations or Gentiles in Matthew 28:19?" *CBQ* 39 (1977) 94-102, especially 99-101.

mercy shown to the poor and outcast of mankind.[206] The reason for this is a surprising Christological one, a startling grounding of all morality in Son-of-Man Christology. Both the good and the wicked are astounded not by the fact that they are being judged by Jesus the glorious Son of Man, nor even precisely by the fact that judgment is rendered according to works (a common Jewish and Christian theme), but rather by the revelation that the glorious Son of Man totally identifies himself with suffering mankind. In the most lowly and despised members of humanity the glorious Son of Man is present. What is done to them, for better or for worse, is done to him. All morality is thus interpreted Christologically, in terms of what we do to the Son of Man in everyman.[207] The "just" (*dikaioi*, v. 36) are indeed, according to Matthew's usage, those who do the Father's will by showing mercy to their neighbor. But this final judgment-scene makes clear that the ultimate reason for the designation "just," the ultimate reason for the command to show mercy, is a Christological reason: all is centered on the person of Christ as Son of Man.[208] It is his presence in suffering mankind which renders invalid the neat distinctions in moral theology between necessary and supererogatory works, between duties toward God and duties toward man. Christian morality becomes simply a matter of unlimited, active love.[209]

---

[206]In my judgment, "the least of these, my brethren" refers to the poor and outcast of all mankind. But this point is hotly disputed. Others see in this group Christians in general, the insignificant and therefore easily neglected Christians, or Christian missionaries.

[207]Once again the proper address to the Son of Man is *kyrie*, Lord (vv. 36, 44).

[208]It may not be mere accident that this affirmation of the union of the Son of Man with suffering mankind comes just before Matthew's fourth prediction of the passion of the Son of Man (26:2).

[209]On this, cf. McKenzie, "The Gospel according to Matthew," 107 (section 177).

CHAPTER NINE

Commentary on the Passion, Death, and Resurrection (Matt 26—28): The Turning Point of the Ages

I. MATT 26:1-30: THE LAST SUPPER

The Christological drama which is Matthew's gospel reaches its climax in his narrative of the passion, death, and resurrection of Jesus. The death-resurrection of Jesus, seen as one great eschatological event, constitutes the turning point of salvation history. All the Jewish limitations of land, people, and Law are torn down as the life-giving death of Christ puts an end to the old cult and the glorified Son of Man comes to his church in proleptic parousia to inaugurate a universal mission.[210] While this may serve as a capsule summary of the function of the death-resurrection of Jesus, the passion narrative of Matthew also contains many supplementary streams of thought.

Before we examine the pericopes of the passion narrative in detail, it might help to clarify our treatment to list the major themes Matthew develops as he narrates the passion.[211] Since Matthew follows Mark closely in the passion narrative, the divergences are all the more significant and indicate clearly what

---

[210]The basis for all these statements was given in Part I in my treatment of salvation-history in Matthew.

[211]In much that follows I am dependent on the magisterial work of D. Senior, *The Passion Narrative according to Matthew* (Louvain: Leuven University Press, 1975).

Matthew's theological interests are.[212] Chief among these interests is a heightened emphasis on Christology. In particular, Matthew emphasizes the prophetic knowledge of Jesus, his dominance over the events of the passion, his status as Son of God, Son of Man, Messiah, and King, as well as his fulfillment of Old Testament prophecy. All these elements underscore the centrality of the person of Jesus. By voluntarily going to his death as Son of Man he ushers in the apocalyptic event, the turning point of the ages. All other theological perspectives in the passion narrative must be understood from this central Christological perspective.

Among Matthew's subordinate themes we can number first the interest in the responsibility of the Jews for the innocent blood of Jesus. The confrontation between Jesus and Israel, growing throughout the gospel, reaches its climactic moment in Israel's fateful choice of Barabbas instead of Jesus. As usual in Matthew, this anti-Jewish polemic actually has a positive, ecclesiological thrust. The death of Jesus, the result of Israel's total rejection of its Messiah, frees the church for its mission to all the nations. Thus, Matthew does not underline the hostility of the Jewish leaders for its own sake. In fact, it too serves his main Christological purpose. It serves as a foil to the majesty and dignity of Jesus. Like the weak Peter, the two thieves, and the passersby at the cross, the Jewish leaders become unconscious witnesses to the Messiah's identity and power. This leads us to a second subordinate theme in the Matthean passion narrative, namely the parenetic or moral value of the characters and events of the story, either by way of example or by way of counter-example. The obedience and fidelity of the Son of God in the midst of his sufferings is, of course, the main parenetic interest. Again, Christology lies at the basis of Christian morality. For a church experiencing persecution and apostasy, Jesus is the paradigm of true righteousness, the paradigm every disciple must follow. But the various laudatory or reprehensible attitudes of Peter, Judas, the woman at Bethany, the disciples, the Gentile soldiers, and the women at the cross all contribute to Matthew's moral exhortation to his church. Now we

---

[212]Throughout his monograph, Senior stresses that even Matthew's additions or changes find some basis or "cue" in Mark.

must see how these themes are worked out in detail.

The conclusion of the Fifth Book of the Ministry and the opening of the passion is announced by the usual formula for ending a discourse and beginning a narrative. But now the formula is significantly altered: "And it came to pass when Jesus had finished *all* these words. . . ." (26:1). The "all" signals that all the instructions and commands of the public ministry, and thus the public ministry itself, have come to a conclusion.[213] Having spoken the apocalyptic discourse, Jesus has nothing left to do except accomplish the apocalyptic event of death-resurrection. And so, unlike Mark, Matthew does not proceed immediately to the Jews' decision to kill Jesus. First Jesus pronounces a fourth passion prediction, one inserted into the Markan context by Matthew. The whole passion is thus put under Jesus' prophetic pronouncement that the Son of Man is being handed over to be crucified, and that in the context of the Passover (Matt 26:2).[214] Only then—almost, as it were, at Jesus' leave—can the Jewish authorities begin their plot to kill Jesus (26:3-5). Jesus' solemn prediction and the calculating plot of the Jews set up, at the very beginning of the narrative, a vivid contrast in roles which will be played out in the subsequent incidents. Matthew's emphasis on the foreknowledge and control of Jesus approaches the presentation of the passion in John's gospel. Jesus marches to his death with sovereign freedom, determined as Son of Man to perform this infinite service for men (cf. 20:28). One example of Jesus' mastery of events is already made clear to the reader here in verses 1-5. Jesus predicts that the passion of the Son of Man will take place during Passover, while the Jews plan to avoid his arrest and execution on the feast. Naturally, Jesus' prediction will prove

---

[213]This is especially true because of the particular pattern Matthew adopted for each book of the public ministry: first narrative, then discourse. Given this pattern, the announcement of the conclusion of the last discourse is necessarily an announcement of the end of the public ministry.

[214]The immediacy of the passion is underlined by the verb *paradidotai*, "is being handed over," in the present tense; cf. the use of the future tense, *paradothēsetai*, in the third passion prediction (Matt 20:18).

true: the Jewish plotting will prove futile.

Jesus' clear foreknowledge is also exemplified in the anointing at Bethany (26:6-13). Jesus knows both the objection of his disciples and the deeper symbolic meaning of the anointing: preparation for burial. The love of this foolishly generous woman contrasts starkly with the death-decree which precedes and the plot of Judas to betray Jesus which follows. As the woman prodigally lavishes money on Jesus, Judas prepares to betray Jesus for money. Judas' agreement with the high priests (26:14-16) places him in sharp contrast not only with the woman but also with Jesus. In a tragic symmetry, both figures are purposefully moving toward the proper moment for beginning the drama of the passion. In a sense, the whole passion has already been presented in 26:1-16; everything that follows will simply be a playing-out of what is presented here. "From that time on" (v. 16) events rush precipitously to their eschatological denouement.

After the Matthean "prelude" to the passion (26:1-16), the next large unit is the narrative of the last supper (26:17-30). In the story of the preparation for the supper (26:17-19), Matthew shifts Mark's interest in the miraculous knowledge and secret instructions of Jesus to the typically Matthean pattern of authoritative command and exact fulfillment of command.[215] The disciples show themselves to be true disciples by exactly fulfilling Jesus' command. In doing so, they deliver a message which is most significant: "My time (*kairos*) is at hand."[216] This Matthean addition harks back to Jesus' prophecy in verse 2 and stresses that Jesus is freely moving toward the eschatological hour of death-resurrection. Jesus sees his final Passover meal as playing a part

---

[215]There is a similar shift in Matthew's redaction of the Markan version of the triumphal entry into Jerusalem. Indeed, the Matthean pattern reaches all the way back to the infancy narrative.

[216]Although *kairos* in the New Testament need *not* mean a critical or decisive moment, the context certainly favors such a meaning here.— Note also that Matthew keeps Mark's introductory phrase: "The teacher (*didaskalos*) says. . . ." While "Teacher" or "Rabbi" in direct address usually occurs in the mouth of unbelievers, Matthew certainly sees Jesus as the one legitimate teacher, and therefore feels no need to strike the Markan use of the word here.

in this eschatological drama. The supper proper divides into two parts: the prediction of betrayal (vv. 20-25) and the institution of the eucharist (vv. 26-30).

A striking example of Matthew's distinction between believer and unbeliever is given in the story of the prediction of betrayal. The innocent disciples address Jesus as Lord (*kyrie*, v. 22), while the guilty Judas uses "Rabbi" (v. 25). Matthew, unlike Mark, has Jesus tell Judas that he is the one;[217] Jesus' foreknowledge and freedom as he goes to his passion are again underlined. Significantly, in this context, the Son of Man title again appears, in connection with the fulfillment of Scripture: "The Son of Man indeed goes his way, as it is written of him." The fourth passion prediction of 26:2 is now re-echoed, with the same stress on the Son of Man who knows where he is going and freely treads the path. Opposed to the *Son of Man* in the same verse is the *man* who would have been better off if he had never been born—as Matthew 27:3-10 will make clear. Besides the main Christological thrust of this scene, there may also be a parenetic note. The Christians of Matthew's church are called to self-examination, especially as they approach the eucharist. Even a supposedly loyal disciple, who is admitted to table-fellowship with his Lord, is capable of treason.

In the institution of the eucharist, Matthew follows Mark closely; most of his changes are due to the liturgical formulas of Matthew's church.[218] The words over the bread indicate that the bread is identified with the whole person of Jesus in his concrete, physical reality ("my body")—a person who freely gives himself to his disciples now in sign as he prepares to give himself for mankind in death. This last point is made clear by the words over the cup. The wine is equated with "my blood of the covenant," that is, my whole life poured out in sacrifice to form a covenant.

---

[217]"Thou hast said it" is a veiled form of affirmation, which throws the responsibility for the question or the meaning of the question back on the person asking the question.

[218]Here I would disagree with Senior, *Passion*, 76-77, who holds that the changes are due to Matthew's own activity, and not to liturgical influence. I do not think that Matthew would presume to alter the words over the cup as they were spoken in his church.

As in Exodus 24:4-8, the blood of sacrifice, shared between God and man in ritual, creates out of death a new common bond of life, a covenant.[219] The blood of Jesus is poured out in sacrifice not just for the disciples around the table, but for "the many." This Semitic phrase means not "the many" as opposed to "all men." Rather "many" means the mass of mankind as opposed to the one suffering servant, the one Son of Man who gives his life as a "ransom for the many" (cf. 20:28).[220] To emphasize that the death of Christ (and its eucharistic memorial) is a sacrifice for sins, Matthew, and no doubt the liturgy of his church before him, adds to the words over the cup the explanatory phrase, "unto the remission of sins." Matthew had pointedly removed this phrase from the description of the baptism of John (Matt 3:1-2 versus Mark 1:4). The baptism of John cannot be a sacrament conferring the forgiveness of sins because the eucharist, the sacramental re-enactment of the sacrificial death of Jesus, does that. Nowhere else does Matthew make it so clear that he views Jesus' death as an expiatory sacrifice. The Son of Man saying about the ransom for many (20:28), the raising of the dead at the death of Jesus, and indeed all the apocalyptic signs receive their deepest explanation here in 26:28. By his sacrificial death, made accessible to the disciples in the eucharist, Jesus overcomes the powers of sin and death.[221]

[219]The phrase "the blood of your covenant [with me]" occurs in Zechariah 9:11, immediately after the prophecy of the meek King coming to Jerusalem on an ass as universal prince of peace (9:9-10). Because of the blood of the covenant, prisoners are released and return from exile is promised. Since Matthew quotes Zechariah 9:9 at the triumphal entry (21:5), he may well intend the allusion to Exodus 24 to be coupled with an allusion to Zechariah 9.

[220]The blood "poured out for many" probably points to the suffering servant of Isaiah 53:12: "He has poured out his soul unto death . . . and he bore the sins of many." The fact that Matthew substitutes *peri* "for the sake of" in place of Mark's *anti* may also be an allusion to Isaiah 53:4 in the LXX: "He suffers for (*peri*) us." But see Senior's caution on this point in *Passion*, 81. The reference to remission of sins, closely tied to the idea of establishing a (new?) covenant, also calls to mind the promise of the new covenant and the remission of sins in Jeremiah 31:31-34.

[221]Consequently, Strecker's attempt to refer the idea of expiatory death to Matthew's tradition rather than to Matthew's own theology is hopelessly wrong; see his *Weg*, 181, 222.

The final verse of the pericope, verse 29, looks across the bloody sacrifice of the physical death to the renewed fellowship Jesus will have with his disciples at the Messianic banquet in the Kingdom of his Father. That Matthew sees that banquet and fellowship proleptically realized in the eucharist is made likely by his addition of "with you" to Mark 14:25. "With you/us" is a favorite theme of Matthew's Christology. Jesus is Emmanuel because in him God has drawn near to his people and is with us (Matt 1:23). He is present with even a few who gather together in his name (18:20). He is with the disciples for all the days of the church's earthly mission (28:20). Since all these references are to a presence of Jesus among believers in the church this side of the parousia, the addition of "with you" in 26:29 makes a reference to the eucharist likely. "From this moment on"—a Matthean addition stressing the pivotal eschatological turning point of the passion—Jesus will not enjoy table-fellowship with his disciples until the sacrificial death is accomplished; then renewed fellowship will be possible at the eucharistic banquet which gives a foretaste of the final banquet after the parousia. In the eucharist, the Son of Man who gave his life as ransom continues to grant forgiveness of sins, fellowship, and a pledge of his parousia. Once again, the Son-of-Man concept serves to bridge different epochs of salvation history and different theological motifs.

II. MATT 26:31–56: PRAYER AND ARREST IN GETHSEMANE

After the supper, on the way to the Mount of Olives, Jesus again shows his prophetic knowledge of his coming sufferings (26:31-35). Citing Zechariah 13:7 freely, Jesus designates himself as the shepherd to be smitten and his disciples as the flock which shall be scattered because of the scandal of Jesus' arrest "this very night." Yet Jesus is not reduced to despair by his prevision. It has all been prophesied in Scripture, and therefore must take place (v. 31). Moreover, the tragedy is only temporary; after the resurrection, the shepherd will again go before his sheep into Galilee. After the passion narrative, Matthew will make good this prediction of Jesus in the gospel's final pericope, 28:16-20. This general prediction of the disciples' failure reversed by Jesus' triumph now becomes specified in a prediction of Peter's triple denial "this very night" (v. 34). In reply, Peter correctly states the proper choice of a real disciple: death with Jesus is preferable to denial of him (cf. 10:32-33, 37-39; 16:24-28). All the disciples profess the same pious thought; yet, the Christian reader, knowing the infallible prescience of Jesus, knows the necessary outcome. All the disciples will be scandalized and scattered, and their chief will become the chief denier. Peter will again show that he can play Satan when he is faced with the cross (cf. 16:21-23). The cross is what tests and proves the genuineness of discipleship and the genuineness of church leadership.

The scene at Gethsemane looms large in Matthew's passion narrative, both for its sheer length (26:36-56) and for the important redactional changes it contains. For convenience sake, the Gethsemane narrative can be divided into the prayer of Jesus (vv. 36-46) and the arrest of Jesus (vv. 47-56). At the very beginning of the whole Gethsemane scene, Matthew sets his tone. Mark began the scene with "they came to the estate" (Mark 14:32). Matthew changes that to: "Then *Jesus* came with them [his disciples] to the estate." Both the centrality of Jesus and his fellowship with the disciples are thus profiled. Christology and moral exhortation will be the twin themes of the prayer-pericope. The perseverance of Jesus in prayer will be contrasted with the sleep of the negligent disciples; even the physical distance between Jesus and the disciples underlines the contrast. Using the words of Psalm 41:6, Jesus expresses his deep sorrow and tries to bridge the gap between himself and the disciples by repeating the "watcher's cry" from the apocalyptic discourse: "Stay awake!" (cf. 24:42, 43; 25:13). But, like the foolish virgins of the parable, even the inner group of Peter and the two sons of Zebedee fall asleep and are unprepared for the eschatological crisis when it comes. Matthew stresses Jesus' desire for union with his disciples by adding his beloved preposition "with": "Remain here and watch *with* me" (Matt 26:38; contrast Mark 14:34).

Using Old Testament imagery, Matthew expresses Jesus' sense of reverence and fear by having him fall on his face (cf.

Matthew's depiction of the disciples at the transfiguration, 17:6). With the first words of Jesus' prayer, Matthew announces his intention of paralleling the prayer Jesus says with the prayer Jesus taught. Matthew changes Mark's "Abba, Father" to "my Father," corresponding to the "Our Father" taught to the disciples in 6:9. Echoes of the Our Father will reverberate throughout the rest of the scene. As does the disciple in the Our Father, so Jesus in his prayer prays for deliverance. More precisely, he prays that the cup, the Old Testament symbol of God's wrathful judgment on the final day, may pass him by. Of course, Jesus himself is not the object of God's wrath. But his sacrificial death for the sins of the many will plunge him into the tribulations of the end-time, which culminate in the cross. Jesus' plea for deliverance is tempered not only by his loving address to his Father, but also by the explicit conditions: "If it is possible . . . but not as I wish but as you wish" (v. 39). The prayer of the Son to his Father is first of all a prayer of obedience. Obedience in suffering is the hallmark of the whole of the passion, the proof that the one who suffers is truly Son.

When Jesus returns to the sleeping trio, Matthew alters Jesus' ironic question to stress the ecclesiological dimension of the scene. On the one hand, Jesus comes to the disciples and asks his question in the plural. And yet Matthew states that the question is addressed to Peter (v. 40). Peter's role as leader and representative, for better or (here) for worse, is a constant concern of Matthew. Peter in the passion narrative shows us the ugly underside of church leadership. True, Peter represents every disciple in his failure to watch and pray in the midst of eschatological trial. Jesus' command to "pray, lest you enter into the [eschatological] test" echoes the Our Father ("lead us not into the test," 6:13) and so applies to every Christian. But, granted Peter's prominent place as leader in Matthew's gospel, a special warning to those in authority cannot be missed. When persecution and even martyrdom beset the church, the church leaders are the most exposed to the test. Filled with the Spirit yet still weak mortals ("flesh"), they are most gravely tempted to fall. In their own eschatological crisis they must hear the command of Jesus as he faces his own martyrdom: "Watch and pray."

Jesus then departs to pray a second time, expressing more intensely his acceptance of the Father's will, since he realizes ever more keenly the inevitability of the passion, as his disciples fail him. This time, the allusion to the Our Father becomes a direct quote: "Thy will be done" (26:42=6:10). Jesus not only teaches his church to pray that God's will be done; he incarnates that prayer in his own life and death—and so becomes the living basis of his church's prayer and conduct. The essence of this filial obedient prayer is that the Father accomplish his saving will in the eschatological crisis, no matter what the cost of suffering be for his sons.[222] The repeated failure of the disciples to measure up to the filial prayer and example of the Son drives Jesus not to despair but to further prayer (vv. 43-44), repeating his act of submission.

Then, with an ironic rebuke, Jesus rouses his disciples to face the eschatological hour as it approaches in the person of Judas.[223] The essence of this hour has been made clear by Jesus from 26:2 onward: the Son of Man is being handed over [ultimately, by the Father] into the hands of sinners. The bloody sacrifice for sin, symbolized at the last supper, begins to be acted out physically. With the arrest, the passion proper begins. And so the Son's obedient submission to the Father's will at this moment of arrest both actualizes all that was said in prayer and sets in motion all that will follow in the passion. Incarnating for his community his teaching of filial obedience, Jesus submits to the divine plan foretold in Scripture and now to be fulfilled in the eschatological hour.

The prayer of Jesus thus flows organically into the arrest of Jesus (26:47-56), the second half of the Gethsemane scene. Jesus'

---

[222]The aorist passive verb *genēthētō*, "be done," has as its implied agent God, not man. The primary object of the petition, both in the Our Father and here in 26:42, is the saving will of the Father, which becomes the eschatological event in the crisis of suffering. Of course, the "doing" of the disciple is not meant to be excluded by this primary reference to God's action; rather, it is presupposed.

[223]Matthew creates a careful parallelism in 26:45-46: "The hour draws near. . . . My betrayer draws near." Sandwiched between the two statements of approaching fate stands the central act of the hour: "the Son of Man is being handed over [by the Father: divine passive]."

words about Judas prove true even as he is speaking them (v. 47). Judas shows his treacherous unbelief by greeting Jesus as "Rabbi" (v. 49). Jesus wastes no time rebuking Judas; rebukes are only for weak but believing disciples (vv. 40–41, 45–46). Showing his command of the situation, Jesus bids Judas to drop the pretense and to get on with the work: "Do what you are here for" (v. 50).[224] *Then,* says Matthew, when Jesus gives leave and not when Judas kisses him, the arrest can take place. But one of the disciples, one of those *with* Jesus, fails to understand God's plan which Jesus is freely accepting. He cuts off the ear of the servant of the high priest. True to his teaching in the sermon on the mount (5:38–42, 44), Jesus rejects man's violence as the tool of God's will, both for himself and for his community. He submits humbly and trustfully to wrongdoers, because he knows full well that as the Son he has the authority to ask the Father for angelic hosts to defend him.[225] Such an appeal to angelic help is, of course, as unacceptable now as it was in the second temptation of Satan in 4:6–7. It would run contrary to God's will which points out the way of the cross as the path the Son must tread, as is clear from the Scriptures.

At this point, Jesus asks a rhetorical question which acts as a rubric for and explanation of the whole of the passion: "How then are the Scriptures to be fulfilled, that it must so happen?" This Matthean insertion links up with the weighty fulfillment vocabulary and theology we have seen in all the formula quotations throughout the gospel. From the conception of Jesus onward, individual events have happened (*ginesthai*) in order that some particular Old Testament prophecy might be fulfilled (*plēroō*) in the life of Jesus. Such a prophecy/fulfillment pattern gave the

---

[224]The elliptical Greek phrase in verse 50, *eph'ho parei*, is notoriously difficult. Suggestions include "for what are you here?"; "it is for this that you are here"; "I know for what purpose you are here"; "it is the kiss for which you have come." Contrary to Senior, *Passion*, 124-127, I think supplying a command ("do") fits best with Matthew's stress on Jesus' command of the situation.

[225]The appearance of the Father, angels, and Jesus in the same verse raises the possibility that we have again the apocalyptic Jewish triad in which Jesus figures as Son of Man. This would certainly fit in with the whole of chapter 26, where Son-of-Man Christology is dominant.

whole life of Jesus a certain eschatological quality. But now, when the eschatological event *par excellence* begins, Matthew no longer thinks of individual prophecies. Now "all things come to pass" (cf. 5:18), and so Matthew simply refers to "the Scriptures" in general, which are globally fulfilled in *the* eschatological event of the death-resurrection. The eschatological or apocalyptic nature of this event is stressed by the formula, "Thus it must come to pass" (*dei genesthai*). The phrase occurs in Daniel 2:28, 29, 45, and Revelation 1:1, (19); 22:6.[226] That cataclysmic event foretold in Scripture for the end-time, the earthshaking breaking-in of the new age into the old, is about to take place in the death-resurrection.

After the important theological insertion of 26:52-54, Matthew rejoins the Markan thread at 26:55. With sovereign control and simple majesty, Jesus rebukes the crowds who heard him teaching in the Temple; they are guilty of duplicity and cowardice. The authority which Jesus demonstrated as he sat teaching blazes out fearlessly in his present challenge to his erstwhile pupils (v. 55). Yet, once again, Jesus refuses to use that authority to escape the eschatological tribulations now unleashed. For a second time, in verse 56, Jesus explains his submission in terms of fulfillment. This time, there is an even clearer allusion to the formula quotations: "But all this has come to pass" repeats word for word the introduction to the first formula quotation in 1:22. And to Mark's laconic "let the writings be fulfilled" (Mark 14:49), Matthew carefully adds the precision: "in order that all the writings *of the prophets* be fulfilled." Prophetic fulfillment, which was the pattern of Jesus' whole life, now reaches its climax in the death-resurrection. With the exception of the fate of Judas, no formula quotation occurs in the passion narrative. What is now being fulfilled is not one particular prophecy but the entire corpus of Old Testament prophecies. That is why, although verses 54 and 56 do not strictly qualify as formula quotations, they perform the

---

[226]Senior, *Passion*, 147-148, is unwilling to accept the full force of this formula, which shows that Matthew does conceive the death-resurrection as *the* apocalyptic event, the turning point of the ages. Verse 54 is not only the climax but also the main purpose of the Matthean insertion, 26:52-54.

function of such quotations for the whole passion narrative to follow. The whole death-resurrection must be read under the rubric of total fulfillment of the prophets, as enunciated in 26:54 and 56.

III. MATT 26:57—27:10: THE JEWISH TRIAL AND THE FATE OF JUDAS

The next scene in the passion is the trial before the Sanhedrin (26:57-68). Matthew again follows Mark and again underscores the Christological thrust of the passage, with a view to his own special brand of salvation-history and eschatology. The false witnesses are mentioned quickly, and then two valid witnesses give truthful testimony[227] about Jesus' power: "I _can_ destroy the Temple of God and after three days build it."[228] Matthew understands this testimony to be true, despite the malice of the witnesses. As Messiah and Son of Man, Jesus does have power over both the Sabbath and the Temple, for he is greater than both (cf. Matt 12:6, 8). This clear affirmation of Jesus' Messianic power leads directly to the confrontation between the high priest and Jesus. Initially Jesus shows his sovereign freedom vis-à-vis the high priest by remaining silent. Then, using a solemn oath-formula, the high priest demands that Jesus tell the Sanhedrin whether he is "the Messiah, the Son of God." By changing Mark's reverent periphrasis "Son of the Blessed One" (Mark 14:61) to "Son of God," Matthew reduplicates the wording of Peter's confession at Caesarea Philippi (Matt 16:16). In fact, since Matthew has the high priest administer the oath in the name of the "living God" (26:63), the wording coincides perfectly. The words Peter, the chief rabbi of the church, proclaimed with belief the high

---

[227]Matthew 26:60 changes Mark's "some bore false witness" (Mark 14:57) to "two said." The number two recalls the proper number needed for valid testimony (cf. Deut 19:15 and Matt 18:16).

[228]Mark reads "I shall destroy (14:58); Matthew changes the prophecy of future action into a declaration of present power: Jesus is the true Messiah who has the power to destroy the old Temple and build a new one—a power which remains even in his passion.

priest of Judaism pronounces with disbelief. Matthew could not make clearer his point that it is high Christology which marks the dividing line between church and synagogue. Belief that Jesus of Nazareth, the lowly one, is the Messiah promised to Israel in the Old Testament, and that moreover he is the truly transcendent Son of God,[229] is what gives the church its identity over against Judaism and necessitates an unhealable breach.

Since Caiaphas' question really represents Matthew's Christology, the reply of Jesus is at first disconcerting. Instead of Mark's straightforward "I am" (Mark 14:62), Matthew has a veiled affirmation: "Thou hast said it" (Matt 26:64). One reason for this indirect "yes" is that it is the way Jesus replies to the three great unbelievers in the passion who ask him a question: Judas in 26:25, Caiaphas in 26:63, and Pilate in 27:11. A second reason, though, is that Matthew now wants to balance the profession of faith of Peter and the church, echoed by Caiaphas, with Jesus' own final self-definition. Using a strong adversative word (plēn, "but," as opposed to Mark's "and"), Jesus proclaims himself as the Son of Man who is soon to be exalted at God's right hand (cf. Ps 110:1) and is to come on the clouds of heaven (cf. Dan 7:13).

Especially noteworthy is the insertion of a favorite phrase of Matthew: ap'arti, "from now on you shall see the Son of Man seated . . . and coming." With this addition Matthew has Christ address his believing community, not the unbelieving Sanhedrin. From the time of the eschatological event of the death-resurrection onward, the believer will see in faith Jesus enthroned as Messianic King, who comes to his church as universal ruler, with all power in heaven and on earth (cf. Matt 28:18). Jesus' promise to the believer of this "seeing" is fulfilled in the last pericope of the gospel, when the eleven do see Jesus the Son of Man coming to them in a proleptic parousia (28:17-18). Matthew thus makes this final self-definition of Jesus also the vehicle of Matthean realized eschatology and of a consoling promise to the

---

[229]Contrary to Senior, *Passion*, 175 n. 5, I think Son of God in Matthew more clearly enunciates the strictly divine, transcendent status of Jesus than it does in Mark.

church. Even as Jesus stands on trial, about to be condemned by the highest authorities of Judaism, he can proclaim with sure prophetic knowledge his imminent exaltation and vindication as King and judge, as Messiah and Son of Man. This will indeed be "seen" "from now on," not by the Jews but by the church. At the solemn climax of the trial before the high priest, Christology and ecclesiology stand out in typically Matthean fashion. The high priest recognizes Jesus' transcendent claim and can have only one reaction to this climactic declaration of chapter 26: "Behold, *now* you have heard the blasphemy." The first charge against Jesus, in Matthew 9:3, was that he blasphemed because he claimed—as Son of Man (9:6)—to have power to forgive sins. Now his own explanation of what he means by Son of Man calls down upon him the final charge of blasphemy, punishable by death (v. 66). Some of the Sanhedrin begin to mock and maltreat Jesus with spittle and blows. But their mockery has an almost Johannine irony: "Prophesy to us, O Messiah." The fulfiller of the Law and the prophets is asked by the Jews who have just condemned him to prophesy. And yet their condemnation proceeds from the final prophecy spoken by this Messiah: the prophecy of his own exaltation and parousia as Son of Man (v. 64)!

The trial scene ends with the denial by Peter (26:69-75), a story already prepared for by the mention of Peter at 26:58. Faced with numerous accusers, Jesus has fearlessly proclaimed the truth about himself. Faced with some servant girls and bystanders, Peter collapses and denies Jesus three times. One should note the charge aimed at Peter: "You were *with* Jesus of Galilee (v. 69). . . . This fellow was *with* Jesus the Nazarene (v. 71). . . . You are *one of them* (v. 73)." Peter is accused of discipleship, of sharing the fellowship of Jesus. And so his denial is a denial not only of Jesus but of his own identity as a disciple. In his growing desperation, Peter moves to an ever more emphatic denial: he does not know what the girl is saying (v. 70); he swears with an oath that he does not know "the man" (v. 72);[230] and finally he

---

[230]The use of the oath contravenes Jesus' own teaching in the sermon on the mount (5:33-37). The eschatological teacher had himself observed his teaching on non-violence in the arrest scene (26:52; cf. 5:38-42, 44). His chief rabbi is not so observant.

strengthens his affirmation of ignorance by placing himself under a curse (v. 74).[231] As soon as Peter pronounces the third denial, the prophecy of Jesus comes true: a cock crows. The personal tragedy, though, is not unmitigated. Peter's reaction to the prophecy of Jesus is not that of the Sanhedrin. He repents and weeps bitterly. Matthew points out to his church that, no matter what the fall, repentance is possible—even for church leaders. The real tragedy is that the other sinful church leader, Judas, does not realize that. The real continuation of the story of Peter's denial is the story of Judas' end in 27:3-10. Matthew puts before Christians, and especially before their leaders, the two possibilities open to sinful Christians: repentance or despair.

Before Matthew narrates the fate of Judas, and indeed as a lead-in to that narrative, he reports the formal conclusion and judgment of the night-session of the Sanhedrin: the highest authority in Judaism decides to put Jesus to death (27:1). Verse 2 then brings us into the second half of the passion narrative, as Jesus is delivered over to Pilate (cf. 20:19).

It is the formal condemnation by the Sanhedrin that moves Judas to be overwhelmed with regret (27:3)—but not, unfortunately, with the genuine repentance of Peter. He tries to rid himself of the blood money by returning the money to the Jewish authorities and confessing his sin of betraying innocent blood. The callous authorities are unmoved; such matters are Judas' affair, not theirs (v. 4).[232] But Judas dramatically affirms their complicity by hurling the thirty pieces of silver into the Temple. Like the traitor Ahitophel in 2 Samuel 17:23, Judas then hangs himself in despair. Jesus' prophecy in 26:24 is thus fulfilled: "Woe to that man through whom the Son of Man is betrayed; it would have been better for that man if he had not been born." Faced with the problem of the money cast into the Temple, the priests are forced to admit it is blood money, and they seek to get rid of it by buying a cemetery for strangers. Ironically, the name of the

----

[231]It is possible, however, that the object of the curse is meant to be Jesus—which would bring the crescendo of curses to a terrifying conclusion.

[232]Pilate will use the same formula of disassociation ("see to it yourselves") in 27:24, in a similar context of being guilty for shedding blood.

field will stand witness against them in future generations. Matthew ends this tragic story by reminding us that even tragedy is under God's guidance of history as outlined in prophecy. In deference to the tragic nature of the story, however, Matthew does not use his usual formula: "This came to pass *in order that* what was spoken might be fulfilled." He simply states the brute fact: "Then was fulfilled. . . ."[233] Although the major part of the citation comes from Zechariah 11:12-13, Matthew refers the prophecy fittingly to the prophet of tragedy and judgment, Jeremiah.[234] Thus, this strange pericope is used by Matthew to confirm the prophetic knowledge of Jesus even as he enters more deeply into his passion, to trace the responsibility for the death of Jesus to the Jewish authorities, and to emphasize the fulfillment of Old Testament prophecies even in such a tragic event.[235]

IV. MATT 27:11–50: THE TRIAL BEFORE PILATE AND THE CRUCIFIXION

Matthew now returns to the Markan thread with the trial before Pilate (Matt 27:11-26). This can be divided into Pilate's interrogation of Jesus (vv. 11-14) and the choice between Jesus and Barabbas (vv. 15-26).

As we return to the Markan story-line, we should notice an interesting shift in Christological emphasis. In the apocalyptic discourse (chaps. 24-25) the dominant title was Son of Man, the natural title for a discourse dealing with the parousia (cf. 24:27, 30

---

[233]The only other example of this avoidance of the formula indicating God's intention is Matthew 2:18, the prophecy of the slaughter of the innocents, which also comes from Jeremiah.

[234]The reference to Jeremiah is not however without basis in the Old Testament citation. Matthew probably has in mind Jeremiah 19:1ff, or, less likely, Jeremiah 32:6-9, or, still less likely, Jeremiah 18:2-3.

[235]Senior, *Passion*, 343-397, wishes to see Matthew 27:3-10 as almost entirely the result of Matthew's creative redaction, working on Markan data, Old Testament texts, and a stray tradition about a field. I would be inclined to think that there was a more developed Judas-legend already in Matthew's tradition.

twice, 37, 39, 44; 25:31).[236] Matthew had inherited the title from the Mark and Q material, but he also exploits and expands its use (e.g., 25:31-46). The Son-of-Man motif is continued in chapter 26 (vv. 2, 24 twice, 45, 64). Indeed, it again dominates the whole chapter, though now it is applied more to suffering and death, though exaltation and parousia are stressed at the climax of the chapter (v. 64). Having stressed sufficiently the role of the Son of Man in his passion-exaltation theology, Matthew, again following Mark, turns in chapter 27 to those titles less amenable to a Christology of suffering: King of the Jews, Messiah, King of Israel, and especially Son of God. By employing the image of the suffering just man and suffering servant from the Old Testament, Matthew gives these titles their proper Christological as opposed to political interpretation. Earlier in the gospel, we noticed how Matthew "bent" titles of glory in the direction of suffering servant and Son of Man. Now such titles of royalty and glory, especially Son of God, receive their definitive "bent" at the cross.

The royal titles begin as soon as Pilate begins questioning Jesus. The first words out of Pilate's mouth in Matthew's gospel are: "Are you the King of the Jews?" (27:11). Matthew reserves this precise form of the King-title for non-Jews, who are looking in "from the outside." The Magi sought out the "King of the Jews" (2:2), and the political overtones of the title unleash Herod's fear and murderous wrath.[237] The infant Jesus was al-

---

[236]The absence of the title Son of Man from the end of chapter 24 (the faithful and unfaithful servants) and the first part of chapter 25 (the ten virgins, the talents) may seem at first glance to argue against the title's dominance in these pericopes. However, they are framed by references to the coming of the Son of Man (24:44; 25:31) and they contain precisely those themes of delay, sudden return, and need for preparation or vigilance which Matthew explicitly associates with the Son of Man (cf. 24:37-44).

[237]Note how Herod immediately equates the foreigners' phrase "King of the Jews" (2:2) with the more "domestic" designation "Messiah" (2:4). Messiah has more religious and prophetic overtones than King of the Jews, and in a number of places in chapter 27 Matthew replaces Mark's "King of the Jews" with "Messiah." But the equation of the two in 2:2-4 shows how easily the more political title infected the more religious one. That is why Matthew must have Jesus answer in-

most killed by secular rulers because of that title. Now the adult Jesus will be. The title which is used in 27:11 for the first time since the infancy narrative will now join with King of Israel and Messiah to form one of the two main Christological threads running through chapter 27 (cf. vv. 11, 17, 22, 29, 37, 42). The other main thread, interwoven and interacting with these explicitly royal titles, is Son of God (27:40, 43, 54).

Granted the political overtones which "King of the Jews" has in the mouth of a Roman prefect, it is hardly surprising that the response of Jesus is again the veiled or nuanced affirmation, "Thou hast said it" (v. 11). What Pilate intends in a political sense is true on a much deeper level. Jesus confirms the truth the interrogator unconsciously utters, while avoiding the misconceptions which distort the interrogator's appreciation of the truth. Both when the Jewish authorities make their accusation (v. 12), and when Pilate seeks some reaction from Jesus (v. 13), Matthew notes Jesus' silence. There may be here something of the suffering servant motif from Isaiah 53:7 ("he opens not his mouth").[238] The impasse of silence leads the governor to seek a resolution through the custom of releasing a prisoner on the feast. A clear choice is placed before the Jewish crowd: Do they want Barabbas or Jesus?[239] Pilate initiates the choice because he knows that the Jews have handed over Jesus out of envy (v. 18). Implicitly, then,

---

directly and why he must take pains to stress in chapter 27 the religious meaning of the royal titles, which undergo transfiguration through suffering.

[238]A possible further connection with the fourth suffering servant song of Isaiah 52-53 is the mention of Pilate's wonder in Matthew 27:14; cf. Isa 52:15.

[239]It would be tempting to see here a clear choice between political and religious messiahship, the revolutionary zealot versus the humble King of peace. But Matthew deletes Mark's description of Barabbas as an insurrectionist (Mark 15:7). The contrast must remain a mere conjecture. Also tempting is the longer reading of a few manuscripts, which give the full name of Barabbas as Jesus Barabbas. The longer reading would highlight the element of clear choice between Jesus Barabbas and Jesus called Messiah. Senior, *Passion*, 238-240, favors the longer reading; but I remain doubtful because the reading is so poorly attested in the manuscripts, especially the Greek manuscripts.

even as early as verse 18, Pilate is presented as recognizing Jesus' innocence, and so he attempts to free him. Pilate is thus carefully differentiated from the Jews, who are depicted as the hostile force urging the death of Jesus.

At this point, Matthew gives the Jewish authorities time to persuade the crowd to choose Barabbas (v. 20) by inserting a piece of special M material in verse 19. Pilate's wife has experienced a troubling dream concerning Jesus, whom she designates as "this just man." This designation, placed just before the condemnation and crucifixion of Jesus, naturally conjures up the figure of the suffering just man in the Old Testament. Jesus is indeed King and Messiah, but far from being a political conqueror he triumphs by his trust in God in the face of unmerited suffering. The phrase kat'onar, "in a dream," has not occurred in Matthew since the infancy narrative (1:20; 2:12, 13, 19, 22), where dreams were the privileged means by which God directed the actions of Joseph or the Magi. Now, at the other end of the life of Jesus, when his life is again in danger, God gives his monitory revelation again, but this time the intended recipient (Pilate) does not respond with the obedience of Joseph—with tragic results. And yet God's knowledge and control of events is thus affirmed. In the face of human calumnies and envy, the Father bears witness to the innocence of his Son. Moreover, a polemical note against the Jews is added. As in the case of the Magi, God's message comes to Gentiles, while the Jews remain obtuse. A Gentile woman pleads for Jesus while the Jewish leaders urge the crowd to plead for Barabbas.

In the end, the Gentile ruler will at least respond to the revelation by disassociating himself from the crime for which "the whole people" willingly take responsibility (cf. vv. 24-25). Matthew emphasizes that the choice is made by the whole group of Jews. After the crowd chooses Barabbas, Pilate goes on to ask about the fate of Jesus-called-Messiah. Matthew states pointedly that all said: "Let him be crucified!" (v. 22). The protest of the unwilling Pilate, implying with a rhetorical question that Jesus has done nothing wrong, is answered simply with a louder shout (v. 23).

At this point, Matthew makes his most important addition to the trial before Pilate. Verses 24-25 create a calculated diptych, a double panel held together by the key word "blood." With a quasi-ritual gesture, Pilate "washes his hands" of the whole affair. Hand-washing as a sign of or means of obtaining innocence or purity is well known from the Old Testament (e.g., Ps 26:6). The symbol no doubt has its roots in magic and cult; and in Exodus 30:19, 21; 40:31 can be found examples of the symbol as a cultic gesture. While Psalm 26 is very much rooted in cultic imagery, the cultic gesture has taken on a moral significance (Ps 26:9-12). Lost somewhere between magic, cult, and morality is the strange ritual in Deuteronomy 21:1-9, prescribed for the case of an unsolved murder. The elders of the people slay a heifer, wash their hands over the victim, and declare that they have not shed "this blood." Especially intriguing is the prayer of the elders in verse 8: "Absolve, O Lord, your people Israel, whom you have ransomed, and let not the guilt of shedding innocent blood remain in the midst of your people Israel." By contrast, Pilate here proclaims his own innocence before an Israel demanding Jesus' blood. Echoes from the fate of Judas ring out, especially the "innocent blood" and "see to it yourself" from 27:4. The responsibility for the bloodshed which the priests, Judas, and Pilate have all tried to shift away from themselves throughout chapter 27 is now willingly accepted by all the people (pas ho laos, v. 25). With a quasi-cultic formula, Matthew states that the whole Jewish people—not just the crowd in front of Pilate—freely accepted responsibility for Jesus' death. What Jesus had threatened and predicted in 23:35 has come to pass: all the just blood of past martyrs now descends upon the Jews, upon "this generation" which rejects Jesus (23:36).

Of course, we have here a fierce polemic by Matthew against the Jews of his own time who have persecuted Jewish Christians and driven them out of the synagogue. But there is a deeper, more theological point here, a pivotal point in Matthew's pattern of salvation-history. This formal rejection of Jesus by the Jews forms part of the "turning point of the ages" which occurs in the death-resurrection of Jesus. The Kingdom of God is taken from this people and given to another people, the church, which will bear its fruits (21:43). The people who will be saved from their sins by Jesus (Matt 1:21, with *laos*) is obviously this new people of God, the church, and not "the whole people" (*laos*) which cries out for Jesus' blood. The blood which is shed for many unto the remission of sins will profit "the many" who form the new collectivity, the church (26:28). It will obviously not save the old collectivity, the Israel which cries out for the shedding of this blood with murderous intent. This blood of Jesus will descend upon them and their descendants[240] with an unintended effect: the status of God's chosen people will be transferred from the Jews to the church. Accordingly, the final pericope of Matthew's gospel will present the exalted Son of Man issuing a command to begin a mission not to Israel, as in chapter 10, but to "all the nations" (28:19).[241] Here, then, in the trial before Pilate, Matthew has created a perfect expression of his own theology, which ties together Christology and ecclesiology within a context of salvation-history. A fundamental choice, involving the confession or the denial of Jesus as Messiah, leads to a fundamental change in the identity of the people of God. That fatal decision is made by the whole Jewish people in 27:25. All Pilate can do in verse 26 is ratify the choice of Barabbas over Jesus.

The mocking by the soldiers (27:27-31) provides something of a dramatic interlude before the crucifixion and also symbolizes the saving effect of the crucifixion. Using the scarlet cloak of an ordinary soldier, a crown of thorns, and a reed as a scepter, the soldiers stage a cruel parody of a coronation. To the mockery of genuflection they add the violence of their spittle and blows. Cen-

---

[240]"And upon our children" in 27:25 could possibly refer only to the next generation, down to the destruction of Jerusalem in A.D. 70. But since Matthew is dealing here with questions of salvation-history and ecclesiology (who is the true people of God?), the wider meaning of "all our descendants forever" is probably intended.

[241]This does not mean that individual Jews are excluded from the mission-mandate of 28:19. Rather, the Jews as a special, separate people have lost their privileged status as the chosen people of God. They have been "declassified" and have become simply one nation among "all the nations." They are included in the universal mission, but with no special position or privilege.

tral to the scene is their greeting: "Hail, King of the Jews!" That King whom the Gentile Magi sought out to adore is now greeted with mock adoration by the Gentile soldiers. All unknowingly, however, they act out what later believing Gentiles will do in earnest, beginning with the soldiers at the cross (27:54). The one the Gentiles now mock as a ludicrous King of a hated race will be worshiped by the Gentiles as Son of God (27:54) and ruler of heaven and earth (28:19).

After a quick mention of the incident of Simon of Cyrene to provide a transition to Golgotha (27:32), Matthew sets about enunciating his Son-of-God Christology in the scene of crucifixion (27:33-44). Matthew has Jesus presented not with wine mixed with myrrh, as in Mark 15:23, but with wine mixed with gall (Matt 27:34). This is meant to recall the agony of the suffering just man in Psalm 68:22 in the Septuagint: "They gave me *gall* for food and for my thirst they gave me *vinegar* to drink." Matthew will complete the allusion in verse 48, with the mention of vinegar. Thus, the whole of the crucifixion is framed by the image of the suffering just man of the psalms. Even in this extremity Jesus shows his sovereign command: "He did not wish to drink" Passing over the actual act of crucifixion with a mere participle, Matthew next alludes to the suffering servant of Psalm 22: "They divide my garments among them, and for my vesture they cast lots" (Ps 22:19).[242] The soldiers then sit to keep watch over Jesus, little realizing that, faced with the apocalyptic events surrounding his death, they will acclaim him Son of God (27:54). The paradox of this crucified Jesus is well summed up in the juxtaposition of verses 37 and 38. On the one hand, the title on the cross proclaims him as King of the Jews, continuing the theme begun at 27:11. It is a mocking declaration which nevertheless voices the unrecognized truth. On the other hand, this King has as his attendants two thieves (v. 38).

The ludicrous contrast between title and apparent reality calls forth the mockery in verses 39-43. Matthew carefully

---

[242]What is remarkable here is that Matthew is satisfied with an allusion woven into the narrative, instead of a formula quotation. This confirms the view that the words of 26:54 and 56 act as a kind of formula quotation for the whole passion narrative.

constructs the mockery out of phrases from Psalm 22 and Wisdom 2. Both texts present the agony of the suffering just man and, most importantly for Matthew, Wisdom 2 stresses the status of the suffering just man as a son of God. The references to Psalm 22:8-9 were already present in Mark. Matthew's most noteworthy additions are the phrases "if you are the Son of God" (v. 40) and "he trusted in God; let him deliver him now if he wants him, for he said: 'I am God's Son' " (v. 43). For Matthew, the deepest mystery of the cross is that Jesus manifests and proves his divine sonship precisely by not saving himself from ignominious death but rather by embracing it in trust and obedience to his Father's will. It would be human to come down; it was divine to remain hanging. This is the astounding "bending" of the title Son of God which Matthew undertakes. Son of God is reinterpreted in terms of trust and obedience in the midst of suffering. The figure of the Son of God becomes meshed with the figure of the suffering just man, as in Wisdom 2, which had already begun to make the equation.[243] This use of Son of God as a temptation or taunt aimed at the suffering one calls up a number of reminiscences from earlier in the gospel. Satan tempted Jesus to turn aside from the path of suffering and the cross and to choose an easy road to kingship (4:1-11). Matthew had Satan introduce his first two temptations with the very words we read in 27:40: "If you are the Son of God. . . ." (cf. 4:3 and 6). For the Satanic mind, divine sonship and voluntary suffering are simply incompatible. It was this same misconception of divine sonship which led Peter to play Satan at Caesarea Philippi. He gladly hailed Jesus as Messiah and Son of God and then vigorously protested when divine sonship was linked with the cross (16:13-23). Now, once again, in what is indeed "the last temptation of Christ," the incompatibility of what Jesus claims to be and what he is actually suffering is thrown in his face.[244] Only the committed believer can gaze on this crucified criminal and see there the Son of God, the King of Israel. And,

---

[243]See, for instance, Wisdom 2:12-13, 16-20.

[244]This contrast between exalted claim and humble status also recalls the scene of the trial before Caiaphas, when Jesus is said to be able to destroy the Temple (compare 26:61 and 27:40) and to be Son of God (compare 26:63 and 27:40-43).

intimates Matthew, the sons of God, the disciples who can make this act of faith in the crucified, must live out their sonship by the same trust and obedience amid sufferings.

The great theme of Son of God, which dominates the scene of crucifixion, also ties that scene together with the following scene, the death of Jesus (27:45-56). As we saw in our treatment of salvation history in Matthew's gospel,[245] Matthew clothes the death of Jesus with a number of apocalyptic signs. The first, inherited from Mark, is the darkness lasting from noon to three o'clock (v. 45). The darkness motif is a typical eschatological and apocalyptic motif; especially interesting is the prediction in Amos 8:9 that "on that day" (i.e., the fearful day of Yahweh) God will make the sun set at noon and will cover the earth with darkness in broad daylight.[246]

Matching the fearful darkness is the fearful cry of Jesus, given in both Semitic and Greek forms: "My God, my God, why hast thou forsaken me?" (v. 46). Having already seen how Matthew uses the psalms of the suffering just man to depict the crucifixion of Jesus, we can safely ignore modern existentialistic interpretations which see the despair or atheism of alienated mankind in Jesus' cry. The Old Testament just man who was severely tested by God in the crucible of suffering saw nothing wrong in complaining loud and clear to the divinity about his apparent abandonment. The sharpness, even stridency, of the lament actually reflects the close sense of intimacy and trust the just man possessed vis-à-vis God. He is on such intimate terms with God that he can voice his complaint in no uncertain terms. The harsh tones of the complaint are meant to arouse God to do exactly what the just man knows God can do, namely, rescue him. In fact, a number of the strong laments in the psalms end with hymns of triumph and thanksgiving for the salvation God has accomplished. Psalm 22 is precisely such a psalm. The words of Jesus thus bespeak both his real anguish and his filial trust in the Father who saves in a way the bystanders do not suspect. The cry

---

[245]Cf. Part I, pp. 33-35.

[246]There may also be an allusion to the plague of darkness in Egypt, when there was darkness over *the whole earth* (or land); cf. Exod 10:22.

will be answered in a preliminary way by the apocalyptic signs at the death of Jesus, and fully at the resurrection.

But the bystanders think of some more immediate rescue. For them, rescue from death means a rescue that prevents death, not the rescue out of death, the rescue of the resurrection. They misunderstand Jesus' cry "my God" (in Hebrew, *Eli*) to refer to the prophet and wonder-worker Elijah, whom, they suppose, Jesus is invoking for miraculous deliverance (v. 47). One of the bystanders wants to offer Jesus some vinegar (a motif from the psalms of the suffering just man) to sustain him, in case Elijah should come. The other bystanders disagree, suggesting that no action be taken until Elijah comes. Their whole conception revolves around miraculous prevention of death, and their tone is one of mockery. No doubt they feel that their skepticism is justified when again Jesus cries out and gives up his spirit.[247]

V. MATT 27:51—28:15: DEATH-RESURRECTION AS THE TURNING POINT OF THE AGES

With the death of Jesus, all salvation history has reached its turning point. This is indicated by the signs and wonders God immediately works in response to Jesus' death.[248] They are not just superficial apocalyptic color, added to a narrative to make it more lively. They are Matthew's way of affirming that, with the death of the Son, a new age has broken into the old. Judaism and its cult are rejected and the way to God is open equally to all men, for the one life-giving sacrifice constituted by the death of Jesus

---

[247]Perhaps Senior, *Passion*, 304-307, puts too much weight on the "again" of verse 50 when he wants to see it as an indication that the final cry of Jesus is also a dramatic prayer, as in verse 46. More probable is his opinion that Matthew's reverent phrase "he gave up the spirit" (contrast Mark's "he expired") expresses the voluntary nature of Jesus' death.

[248]Although it is common to speak of verses 51-54 as apocalyptic "signs," that label really does not do justice to what Matthew calls in verse 54 *ta ginomena*, "the things which happened." Especially in the case of the raising of the dead we are dealing not with apocalyptic *signs* but apocalyptic *events*, end-time *events* retrojected into the historical event of Jesus' death. The end-time is happening now.

has obtained remission of sins "for the many." We have already explored the details of 27:51-54 in Part I, when we saw Matthew's outline of salvation-history. Here we need only recall that the life-giving death of Jesus is portrayed as spelling the end of the sacrificial cult in the Temple (v. 51a, the rending of the veil), marking the earth-shaking beginning of the new age (v. 51b, the earthquake), causing the dead to rise in a proleptic final resurrection (vv. 52-53, the tombs are opened and the dead come forth), and bringing the community of the Gentiles to the Easter faith that Jesus is the Son of God (v. 54). At the cross, death and sin are conquered in principle, and the Old Testament restrictions of race, cult, and law are thrown down in favor of a faith preached to all the nations. This is the point of Matthew's redaction of Mark 15:39 in Matthew 27:54. It is no longer simply the centurion but also those with him standing guard over Jesus (cf. v. 36) who, at the sight of the apocalyptic events, make their profession in Jesus as Son of God.[249] The unclean Gentiles, the very crucifiers of Jesus, now are seized with reverent fear and express that faith which is proper to the disciples (cf. the same words in the mouths of the disciples in 14:33). The gathering-in of the Gentiles into the church, which the exalted Son of Man commands in 28:19, is anticipated here at the cross. The cosmic turning of the ages is reproduced on the personal level of conversion (a "turning"), as the soldiers look on the criminal they have crucified and proclaim him the transcendent Son of God. What the Jews said mockingly and conditionally before Jesus' death the Gentiles now declare as a fact of faith: "Truly this was God's Son."

After this climax, Matthew spends the rest of chapter 27 preparing for the resurrection stories in chapter 28. We can conveniently divide the material into three sections: the women at the cross (27:55-56); the burial of Jesus (27:57-61); and the guards at the tomb (27:62-66). In verses 55-56, Matthew mentions the many faithful women who had followed Jesus *from* Galilee (contrast Mark's *in Galilee*). They are the true disciples who have followed

---

[249]As can be seen from Matthew 27:35-36, these soldiers are the very people who nailed Jesus to the cross and divided his garments. Matthew's missionary and parenetic thrust is clear: conversion and repentance are possible for anyone.

their master up the way of the cross; not even after his arrest have they deserted him. While their past function was *serving* Jesus, now their key function is simply *seeing* (v. 55). From among their number, the two Marys are to be the living link between death, burial, and resurrection. These women who have seen the death will also be witnesses at the burial, and the first witnesses at the empty tomb. In 28:1, Matthew changes Mark, to read that the two Marys come to *see* the tomb.[250] These two faithful women thus form the bridge of witness from Good Friday afternoon to Easter Sunday morning.

Beginning with the mention of the women, but even more so with the burial of Jesus and the setting of the guard, there are numerous connections with the stories in chapter 28. In a sense there is a certain leap-frog effect. The burial of Jesus (27:57-61) goes together with the empty tomb story (28:1-10), which in turn leads to the appearance of the exalted Son of Man (28:16-20). Dovetailed with these stories is the tradition of the guards at the tomb. The story of the setting of the guard (27:62-66) has its real continuation in the lie concocted by the guards and the Jews in 28:11-15. The mention of the guards in 28:4 acts as a linchpin joining the two cycles of stories together.[251]

In the story of Jesus' burial (27:57-61), Matthew changes the figure of Joseph of Arimathea. Perhaps he felt that Joseph's being "a prominent member of the council [the Sanhedrin; so Mark 15:43]" put him too close to the faithless leaders who condemned Jesus to death. What prompted Matthew's description of Joseph as "a rich man" is less clear. A reference to the burial of the suffering servant is not impossible, since in both the Hebrew and the Greek versions of Isaiah 53:9 "the rich" are mentioned in some connection with the servant's burial.[252] Instead of Mark's

---

[250]The same verb for seeing (*theōreō*) is used in 27:55 and 28:1.

[251]For further considerations of structure, cf. C. H. Giblin, "Structural and Thematic Correlations in the Matthean Burial-Resurrection Narrative (Matt XXVII.57-XXVIII.20)," *NTS* 21 (1974-75) 406-420. Perhaps Giblin does not take enough account of the elements binding the death-scene to the empty-tomb story.

[252]Admittedly, the sense of the text is clear in neither the Hebrew nor the Greek. The reference to Isaiah 53:9 has been sustained with an appeal to the Qumran text of Isaiah by W. Barrick, "The Rich Man from Arimathea (Matt 27:57-60) and 1 QIsa^a," *JBL* 96 (1977) 235-239.

vague "he was awaiting the Kingdom of God," we read in Matthew that Joseph was himself a disciple of Jesus.[253] Like the woman who anointed Jesus *for burial* in Matthew 26:6-13, Joseph performs his good work of mercy toward the body of Jesus and then disappears. Matthew stresses that the grave is new, that a *large* stone was rolled in front of the door, and that the two Marys were witnesses of the exact spot—all apologetic points to forestall later charges of confusion or fraud.

The apologetic motif is stronger still in the story of the posting of the guards (27:62-66). The story no doubt arose as the answer of Matthew's church to Jewish claims that Jesus' disciples stole his body and then proclaimed he had risen.[254] Matthew's apologetic answer begins by portraying the high priests, and notably also the Pharisees, as breaking the Sabbath in order to negotiate with Pilate, the hated Gentile ruler. They are driven to such extremities by their fear of Jesus' prophecy that he would rise after three days. The great irony here is that the Jewish rulers take more account of Jesus' promise after his death than do his disciples.[255] The weary Pilate assigns them a guard and adds what for Matthew is a deeply ironic command: "Secure the tomb *as best you know how*." Roman and Jewish rulers might combine to prevent the resurrection, but all in vain. The seal on the tomb will prove no more effective and definitive than the seal on the stone which blocked the lions' den into which Daniel was thrown (cf. Dan 6:18).

After the Sabbath, as the first day of the week is beginning,

---

[253]At this point we note one of the strange parallels Matthew has at times with John. While Luke follows Mark here, John 19:38 says that Joseph was a disciple of Jesus.

[254]An interesting side point here is that the Jewish charge (older than the answer of Matthew's church and therefore much older than Matthew's gospel) presupposes that the tomb was empty on the third day. Apparently nowhere in the early disputes over the resurrection of Jesus is the charge ever made that the body was still in the tomb on Easter Sunday.

[255]Naturally, since this story is a later apologetic development, one should not raise historical questions about how the Jewish rulers learned of Jesus' prophecy. To appeal to 12:40 is to look for historical probability where it is not to be found. The stress on the words "three days" and "be raised" serves neatly to introduce chapter 28.

the two Marys come to see the tomb, no doubt to mourn.[256] As the two women were present at the earthquake and other apocalyptic events surrounding the death of Jesus, so now they witness another earthquake, accompanied by the angel of the Lord, who descends from heaven to interpret the apocalyptic events.[257] The angel shows his supernatural power by rolling back the huge stone. He then sits upon it to symbolize God's triumph over death in the resurrection of Jesus (v. 2). The use of images like lightning and snow to describe the angel confirm him as a stock figure of apocalyptic (v. 3). The guards posted to guard the dead Jesus are themselves struck down with fear like dead men (v. 4), while the angel announces that the once dead Jesus is risen. The motifs of earthquake, fear of the guards, death, and resurrection bind this scene to the scene of the death of Jesus. Matthew thinks in terms of one great apocalyptic event, the death-resurrection as the turning point of salvation-history. This event should indeed instill fear in the faithless guards. But for the faithful women the angel speaks words of joy, not fear (v. 5).

His message is terse and can be summed up in four points: (1) the introductory command common to appearances of God to men in the Old Testament: fear not; (2) the explanation why fear should give way to joy: the basic proclamation of the resurrection; (3) a demonstration of this proclamation: the empty tomb is pointed out; (4) the commission to communicate to the disciples (a) the good news that he is risen, (b) the command to go into Galilee, and (c) the promise that "there you shall see him."

The women hasten from the tomb to fulfill their commission, since their joy outweighs their fear (contrast Mark 16:8). On the

---

[256]The story of the sealing of the stone and the posting of the guards leaves no place for Mark's reason for the visit: "to anoint him" (Mark 16:1).

[257]Cf. my treatment of 28:2-3 under salvation-history in Part I. The phrase "angel of the Lord" takes us back to the infancy narrative (1:20; 24; 2:13, 19). The many correspondences between chapters 27-28 and chapters 1-2 remind us that Matthew's infancy narrative is really a proleptic passion narrative.

way, Jesus meets them and wishes them his Easter joy.[258] They reverently approach, seize his feet (to kiss them?), and prostrate themselves in worship. Jesus repeats almost word for word the message of the angel. As a result, many commentators dismiss this short resurrection appearance as a mere variant which has no real function in the narrative. Yet Matthew uses the cameo scene to make three important points.

1. The risen body is real; it can be touched. This fits in with one of Matthew's main concerns: the identity of the earthly Jesus and the risen Lord. The Jesus who taught on the mountain in Galilee is the same Jesus who, on a mountain in Galilee after his resurrection, commissions his disciples to teach his commandments to all nations. In a sense, just as Son of Man was *the* dominant Christological title in chapters 24-26, and just as Son of God was *the* dominant Christological title in chapter 27, so "Jesus," the simple name of the man from Nazareth, is the dominant "title" for the resurrection narratives in chapter 28. Precisely where we would expect a heaping-up of the loftiest Christological titles, Matthew suddenly stops using titles and refers throughout the chapter simply to "Jesus" (vv. 5, 9, 10, 16, 18). Jesus the crucified is Jesus the risen: that is the message not only of the angel in verses 5-6 but also of the whole chapter. Matthew does indeed allude to the Son of Man in 28:18, and the title "Son" does occur obliquely in the baptismal formula of 28:19. But the major Christological "title" of the resurrection chapter is simply "Jesus."

2. This same Jesus reconstitutes the fellowship he had with his disciples during the ministry, a fellowship broken by their flight after his arrest. As in 12:49, so here in 28:10, he calls his disciples "his brothers." They are again called into fellowship, again called to do the will of Jesus' Father (12:50), again called to be members of the family and people of God. They are again called to be the church. Thus we are prepared for the final

---

[258]The Greek *chairete* ("all hail!") is the normal Greek greeting, but coming right after the mention of the "great joy" (*charas megalēs*) of the women, it probably carries a deeper sense. Compare Matthew 28:9-10 with John 20:14-18.

enunciation of the bond between Christology and ecclesiology in 28:16-20.

3. A final point, more implicit than expressed, is that, although this is the same Jesus, the women may not hold on to him or to their old relationship with him. The risen Jesus appears to a person only to send that person away, to send him or her on mission to others, yes, to all the nations—the same Jesus, but a new mission.

Just as the loving burial of Jesus, accomplished by Joseph and witnessed by the women, had its counterpart in the plan of the Jewish leaders to seal the stone and set a guard, so too the good news of Jesus' resurrection imparted to the same women has its counterpart in the bad news of the theft of Jesus' body, concocted by the same Jewish leaders (28:11-15). Since all political, military, and religious means have failed to vanquish Jesus, his enemies are reduced to lies and bribery to squelch the news of his victory. Unable to prevent the resurrection, they are reduced to hindering belief in it.[259] As with Judas, so with the soldiers, their ultimate weapon is money. It is a powerful tool of teaching. Almost in a parody on his own vocabulary of teaching and doing, Matthew dryly remarks of the soldiers: "They did as they were taught" (28:15). The counter-teaching, the lie, the word (*logos*) which reviles the word of the gospel, has been spread among the Jews[260] down to Matthew's own day.

VI.   CONCLUSION TO PART TWO: PROLEPTIC PAROUSIA

We come at last to the final pericope of the gospel, which we

---

[259]Grundmann, *Das Evangelium nach Matthäus*, 572, sees here another contact with the infancy narrative. In both cases, leaders of the Jews hear disturbing reports about Jesus, try to take measures against him, and fail to achieve success.

[260]Matthew may be using the term "Jews" rather than "Israel" in 28:15 with a precise theological purpose. After the death-resurrection, Israel, the privileged chosen people of God, is no more. The Kingdom of God has been transferred to the church (21:43). What is left is the Jewish nation, which is simply one of the nations of this world.

have already examined for its message in regard to salvation-
history.[261] Having worked through the whole of the gospel, we
can appreciate now much more Otto Michel's famous dictum:
Matthew 28:18-20 is the key to the understanding of the whole of
Matthew's gospel.[262] The great concluding scene of 28:16-20 is
made up of a narrative framework (28:16-18a) and a chain of three
sayings (28:18b, 19-20a, 20b).

In verse 16, the story begins by a link-up with the public
ministry, the passion narrative, and the commission to the
women in 28:7, 10. The *eleven* disciples go into Galilee (v. 16).
The disciples, whom Matthew more or less equated with the
twelve, were the core group of Jesus' followers, the symbol of
church members and especially of church leaders. But Judas
turned traitor, so now Matthew must speak of the eleven disciples. Restored to fellowship as "brothers" by the risen Jesus
(28:10), they obey the command of the one they deserted in the
passion, thus reverting to the obedience they showed just before
the passion proper began (cf. 21:1-7; 26:17-19). They return, as
directed, to Galilee, the place of Jesus' humble earthly ministry
and of his eschatological teaching. They go to the mountain, the
typically Matthean place of revelation.[263] Despite the emphasis
on seeing in the commands of 28:7, 10, the action of seeing Jesus
is passed over in a participle, with no description of how Jesus
looks. The emphasis in verse 17 is rather on the perennial tension
in the life of discipleship: "they worshiped him, but some hesi-
tated."[264] There is no explanation of why this doubt arises or how
it is overcome because the tension between worshiping belief and
hesitant smallness of faith (*oligopistia*) is the very structure of

---

[261]See Part I, under salvation-history, pp. 37-38.

[262]O. Michel, "Der Abschluss des Matthäusevangeliums," *EvT* 10
(1950) 21. My only modification of that statement would be to broaden it
out to the entire pericope, 28:16-20.

[263]However, the phrase, "the mountain whither Jesus had ordered
them [to go]" is not explicable by what Matthew has said earlier in
chapter 28. The phrase probably indicates that behind 28:16-20 is some
earlier tradition.

[264]I prefer to take *hoi de* in 17b as "but some." The phrase, however,
could refer to all the eleven: "but they."

discipleship in this present age, this "mixed-bag" condition in the church and in the world.[265]

In verse 18a, Jesus seizes the initiative by approaching his prostrate disciples and addressing to them his three words of declaration (v. 18b), command (19-20a), and promise (20b). In 18b he makes a *Christological* declaration, explaining the meaning of the death-resurrection for himself. By the death-resurrection he has been exalted to God's right hand as the Son of Man, the cosmocrator who has authority over heaven and earth.[266] The prophecy of Daniel 7:13 and the prophecy of Jesus in 26:64 are now fulfilled. *From now on* (cf. the *ap'arti* in 26:64) the exalted Son of Man sits at God's right hand, sharing his cosmic rule. And from now on, the Son of Man comes to his church in a proleptic parousia. Far from ascending *from* his church, as in Luke 24:51 and Acts 1:6-11, the risen Jesus comes *to* his church, to remain with it all days until the end of the age, until the full, visible parousia which will bring the present age to a complete end. By his death-resurrection, Jesus has put off the restrictions of the territory, religion, race, and Law of the Jews. Although he exercised authority (*exousia*) during his public life, by his death-resurrection he has received from the Father all authority (*pasa exousia*) over the whole cosmos. This is the picture of the Son of Man in the explanation of the parable of the wheat and the tares (13:36-43), a picture not verified fully of the earthly Jesus during his public ministry. Clearly, then, the death-resurrection is first of

---

[265]I would not agree with the position of Bornkamm in "Der Auferstandene und der Irdische," in G. Bornkamm-G. Barth-H. Held, *Überlieferung und Auselgung im Matthäusevangelium* (fifth edition; Neukirchen: Neukirchener Verlag, 1968) 290. Bornkamm understands verse 17 in reference to the doubts of the later church about the reality of the resurrection. Doubts are overcome, says Matthew, not by seeking any material assurances (—then what of 28:9-10?), but simply by the word of the Exalted One. Yet Matthew never indicates that the doubt is overcome. *Distazō* rather refers to hesitation in the face of a panic-producing crisis; it is that small faith (*oligopistia*) which marks every disciple in this world.

[266]In defense of an allusion here to the Son of Man and Daniel 7:13, cf. my article, "Salvation History in Matthew: In Search of a Starting Point," *CBQ* 37 (1975) 210-212, especially 212, notes 17 and 18.

all a Christological turning point. It means the definitive exaltation of Jesus as Son of Man, ruler of the universe and of the
universal church.[267] Matthew 28:16-20 is not merely an
ecclesiological statement; it is first of all Christological.

Now that this Christological turning point has taken place, it
functions as the basis for the ecclesiological turning point. On the
basis of his exaltation ("Going *therefore*"), the Son of Man commissions his disciples to (a) make disciples of all the nations, in
verse 19a; (b) baptize them with the Trinitarian formula, in verse
19b; (c) teach them all the commands which Jesus uttered during
his public ministry, in verse 20a. This commission, which neatly
falls into three parts, constitutes a threefold rescinding of the
limitations of Jesus' public ministry. Making disciples of all the
nations revokes the limited mission to the land and people of
Israel (cf. 10:5-6; 15:24). Using Trinitarian baptism as the initiation rite for all nations implicitly does away with circumcision as
the key initiation rite introducing the convert into the people of
God. And once the convert enters the church, what is normative
for his Christian life is not the Mosaic Law as such, but the
commands of Jesus—be they in conformity or in conflict with the
Mosaic Law. In short, what we have in verses 19-20a is nothing
less than the founding of the church by the risen Jesus. All the
ecclesiological instructions and promises in the body of the gospel
now reach their proper term.

Yet even here, at the heart of this ecclesial pronouncement in
19-20a, Christology is at the basis of the church's existence and
activity. The baptism Matthew's church practices[268] is one of the
most solemn and weighty expressions of "high Christology" in
the New Testament. To put the Son on the same level with the
Father and the Spirit in a terse triadic formula is to profess the
Son's divinity in a manner that is surpassed only by the fourth

---

[267]Note the emphasis on universal authority and mission, and on
unrestricted teaching and time, by the repetition of the adjective "all"
(*pas*): all authority . . . all nations . . . all I commanded . . . all days.

[268]The attempts to see the Trinitarian formula in 28:19 as a secondary addition to the Matthean text fail for lack of solid evidence; cf. B.
Hubbard, *The Matthean Redaction of a Primitive Apostolic Commissioning* (Missoula: Scholars' Press, 1974) 151-175.

gospel and the Epistle to the Hebrews.[269] For Matthew's church, then, baptism plunges one into the mystery of the communal life of Father, Son, and Spirit, and therefore constitutes all those so baptized as members of the family or people of God, as disciples and therefore as brothers of Jesus (cf. 28:10). Again, Christology and ecclesiology, high estimation of the person of Jesus and lofty definition of the church, go hand in hand.

But Matthew, of course, is not about to let lofty conceptions of the church obscure the cost of discipleship and the church's exposure to future judgment. The baptized life is a life lived according to justice, which means according to God's will, which in turn means according to the commandments taught by the earthly Jesus. Because the one and the same Jesus—the one and the same Son of Man—enjoined these commandments during his public ministry, enjoins them now on his church after the resurrection, and will judge *all* men according to these same commands, lofty ecclesiology, based on high Christology, also means lofty obligations. In morality as well as in mission and cult, Christology grounds the church's life and action.

This point is summed up perfectly in the concluding promise of the gospel in 28:20b: "And behold, I am with you all days, even to the consummation of the age." This Emmanuel (1:23) who once called disciples to follow and be with him during his public ministry, who promised that he would be in the midst of two or three gathered together in his name (18:20), this God-with-us now promises not a local presence in a particular territory like Palestine or during some set time period like the public ministry. He promises his universal presence to his universal church, throughout the whole of human history, till he comes again in glory to hold his final judgment, according to the commandments he and

---

[269]One must beware of using "the Son" in 28:19 to prove that the whole pericope is dominated by Son-of-God Christology, for four reasons. (1) As we have seen, the absolute use of the term Son is not to be equated automatically with Son of God; it can also have reference to the Son of Man. (2) This is especially the case in triadic formulas, as we have seen in 16:27 and probably 24:36. (3) This reference to the Son of Man is reinforced by the allusion to Daniel 7:13 in Matthew 28:18. (4) At any rate, the title occurs only in a quotation of a cultic formula; it should not be allowed by itself to define the dominant Christology of the pericope.

his church have taught. The church which he now establishes and immediately sends on universal mission is sustained by his energizing presence until the end of the world, whenever that may be.[270] The church proceeds from the risen Son of Man, is sustained in its mission, cult, and teaching throughout history by this Son of Man, and in the end will arrive at his judgment seat for the final hearing. The final pericope of Matthew's gospel, 28:16-20, is also the final, eloquent statement of what we have seen throughout the gospel. Christology and ecclesiology are bound inextricably together at the heart of Matthew's theology.

We can now look back—somewhat winded—at the twenty-eight chapters of Matthew's gospel which we have just traversed. I think we can safely say that the following propositions, enunciated briefly at the beginning of Part II, have been firmly established:

1. In Matthew's gospel, Christ is presented not only as *a* teacher (e.g., chaps. 5-7); he is *the* teacher of Christian morality (e.g., 23:8, 10).

2. Not only does he teach Christian morality; he also embodies and grounds the life he teaches. That is to say, he exemplifies his own message of obedient trust in the Father and love for all men throughout his life and finally in his death (e.g., 3:15; 4:1-11; 8:17; 12:18-21; 26:36-56; 27:34-44). Moreover, by his death-resurrection, he defeats once and for all the powers of sin (26:28) and death (27:51-53; 28:2-7) and thus opens up for the disciple a new existence:

(a) an existence plunged into the life of Father, Son, and Spirit (28:19), where all are brothers of Christ (12:49-50; 23:8);

(b) an existence lived under the dominion of the exalted and now reigning Son of Man (28:18; 13:37-38);

(c) an existence molded according to the teaching of the earthly Jesus (28:20a; 7:21-27);

---

[270]One can see then how the "delay" of the parousia no longer creates a problem for Matthew. A proleptic parousia has already taken place *for the church*; Jesus remains present to his church, empowering it for mission. Actually, the return of Jesus at the end of the gospel is the Matthean equivalent of Luke's sending of the Spirit on Pentecost and John's indwelling by the Paraclete.

(d) an existence and mission sustained by the perduring presence of the risen Jesus (28:20b; 1:23; 18:20).

3. Matthew, however, does not lapse into a me-and-Jesus approach. Inextricably joined to Jesus is his people, the church (1:21; 16:17-19; 18:15-20). An individual belongs to the Kingdom of God by belonging to that people to whom the Kingdom has been transferred from Israel (21:43). The final Christological declaration, missionary mandate, and promise of presence (28:18-20) are given not to scattered individuals, but to the eleven (28:16), who typify not only Christians in general but more especially the leaders of the later church. Ecclesiology is not interjected haphazardly into the gospel by Matthew. In pericopes which stem from Mark, we see a careful attempt to balance the original Christological message with an ecclesiological one (e.g., Caesarea Philippi, the parable of the evil farmers, the cry of the crowd before Pilate, the healing of the paralytic, the walking on the water). The same emphasis is clear in Matthew's special material (1:21; 18:20; 28:16-20). The nexus between Christology and ecclesiology is one of the most typical characteristics of Matthew's gospel, yes, even its specificity. Luke was free to develop his ecclesiology in a separate book, the Acts of the Apostles. Matthew wrote his Acts in the gospel; his ecclesiology had to be fully developed in the same book as his Christology.

4. Granted this nexus, one must specify what is the place of the church vis-à-vis the Christian morality taught by Christ. If Christ is *the* teacher and *the* basis of Christian morality, what is the church? Matthew 16:17-19; 18:15-20; and 28:16-20 show that the church's function is to hand on, explain, and enforce the teachings of Jesus. This function of teaching, while spoken of and promised during the earthly ministry of Jesus, was not actually exercised by the eleven until after the death-resurrection (contrast 10:1, 7-8, with 28:20a). This power to teach and interpret is at once all-inclusive and yet restricted. It includes all that *Jesus* commands (28:20), not all things under the sun. Peter's power is all-inclusive: what you bind on earth shall be bound in heaven (16:19). And yet the rabbinic terminology of binding and loosing moves in a certain thought-world. Peter is to play chief rabbi, interpreting the sayings of Jesus. His power covers the whole of this area, but does not extend to all things knowable.

5. A corollary of our investigation concerns the use of the titles Matthew employed to construct his Christology. A first, rather embarrassing result is that Matthew is quite capable of making important Christological statements without titles— witness the sermon on the mount or the predominance of the simple name Jesus in chapter 28. Among the titles Matthew does use, I think we saw sufficient evidence to modify the thesis of Kingsbury. According to Kingsbury, Son of God is the central title of Matthew's gospel. It is the most comprehensive title, superior to all others, although Son of Man does supersede Son of God at the parousia.[271] At least on this side of the parousia, then, Son of Man tends to fall under the shadow of Son of God. I think our survey of the whole gospel makes this position questionable. From all we have seen, I would recall just a few points.

(a) Statistics alone make such a reduced status for Son of Man doubtful. Son of Man occurs in Matthew thirty times. These are explicit appearances, which do not take into account the addresses "Lord" and other indirect expressions which have as their ultimate referent the Son of Man. By contrast, Son of God—in that full, exact form—occurs only nine times. To these occurrences of Son of God may be added the address, "my Son," which appears three times.[272] The absolute use, "the Son," occurs five times, three times in one verse (11:27). From all that we have seen, it is clear that one should not make the mistake of automatically equating the last category with the full title Son of God. But, however one combines the occurrences, Son of Man has an overwhelming statistical preponderance in the gospel.

(b) Statistics alone, however, prove little. More important is the question of the range and depth of meaning of any given title. We have seen throughout the gospel that Son of Man has the widest conceivable span of meanings: humble servant of the pub-

---

[271]There is something of a shift on this point within Kingsbury's book. In the beginning of the work, the superiority and centrality of the Son of God over every other title is strongly stressed. In the recapitulation, however, more weight seems to be allowed to Son of Man than one would have expected from the beginning of the book (cf. pp. 162-163).

[272]Somewhat similar, though in a class by itself, is the use of "his son" and "my son" in the parable of the evil tenants of the vineyard (21:37).

lic ministry, possessor of the divine power to forgive sins during the public ministry, friend of sinners who is exposed to reproach, mockery, and blasphemy, Lord of the Sabbath, the suffering, dying, and rising servant, the cosmocrator, the judge of the last day, coming in his glory and accompanied by his angels. What is even more interesting is that these meanings do not simply stand juxtaposed in a hodgepodge manner. They form a continuum of meaning, an arch of tension spanning public ministry, passion and exaltation, rule of the world, and final judgment. And the span not only ties together the various aspects of Son of Man, but also ties together the Son of Man with the church. The earthly Son of Man who serves the lowly by healing them, who forgives the sinful and welcomes the outcast to table, is also the Son of Man who dies and rises for the sins of the many, who comes in proleptic parousia to order the teaching of all he has commanded, and who will come again to judge according to what he has commanded.[273] Despite all its variegated applications, the Son of Man concept forms a meaningful whole. It cannot be partly swallowed up by Son of God with the parousia left over as an undigestible morsel.

On the other hand, I am not arguing for the opposite excess, the subsuming of the Son of God under the Son of Man.[274] Son of God is too pivotal a title in the infancy narrative, the temptation narrative, at Caesarea Philippi, at the trial before Caiaphas, and at the cross, to be absorbed by any other title. What the data impose upon us is the abandonment of talk about *the* central title in

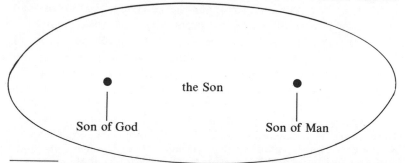

the Son

Son of God   Son of Man

---

[273]This point could be expanded still further by noting all the satellite titles and concepts that are associated in the gospel with Son of Man, e.g., prophet, servant, teacher.

[274]This is the mistake of Lange, in his book *Erscheinen*.

Matthew's gospel, along with the implicit image of a circle with one center. Instead, we should think of an ellipse with two foci, Son of God and Son of Man, with *the* Son floating somewhere in between.

We can certainly say that Matthew's dominant Christology is a Son-Christology. But that should not be automatically equated with a Son-of-God Christology. Matthew's position is broader and more complex than that.

In conclusion, I think I have established my five major propositions. In doing so, I have laid the basis for an attempt to understand Matthew's basic approach to Christian and ecclesial morality. But now it is time to move on from basics to specifics. In Part III we shall examine some specific questions of Christian morality. In the present section I purposely did not go into great detail about the sermon on the mount, especially 5:17-48, because I wanted to keep this prime statement on Christian morality for a detailed discussion in Part III. It is to this discussion that we now turn.

PART THREE

REMODELING MORALITY

The Eschatological Demand of Christ

CHAPTER TEN

The Programmatic Statement on Christ and the Law in Matthew 5:17-20[1]

I. INTRODUCTORY REMARKS

In Part II we saw the Christological-ecclesiological basis of morality in Matthew's gospel. In the course of the mini-commentary presented to substantiate this Christological-ecclesiological basis, I purposely skimmed over the key section on Law and morality, Matthew 5:17-48. It is to this section that we now return to see what specific moral demands Matthew rests on the basis he has constructed. The general contours of Christian discipleship (life caught between faith and wavering, the stress on mercy and love as the cutting edge of interpretation of the Mosaic Law, the rejection of casuistry and formalism) came out clearly in the mini-commentary and need not be repeated here. Our concern will be solely the concrete moral demands that "flesh out" the general contours of discipleship.

Matthew devotes a pivotal section of the sermon on the mount to a programmatic statement on Christ and the Law (5:17-

---

[1]Space does not allow for detailed proof of all the assertions made here. For a more thorough analysis, see my *Law and History in Matthew's Gospel*, 41-124.

20). From this statement of principle he draws six conclusions or applications (the antitheses, 5:21-48). The composition of this whole section by Matthew out of various sources is most carefully done. Whatever be the results of the effort, Matthew is obviously attempting to make a major statement about Christ, the Law, and Christian morality. The presumption must be that his thought is as ordered as his structures, unless the contrary is proven.

As regards the larger context, Matthew ably situates his unit on the Law in the wider framework of the sermon. Matthew begins the sermon with the nine beatitudes (5:3-12), in which comfort for the necessarily passive and afflicted (poor in spirit, those who mourn, the meek, the persecuted) is interwoven with a call to positive moral action (the merciful, the pure of heart, the peacemakers). The objective third person plural gives way to the second person plural in the ninth beatitude, which provides a neat transition to the parables on salt and light, each of which is introduced by the urgent reminder, "*You are* the salt of the earth (5:13). . . . *You are* the light of the world (5:16)." The paradox of discipleship is clear. Those persecuted and despised by this world are the most important for the true welfare of the world. The disciples' mission is to live against the world for the world.

The second person plural is continued in 5:17, but otherwise a clear break occurs. Exhortation gives way to stern admonition ("do not think that. . . .") and the new topics of (1) the Mosaic Law and (2) the relation of Jesus and the disciples to the Law are introduced. The topics are treated in principle in verses 17-20 and then are applied in verses 21-48.

Matthew 5:17-20 provides a perfect study in Matthean tradition and redaction. The basic stock of verses 17-19 probably stood in the Q-tradition, perhaps even in the present order. Matthew added material to each verse to make it speak to his own concerns, and then rounded out the whole statement by creating verse 20, which also acts as a heading of and provides a transition to the antitheses. Let us take each verse of 5:17-20 in order and see what it says about Matthew's view of Christ, Law, and Christian morality.

II. MATT 5:17: FULFILLING THE LAW AND THE PROPHETS

"Do not think that I have come to destroy the Law or the prophets; I have not come to destroy but to fulfill." The continuation of the second person plural shows the verse is addressed to Jesus' disciples. They are warned not to entertain the idea that Jesus is a destructive revolutionary in relation to the Law and the prophets. The fact that the disciples have to be warned about such a conclusion signals that something startling about the Law is about to be taught—both in verse 18 and in the antitheses. The warning of verse 17 thus points forward, not backward to the beatitudes or the parables of salt and light. When the disciples hear Jesus revoking major social and religious institutions of the Law (divorce, oaths, legal retaliation), they are not to imagine that Jesus is simply destroying the whole of Old Testament revelation (the Law and the prophets).

According to verse 17, then, what is at stake here is the proper understanding of Jesus' eschatological mission, summed up in the solemn formula, "I have come" (*ēlthon*). This formula, found elsewhere in the New Testament, but especially important in the Synoptics, expresses some precise purpose of the eschatological figure's coming, often in terms of a surprising reversal of expectations (e.g., "I have come to call not the just but sinners"). In our context, verse 17 reverses the expectations which the radical antitheses might arouse. Despite what Jesus is about to teach, he is not simply obliterating the Law and the prophets. He has come not to annul them, but to *fulfill* them (*plērōsai*). With the word "fulfill" we touch a central point in Matthew's approach to Christ's moral teaching. "To fulfill the Law and the prophets" must not be reduced in meaning to a banal "doing" or "observing." "To fulfill" is not the usual verb employed in Greek for the idea of putting a law into practice. It is never used that way in the Greek Septuagint, which however does speak of the prophetic word of the Lord being fulfilled. Matthew himself supplies no clear example of "fulfill" in the simple sense of doing or obeying a law.

This Matthean usage (or better, lack thereof) is all the more surprising if we compare it with Paul's. Paul, for all his interest in prophecy, does not use *plēroō* (fulfill) for the fulfillment of prophecy. Yet he does use *plēroō* for the fulfillment (or summing-up) of the Law by love (Gal 5:14; 6:2; Rom 13:8-10; 8:4). Matthew's usage seems just the opposite. He does not use "fulfill" in the traditions which come closest to Paul's teaching on love (Matt 22:34-40, the great command of love; 7:12, the golden rule; 19:18-19, love of neighbor added to the commands of the decalogue). Instead of concentrating on Law and commands, Matthew uses the verb "to fulfill" overwhelmingly in contexts connected with the fulfillment of prophecy. The verb "to fulfill" occurs sixteen times, twelve of which are found in phrases introducing an Old Testament formula quotation (e.g., "now all this came to pass that what was spoken through the prophet might be *fulfilled*, saying. . . ."). To these twelve cases (1:22; 2:15, 17, 23; 4:14; 8:17; 12:17; 13:35; 21:4; 26:54, 56; 27:9), we should add the case of "to fulfill" expressed by the compound verb, *anaplēroō*, in Matthew 13:14. Most of the other occurrences of "to fulfill" (5:17; 13:48; 23:22) have at least some vague connection with prophets, eschatological fullness, or the final consummation.

It may be no accident that the first words of Jesus recorded by Matthew in his gospel—words addressed to the Baptist before Jesus' baptism—express his sense of mission in terms of fulfillment: "Let it be so for now; for thus it befits us to fulfill all justice." This statement should not be reduced to the simple thought that "we should do God's will." Besides meaning moral conduct in accordance with God's will (Matt 5:10, 20; 6:1), "justice" (or "righteousness," *dikaiosynē*) also means God's saving activity or gift of salvation in the end-time (5:6; 6:33; possibly 21:32). It is quite interesting that none of the passages with "justice" in the sense of moral action carry the verb "to fulfill," nor does any of them refer to the action of Jesus, but rather to that of his disciples. Add to all this the fact that the theophany after the baptism in 3:16-17 alludes to Messianic prophecies (Isa 42:1; 44:2; Ps 2:7; Gen 22:2; Jer 31:19-20), and one begins to suspect that the fulfillment of all justice in 3:15 is also involved in the fulfillment of prophecy. When Jesus came to John to be baptized, the latter protested that he needed the baptism of Jesus, the one who baptizes with the spirit of the end-time (cf. 3:11). Jesus answers that John must allow this strange reversal of expected roles for the moment, for both of them are bound to be the proper instruments of God's saving action, marked out beforehand in prophecy and now being fulfilled. Each must carry out his assigned role in this critical time of fulfillment.

In short, there is no reason in Matthew's gospel to take the verb "to fulfill" in 5:17 as meaning anything but "to fulfill prophecy." This means the whole verse and the whole Law-question must be understood in the light of Matthew's great concern for the fulfillment of prophecy. In Matthew, the Law must be seen in a prophetic light and must be interpreted in analogy with the interpretation of prophecy. This view is very much strengthened by a Q-statement on the Law and prophets, found in Luke 16:16 and Matthew 11:13. Luke 16:16, no doubt the more original form, reads: "The Law and the prophets [lasted] until John [the Baptist]." Matthew rewrites that straightforward statement to produce the startling affirmation: "For *all the prophets* and the Law *prophesied* until John" (Matt 11:13). Two points are especially noteworthy in the changes Matthew has introduced. First, Matthew has turned around the customary sequence "Law-prophets"; the order "all the prophets and the Law" is simply not found in the whole of the Septuagint Old Testament or in the rest of the New Testament. Matthew is standing the accepted canon of the Old Testament on its head. For the Judaism of the time, the Mosaic Law was *the* determinative part of the canon, the "canon within the canon." For observant Jews, the prophets were important first of all as the protectors and authorized interpreters of the Law. Matthew is saying just the opposite. In Matthew's view, the prophets are the "canon within the canon." The Law is to be seen by Christians in a way similar to the way in which they view the prophets.

This message is driven home by Matthew's second change, the insertion of the verb "prophesied." The word "Law" never acts as the subject of the verb "prophesy" in the Septuagint or the rest of the New Testament. And the past tense of the verb "prophesied" is most important for understanding how the Law is to be understood in analogy with prophecy. In both cases, the high point of their importance is over. For example, it is quite true that the prophets still witness to Christ within the Christian church. But, under the old covenant, as long as the Messiah had not yet come, the prophets had as their primary and indispensable function the task of pointing forward to the life of the Messiah, something which still lay in the future. When that Messianic future became the present, and for Matthean Christians the sacred past, the prophets lost their key position as sign-pointers to the Messianic future. They rather witnessed to what had been fulfilled in the facts of Christ's life. The central position in the life of faith which the prophets once held in the eyes of the Jews has now been taken over by the Fulfiller of the prophets, Jesus Christ. The Jews at the time of Jesus would have asked: What is the relation of this Jesus to the prophets, who stand at the center of our faith? The Christians of A.D. 90 would have asked: What is the relation of the prophets to Jesus Christ, who stands at the center of our faith? A Copernican revolution has taken place; the center of the religious universe is no longer where it was.

The same holds true, analogously, of Matthew's view of the Law. In Matthew's mind, the Law, in both its ethical and prophetic utterances, pointed forward to the Messianic events and teachings of Jesus. This is why it can be the subject of the verb "prophesied." But, again, once the Fulfiller came, the prophetic pointer could no longer be the center of attention or the decisive norm. The Jews at the time of Jesus would have asked: What is the relation of this Jesus to the Mosaic Law, which stands at the center of our faith? The Christians of A.D. 90 would have asked: What is the relation of the Mosaic Law to Jesus Christ, who stands at the center of our faith? Another Copernican revolution had taken place.[2]

This is brought out by the introductory formula in the six

---

[2]Many of the problems in the whole question of "Jesus and the Law" arise from a failure to distinguish between the burning question in the mind of Jews at the time of the historical Jesus and the burning question in the mind of second- or third-generation Christians, now separated from the Jewish synagogue. The redactional question of Matthew is not the question of some Pharisee in A.D. 30. Too much baptismal water has gone under the bridge in the meantime.

antitheses: "It was said [by God on Sinai] . . . but I say to you."
And in three out of the six antitheses, Jesus dares to revoke institutions sanctioned by the Mosaic Law. It is not by accident
that the sermon on the mount concludes not with a call to obey
the Mosaic Law but with a demand to obey the words of Jesus as
the norm of final judgment (7:24, in the parable of the two
houses). Doing the words of Jesus (7:24) is the same thing as
doing the will of his Father (7:21). The person and the words of
Jesus are the criteria for moral action now and for judgment on
the final day (10:32-33, 37-39; 19:8-9; 19:18-19). That is why Matthew can end his gospel not with a call to obey the Mosaic Law
but with a call to universal mission, with baptism instead of circumcision as the rite of entrance into the people of God, with the
commands of Jesus as the content of Christian moral teaching,
and with the presence of the risen Jesus as the sustaining force of
Christian morality (28:16-20).

We can see, then, that, when we say that Matthew interprets
the Law in analogy with prophecy, we do not simply mean that
Matthew stresses the prophets' message of mercy and
compassion—though that is certainly true. But, beyond that,
Matthew gives the Law a prophetic function which is tied to a
definite period of salvation-history, a function which is superan-
nuated by the coming of the Fulfiller. The Law question in Matthew ultimately receives a Christological and ecclesiological solution. That is why we have stressed the connection of Christ,
church, and morality. The Son, Jesus Christ, is the only one who
can teach the sons (the church) how to do the will of the Father
perfectly (cf. 5:43-48 and 11:25-30). For the new people of God
which is the church, Emmanuel, God-with-us, not only frees us
from our sins but also teaches us the positive "justice" God
wishes. He dwells in the midst of Christians in prayer just as the
divine presence was thought to dwell in the midst of those discuss-
ing the Law (cf. 18:20; also 1:23; 28:20). The high Son-
Christology of Matthew, tinged as it is with Wisdom-Christology,
means that the Torah cannot hold center stage for the Matthean
church. Only the Lord of the church can do that. The transcendent person and mission of Jesus Christ, interpreted in the context of Matthew's view of salvation-history, eschatology, and the
church, form the key to the Law question in Matthew.

III.   MATT 5:18: NO CHANGE UNTIL ALL COMES TO PASS

This interpretation is confirmed by *5:18*: "(a) For amen I say to you, (b) until heaven and earth pass away, (c) not one yod or decorative stroke shall pass from the Law, (d) until all things come to pass." In 5:18, Jesus explains further the relationship he has to the Law and the prophets inasmuch as he is their Fulfiller.[3] Jesus introduces his statement with "Amen," literally, "firmly, surely, certainly." While this Hebrew word is used in the Old Testament at the end of prayers, wishes, and statements to affirm, strengthen, or respond to them, Jesus seems to have been the first to have used Amen at the beginning of an affirmation. It seems to carry the idea that Jesus enjoys direct knowledge of the apocalyptic events of the end-time and the laws which govern them, and therefore he alone can testify to his disciples concerning them. The very formula "Amen I say to you" (5:18a) thus introduces something of a prophetic-apocalyptic note into 5:18 from the beginning.

The apocalyptic tone is immediately taken up by the image of heaven and earth passing away (5:18b). Granted the apocalyptic atmosphere of the first century A.D., the prophetic-apocalyptic context of the whole of chapter 5 and of the whole of Matthew's gospel, we should be careful not to reduce "till heaven and earth pass away" to a bland "never." Rather, it states that the truth expressed in the main clause (5:18c: not the slightest element shall pass from the Law) is restricted temporally. Not the slightest part of the Law[4] shall pass away until the apocalyptic

---

[3]It should be noted that just as 5:17 mentions Law and prophets, so does 5:18, at least in Matthew's redaction. While the body of the verse deals with the Law, the last clause (5:18d) deals with the fulfillment of prophecy: "until all things come to pass."

[4]The Greek text speaks of the "iōta" and "horn" (or "hook") of the Law. The first word seems to represent the Hebrew yod, the smallest letter in the so-called "square" alphabet. The "hook" probably refers to a type of ornamentation used in a particular kind of script, the so-called "Herodian book-hand." Most interestingly, the yod or the hook was used in rabbinic stories about the Book of Deuteronomy accusing King Solomon of trying to change the Law. The point of all these stories is the eternal validity of the Law in all its parts.

event of the passing away of the old world. Like heaven and earth, the Law was a pillar of stability in the present age. But, as in the case of the physical cosmos, this stability holds true for the Law only during the present age. The use of "yod" and "stroke" indicates that the *written* (not oral) Law is being considered, and more precisely the Pentateuch, seen as an inviolable whole. Both in its legal and prophetic content, the Law will not pass away, even in its smallest parts—*until*. Here, in 5:18d, we meet a second "until" clause, paralleling the one in 5:18b.[5] The Law will remain valid in all its parts "until all things come to pass" (*heōs an panta genētai*). The verb for "come to pass" (*genētai*) is frequently used by Matthew in the middle voice to express the coming to pass of some event; indeed, it is used that way in some of the introductions to formula quotations (Matt 1:22; 21:4; 26:54-56). Matthew does not use the middle voice of this verb to express obedience to or the observance of the Law. Therefore, it becomes impossible to translate *panta* as "all the commands of the Law [summed up in the command of love]." *Panta* ("all things"), with *genētai* as its verb, must mean "all events," and, in context, "all events prophesied."

Taking all this together, we might paraphrase 5:18 as follows: "As *the* apocalyptic seer, I can assure you of this: until the old heavens and the old earth pass away at the end of the world, not the slightest part of the Law will pass away, until all the events prophesied in the Old Testament come to pass." The general sense of 5:18 is thus clear, as well as the fact that it continues the theme of the fulfillment of the Law *and the prophets* begun in 5:17. But what precisely does Matthew mean by this verse, with its two apparently redundant clauses expressing the proviso of "until"? To delve deeper into Matthew's understanding of this verse, we must compare 5:18 with a number of other similar verses in the Q and the Markan traditions.

First, there is the parallel to Matthew 5:18 in Luke 16:17:

---

[5]*Pace* E. Schweizer, any attempt to make *heōs an* mean "in order that" in 5:18d runs up against the clear usage of New Testament Greek.

Matthew 5:18	Luke 16:17
a) For amen I say to you:	a) It is easier for heaven and earth to pass away,
b) until heaven and earth pass away,	b) than for one stroke of the Law to fall.
c) not one yod or stroke will pass from the Law,	
d) until all things come to pass.	

Since Luke's form is shorter and simpler, we might at first glance be tempted to say he represents the earlier form of the saying. Yet both Matthew and Luke have clearly reformulated an earlier saying, each for his own theological purposes. When we strip away from Matthew 5:18 what is clearly Matthean redaction, we are left with what is probably the earliest form of the saying available to us. Matthew 5:18a ("For amen I say to you") may safely be assigned to Matthew's redaction, since it is totally lacking in the Lukan parallel and since the precise formulation found in Matthew 5:18a occurs only in Matthew. Since both 5:18b and 5:18d are dependent temporal clauses beginning with *heōs an* ("until") and followed by the aorist subjunctive, some sort of conflation or addition seems to have taken place. Since 5:18b is paralleled in Luke 16:17 while 5:18d is not, and since 5:18d reflects Matthew's own interest in the coming to pass of all prophesied events, 5:18d is also probably a Matthean addition. Thus what remains are two different versions of an earlier Q-saying:

Matthew 5:18	Luke 16:17
b) until heaven and earth pass away,	a) it is easier for heaven and earth to pass away,
c) not one yod or stroke will pass away from the Law	b) than for one stroke of the Law to fall

Looking at these two forms, we see that Matthew 5:18bc is

---

[6]Another reason for thinking 5:18bc is the most primitive form is that it contains a chiasm which is obscured by the changes or additions made by Matthew and Luke.

the more stringent form of the basic statement, and so probably represents the most primitive form of the saying accessible to us.[6] Luke modifies the statement to avoid the whole consideration of a temporal limit to the Law's validity. Luke recasts the saying to set up a comparison between two events which could occur only with extreme difficulty: the passing away of heaven and earth and the falling of a stroke from the Law. But let us remember: Luke is describing and comparing events that are difficult, not impossible. Luke readily takes over Mark 13:31 in Luke 21:33: "Heaven and earth shall pass away, but my words shall not pass away." Thus, Luke does not speak of some impossible event when he mentions the passing of heaven and earth in 16:17. That is an event which will surely occur, but with much anguish and conflict.

The comparison set up in 16:17 suggests that something similar holds true for the passing of some part of the Law. That a change in the Law is not an impossible event is made clear by the very next verse, 16:18, which abrogates divorce. Such a change in the Law will come, however, with conflict, anguish, opposition, and violence. Such is the context of these sayings in Luke. The Pharisees have laughed at Jesus (16:14), and Jesus' response is a denunciation of the Pharisees: although they be honored by men, they are an abomination to God. The Law and the prophets have lasted up until the Baptist. But now the preaching of the gospel has begun and is accompanied by violence. The context is thus colored by themes of the opposition, change, and violence which mark the ministry of Jesus. Luke's formulation of 16:17 takes up these themes when it compares the difficulty of the passing of the Law with the cosmic catastrophe of the end-time. The fierce hostility faced by the "law-free" preaching of Stephen and Paul in Acts will verify what Luke states in 16:17.

Over against Luke 16:17, then, Matthew 5:18bc represents the more stringent and primitive form of the saying. We may not be able to be sure whether, in the earliest Jewish-Christian form of the saying, "till heaven and earth pass away" may have been simply a rhetorical way of expressing "never." But in Matthew's own eyes, the phrase in 5:18b probably refers to a future apocalyptic event which *will* occur. We need only compare 5:18bc with Matt 24:35, in Matthew's apocalyptic discourse:

5:18b Until heaven and earth pass away,	24:35a Heaven and earth shall pass away,
5:18c not one yod or stroke will pass from the Law;	24:35b but my words shall not pass away

For Matthew, then, the passing of heaven and earth is an event sure to take place in the future, since it has been predicted by Jesus. Thus, 5:18 seems to set a time limit for the Law's inviolable validity. Time limits are no strangers to Matthew's thought world. As we saw in Part I of this book, the death-resurrection acts as the limit to Jesus' restricted ministry to the land and people of Israel. It would be quite easy, then, for Matthew to read 5:18bc as stating a time limit as well. And, as to the question of which time limit is meant, Matthew's outline of salvation-history provided a ready-made answer. In the original primitive saying, the passing of heaven and earth may have referred literally to the final, cosmic catastrophe. But Matthew knows important changes in the Law will take place once the universal mission begins at the end of the gospel. To bring the "passing" of 5:18b into harmony with his own view of Law and salvation-history, Matthew tacks on 5:18d: "until all things come to pass." Matthew is again looking at the apocalyptic discourse as he reworks 5:18:

5:18a For amen I say to you:	24:34a Amen I say to you:
c not one yod or stroke shall pass from the Law	b this generation shall not pass away
d until all things come to pass	c until all these things come to pass

Matthew 24:34b shows us a perfect example where the phrase "shall not pass away . . . until all [these things] come to pass" (*ou mē parelthē . . . heōs an panta tauta genētai*) does not mean: "this will never happen." This generation *will* pass away; the interest of the saying centers on what will be the time limit. In the context of the eschatological discourse, "until all these things come to pass" obviously refers to the fulfillment of prophesied events in an apocalyptic context. In adding 5:18d to the original

saying, Matthew states that the fulfillment of prophecy in a apocalyptic context will be the time limit up until which any change in the Law will be impossible. Now, the only prophecies mentioned up until 5:18 in Matthew's gospel have been Old Testament prophecies describing individual events in the sacred past of the "life of Jesus." This is in keeping with Matthew's use of formula quotations, which are always used for the earthly life of Jesus, never for the future of the church or for Christ's final coming in judgment.

Putting all of this together, we can see a clear line of thought in 5:18. The smallest commandment in the Mosaic Law will remain in force (18c) up until a set eschatological time limit in salvation-history (18b). Taken by itself, 18b would refer literally to the end of the universe. But 18d reinterprets this eschatological event as the whole life of Jesus ("all things"), which fulfills Old Testament prophecies. This fulfilling activity reaches its climax and completion in the death-resurrection of Jesus, seen as the "turning of the ages." Before this turning point, Jesus' mission and impact were kept within the holy land and the holy people of the Mosaic Law. In keeping with this, Jesus remained faithful to the Law. But after the Old Testament prophecies reach their culminating fulfillment in the death-resurrection, the exalted Son of Man comes in proleptic parousia to order a universal mission with baptism in place of circumcision. The Mosaic Law is no longer binding as a whole because it is *Mosaic*. What binds a Christian is binding because it is what Jesus commanded—whether or not that coincides with what Moses commanded. Thus, 5:18d does not merely repeat 5:18b, despite the repetition of the conjunction "until." Matthew 5:18d tells us that the great turning point of the ages, *the* apocalyptic event (5:18b), occurs at the death-resurrection of Jesus, when all Old Testament prophecies are fulfilled. Reciprocally, 5:18b tells us that 5:18d, the fulfillment of all prophecies, is *the* apocalyptic event ushering in a new age.

On the whole, then, Matthew has carefully added to an originally stringent saying on the Law to bring it into his own ordered pattern of salvation history. He has provided the theoretical basis for what happens in the six antitheses (5:21-48): at times the Mosaic Law is simply deepened, at times it is revoked.

IV.   MATT 5:19: FIDELITY IN TEACHING AND DOING

From the lofty programmatic statement in 5:17-18 some practical consequences about teaching and doing are drawn in *5:19*: "Therefore, whoever rescinds one of these least commandments and so teaches men shall be called least in the Kingdom of heaven. But whoever does and teaches, he shall be called great in the Kingdom of heaven." The adverb "therefore" signals a shift in tone and in subject-matter. Verses 17-18 made a pronouncement about Christ, his relationship to Law and prophets, and the apocalyptic terminus of the slightest parts of the Law. Verse 19 . now draws a practical conclusion for teachers.

The connection between verse 18 and verse 19 lies precisely in a concern over the smallest parts of the Law, referred to in verse 18 under the metaphor of yod and stroke, and expressed clearly in verse 19 as "one of these smallest commandments."[7] Since elsewhere in Matthew the noun "commandment" (*entolē*) refers to Old Testament precepts and not to commandments of Jesus, "one of these least commandments" should be taken in the same sense, especially given the connection with verse 18. The "least commandments" are the precepts of the Mosaic Law deemed to be of no great significance.[8] With a play on words known as paronomasia, verse 19 declares a tit-for-tat recompense on the last day. Those teachers who rescinded the very insignificant commandments and taught men to follow their example shall receive a very insignificant rank in the Kingdom on the last day.[9] One must admit this is a strangely weak threat, but then the transgression in verse 19 is far below the dissolving of Law and prophets envisaged in verse 17.

---

[7]The demonstrative adjective "these" should be taken with its full force, and not dismissed as a Semitism which is to remain untranslated.

[8]An elative sense ("very significant") rather than a strict superlative sense (*the* most insignificant one) is probably intended.

[9]The future verb "shall be called [by God]" refers to God's declaration at the last judgment. And what God says, will be. There are no grounds for interpreting "shall be called least *in* the Kingdom" as "shall be excluded *from* the Kingdom."

The positive part of verse 19 (whoever does and teaches) fits in perfectly with Matthew's stress on the need to *do* as well as speak the will of God (e.g., 7:15-20, 21-23, 24-27; 23:3). Notice that all these passages refer to Jews or Christians in general, and not to Jesus in particular. Jesus *fulfills* the Law and prophets (5:17); others *do* various commandments of the Law. The Fulfiller of the Law and the prophets must not be confused with ordinary men and their obligations vis-à-vis the Law. And it is this shift from Jesus to ordinary men which gives us the clue to the place of verse 19 within the overall structure of 5:17-48. Matthew 5:17 began with the disciples very much on the sidelines ("do not think. . . ."); the center of attention was Jesus and his relation to the Law. By the time we reach 5:20, Jesus is on the sidelines ("for I say to you") and the disciples are very much to the fore ("unless *your* justice exceeds that of the scribes and the Pharisees, *you* shall not enter the Kingdom of heaven). It is in verse 19 that the transition from the topic of Jesus-and-the-Law to the topic of men-and-the-Law takes place. Then, in the antitheses, both Jesus and the disciples will play important roles: Jesus as the source of authoritative teaching, deepening and at times revoking the Law, and the disciples as the recipients and observers of this new teaching.

Matthew 5:19 serves to emphasize Matthew's great concern with both correct teaching and zealous doing. On the level of the sacred past of Jesus, the verse voices Jesus' fidelity to the Mosaic Law during his public ministry, a fidelity he inculcates in others (cf. Matt 23:2-3). On the level of Matthew's church, the verse exhorts the Christian disciple—and especially the Christian teacher—to be scrupulous in the teaching and doing of the commandments of the Law, as reinterpreted by the Fulfiller of the Law. This second meaning—exhortation to Christians—is carried forward by the culmination of 5:17-20, v. 20. Verse 19 thus fulfills well its function of providing a transition from the first theme of Christology-and-Law to the second theme of disciples-and-commandments.[10]

---

[10]Despite the fact that 5:19 functions fairly well in its present context, some tensions remain unresolved. (1) The strange threat of being declared least *in* the Kingdom does not seem to fit well with the absolute

V. MATT 5:20: THE MORE ABUNDANT JUSTICE

With *5:20* we reach both the culmination of the programmatic statement begun in 5:17 and the immediate introduction to the six antitheses (5:21-48): "For I say to you that unless your justice exceeds that of the scribes and Pharisees, you shall not enter the Kingdom of heaven." Verse 20 addresses the disciples, who were last referred to directly in 5:18a. They are now put squarely on center-stage, and will remain there until the end of the antitheses. What is demanded of the disciples is "justice," a word almost unique to Matthew among the Synoptic gospels. While the word can at times mean God's saving activity (so 5:6; 6:33), the reference here is obviously to the word's other meaning, namely, the moral activity which does God's will, the truly Christian morality which corresponds to the will of the Father, as revealed to the sons by the Son. True disciples are not simply to practice such justice. Such justice is to abound, to exceed, to spill over, to overflow (*perisseusē*). Their morality is to show an exuberant richness and abundance proper to the new age of salvation, to the last days, to the "eschaton" Jesus has brought and taught.

This eschatological abundance can have nothing to do with the Pharisees' scrupulous performance of the minutiae of the Law, all with a view to piling up merit. No, the "extra," the "plus," the superabundance of Christian justice cannot lie in a bigger and better Pharisaism, but in a new eschatological quality to one's moral action. This eschatological quality is best described by the antitheses which follow. There we see a total obedience to God, a radical giving of self to God and neighbor in

---

statement in verse 18 and the absolute exclusion threatened in verse 20. (2) The play on words in "*least* commandment . . . shall be called *least*" is not paralleled in the shorter, positive part of the statement; the adjective "great" is in the positive degree and is not used twice. These tensions may be due to the fact that a primitive form of 5:17-19 existed in Q, was taken over by Matthew with modifications, was joined by him to his own creation (v. 20), and then was put at the head of the six antitheses. On the whole, verse 19 fits this new, wider context, but some tensions resulted. It may also be that the short, positive part of verse 19 comes from Matthew's own hand, balancing the negative statement in the tradition.

both interior dispositions and exterior actions. The fonts of morality are cleansed in the depths of man's spirit so that the waters of concrete actions may run clear and abundant. The true ultimate purpose of the Law is ruthlessly pursued, even when this means rescinding some concrete elements of the Law. This eschatological abundance which can even include annulment is possible because Jesus the Son has brought the end of time in himself, in his teaching, and finally in his death-resurrection. Because Jesus gives his disciples the eschaton, he can demand eschatological morality from them. What is new about Christian morality, Christian justice, is ultimately Christ himself, the eschaton in person. The emphasis in this superabundance of Christian morality is therefore on a new quality of action made possible by Christ, though the new quality will obviously have its impact on the quantity of loving deeds performed.

This eschatological morality is sharply contrasted with the legal justice taught and practiced by the "scribes and Pharisees," the official representatives of Jewish theology and piety.[11] Only this eschatological, Christian justice will fulfill the condition for entrance into the final Kingdom. This image of entrance, dependent on the fulfillment of some condition, is based on two Old Testament images: (1) entrance into the promised land (Deut 4:1) and (2) entrance into the Temple (Pss 15; 24; 118:19ff) or into the holy city (Isa 26:2f). Here, of course, the entrance is not into any earthly place, not even into one of the earthly stages of the Kingdom, but rather into the Kingdom at the end of time. By implica-

---

[11]Matthew uses the precise formula "the scribes and the Pharisees" nine times. Neither Mark nor Luke consecrates this formula as *the* designation of the official teachers of Judaism who are hostile to Jesus and his disciples. This frozen formula reflects the experience of Matthew and his church; it is not to be taken as an historically accurate picture of conditions at the time of Jesus. During Jesus' life, the scribes (professional lawyers and theologians) were often Pharisees, but some were Sadducees. The Pharisees were a free association of pious Jews who banded together for diligent study and strict observance of the Law, both written and oral. Most Pharisees were not specially trained scholars, but rather devout laymen. Since the scribes of the Pharisaic tradition had gained the leadership in Judaism after A.D. 70, Matthew equates "scribes and Pharisees" with Jewish leadership in general.

tion, only the Christians who do God's will revealed in Christ, and *not* the Jewish leaders, will enter the Kingdom. A stronger rejection of Pharisaic teaching and a more urgent call to Christian endeavor could hardly be imagined. Typically, Matthew summons Christians to stringent moral action by stressing the stringent judgment which lies before them. The good news of God's love and mercy is not an invitation to smug laziness.

Verse 20 plays a pivotal role in Matthew's composition.[12] It sums up the concern about Law and morality in verses 17-19 and translates it into the question of Christian "justice." This in turn acts as the rubric over the six antitheses which follow, the six concrete examples and applications of this Christian justice. The superabundant, eschatological justice Jesus demands bursts the narrow bonds of the teaching of the scribes and Pharisees and pushes the Law back to its ultimate intention, even when this involves abrogating the letter of the Law. The stringency of verse 20 is thus not that of Jewish Christianity narrowly understood, but rather that of the radical Jesus, who will allow his disciples no half-measures (cf. Matt 8:18-22). Verse 19 could be more lenient in tone, since it was concerned only with Christian teachers and with their fidelity to minor matters. Verse 20, by contrast, deals with the indispensable moral activity of every disciple; and so the sanction is much graver. There is no room here for a two-tier morality, that of the ordinary Christian and that of the spiritual elite. One is either a committed disciple or one does not enter the Kingdom at all.

---

[12]This fact, along with the heavy Matthean terminology and the links to other parts of the sermon on the mount, makes it likely that verse 20 is a creation of Matthew.

CHAPTER ELEVEN

Practical Concerns: The Six Antitheses

I.   THE ANTITHESES (MATT 5:21–48)

All the theoretical statements about Law in 5:17-19 converge on one practical concern: justice, the doing of the Father's will (5:20). What that justice means in practice is explained in the six antitheses which follow immediately upon 5:20. It is to these concrete statements on the morality Christ demands of his disciples that we now turn, to complete our treatment of Christ, church, and morality in Matthew. As we treat each antithesis, we will focus upon the major moral message it contains, without concerning ourselves about minor problems of exegesis.[13] Paramount for us will be the extent of the "radicalism" in the "justice" Jesus demands for entrance into the Kingdom. Does the radical nature of a given antithesis merely deepen or extend the letter of the Law, or does it revoke the letter of the Law? As we shall see, the answer differs from antithesis to antithesis.

Before we examine each antithesis separately, we should review a few key features of the antitheses in general. The clear grouping of six antitheses (5:21-26, on murder; 5:27-30, on adultery; 5:31-32, on divorce; 5:33-37, on oaths and vows; 5:38-42, on retaliation; 5:43-48, on love of neighbor) is obviously the work of Matthew. But how much of the material came to Matthew in antithetical form, and where exactly it came from, is disputed

---

[13]E.g., for disputes on the meaning of *raka* and *mōre* in 5:22 and on theories of the growth of the first antithesis in the pre-Matthean tradition, see the standard commentaries on Matthew.

among scholars. Many writers group together antitheses #3, 5, 6 (on divorce, retaliation, love of neighbor) because they are also present in Luke, without a full-blown antithetical formula. From this is deduced the hypothesis that the core of these three antitheses came from Q, which contained them without an antithetical formula. But such a deduction is not absolutely certain. Luke 6:27, on love of enemies, begins: "But I say to you who are listening." Luke may possibly be preserving a relic of a fuller antithetical formula such as the Matthean parallel has: "You have heard that it was said. . . . But I say to you" (Matt 5:43-44). Another difficulty for this neat deduction about the Q-material is that the core of the fifth antithesis, on retaliation (Matt 5:38-39a), does not have a parallel in Luke, though the further Matthean material does. Strictly speaking, then, the fifth antithesis proper is not Q-material.

Apart from the core of the fifth antithesis, the material proper to Matthew comprises most of the subject matter in antitheses #1, 2, 4 (on murder, adultery, and oaths). It has often been asserted that these three antitheses had their antithetical form before they came to Matthew. This is affirmed on the basis that the commands after the "but I say to you . . ." are much more understandable in an antithetical framework. For example, the statement "everyone who looks on a woman so as to desire her has already committed adultery with her in his heart" is more readily intelligible if it comes right after "you have heard it said: you shall not commit adultery."[14]

Diversity marks the antitheses not only with regard to sources but also with regard to content. All the antitheses share a certain legal air because of the citations from the Pentateuch and because of the legal literary forms used to enunciate Jesus' own teaching. Yet, when we take a closer look at the content of the antitheses and their use in the early church, we see that certain subjects belonged to the area of general moral exhortation, while

---

[14]While this line of reasoning does not settle the question once and for all, its position is preferable to that of I. Broer, who holds that the antithetical formula is totally the work of Matthew; cf. his "Die Antithesen der Evangelist Mattäus," *BZ* 19 (1975) 50-63.

other matters formed part of the primitive church's law and discipline. On the one hand, church preaching might strenuously exhort Christians to avoid all internal anger, impure thoughts, and hatred of enemies, but such obligations were hardly enforceable by church sanctions; and we find no such attempt to enforce them. On the other hand, the early church did treat Jesus' prohibition of divorce as a concrete rule of discipline to be enforced by the church. The multiplicity of forms of the divorce-prohibition in the New Testament, and, indeed, Matthew's so-called "exceptive clause" (5:32; 19:9), show that the prohibition was understood as a rule of life to be applied to and enforced in concrete situations.

We must consequently be careful about blanket statements which supposedly hold true of all the antitheses. It may well be that, in Matthew's church, the prohibitions of divorce, oaths, and court actions (antitheses #3, 4, 5) were enforced as church discipline. On the other hand, the prohibition of internal anger, impure thoughts, and hatred of enemies (antitheses #1, 2, 6) were hardly amenable to similar external control by the church. And it may not be pure coincidence that the antitheses which were matters of church discipline (#3, 4, 5) are also the ones which will be shown to include an element of revocation of the Mosaic Law. Precisely where the teaching of Jesus becomes so radical that it annuls the letter of the Law, precisely there the church feels a need to enforce Jesus' eschatological teaching and living by public sanction. The eschatological community has to undertake positive steps to assure the living of the eschatological "life-style," at least within its own bailiwick. The moral theologian must therefore tread lightly as he tries to express the meaning of the antitheses for the life of the church today. What may be true of one antithesis need not be true of another. /

Faced with this great diversity of material, Matthew seized upon the basic antithetical formula as his chief tool for creating some sort of literary unit. The full formula occurs in 5:21 and 33: "You have heard that it was said to the men of old. . . . But I say to you." A medium formula occurs in 5:27, 38, 43: "You have heard that it was said. . . . But I say to you." And a short formula occurs at 5:31: "It was said. . . . But I say to you." The variation seems simply rhetorical; in each case the idea contained in the full formula is implied. What is that idea? The "you" of the audience is no doubt primarily the disciples (cf. 5:1, and all the second person plural references which follow). The "hearing" could include both hearing the Scriptures read in the synagogue and hearing the explanations of the texts given by the Jewish teachers. Since each antithesis begins with a citation (or paraphrase) of one or more text from the Pentateuch, the written Law seems to be what is first of all referred to, though the accompanying interpretations of the rabbis are hardly excluded. This stress on the word of the written Torah is confirmed by the key verb, "it was said" (*errethē*). We have here the Semitic usage of veiling the name and action of God by casting the verb into the passive voice, the so-called "divine passive." "It was said" actually means "God said, when he gave the Law." Since the formula always introduces a citation or paraphrase of the written Torah, and since the aorist passive forms of the verb "to say" (*errethē*, *rēthen*) are used by Matthew only of God's speaking, the primary reference cannot be to the oral traditions of the rabbis. Consequently, "the men of old" must refer first of all to the Israelite generation journeying with Moses in the desert, though a further reference to later teachers of the tradition (e.g., the "scribes and Pharisees" of 5:20) need not be excluded.[15]

Only now can we understand the full force of the other half of the basic antithetical formula: "But *I* say to you." What is being contrasted here is not an act of hearing and an act of saying,[16] but rather two acts of saying: one by God in the Old Testament, and one by Jesus in this eschatological hour. There is some sort of contrast or tension between the word of God as expressed in the Torah and the word of God as expressed by Jesus. Where there is any conflict, the Torah must yield to Jesus as the definitive norm for the disciple's living of God's will. The Christian morality specified in the six antitheses thus takes on a peculiar double move-

---

[15]The attempt to make the dative *archaiois* ("men of old") a dative of agent ("by the men of old") offends both general Greek usage and Matthew's own particular style.

[16]Accordingly, rabbinic parallels that contrast hearing and saying are beside the point, *pace* D. Daube and W. D. Davies.

ment. On the one hand, it moves in the direction of deepening, radicalizing, spiritualizing the commands of the Torah. Yet, on the other hand, it also at times rejects the letter of the Torah, indeed some of its important institutions, when these run counter to God's true will. And what *is* God's true will is decided in every case by the eschatological authority of Jesus the Son, who claims direct and intuitive knowledge of God's will, and who thus can claim to be in his own person the ultimate norm of morality for the Christian. We must now examine more closely these two moments or movements in Christian morality: "mere" radicalizing of the letter of the Law, and radicalizing which annuls the letter. Fortunately, Matthew, the great lover of neat patterns, has given us three antitheses which fall into the first category and three which fall into the latter.[17]

II. RADICAL MORALITY THAT DOES NOT ANNUL THE LAW

The three antitheses (#1, 2, 6) which radicalize the Law without annulling it follow a "not only-but also" pattern. Jesus affirms the command of the Law but demands more.

(a) The antithesis on murder (5:21-26) obviously does not abrogate the prohibition of murder. Rather, anger and harsh words are just as bad.[18] In mock imitation of the hair-splitting casuistry of the Pharisees, Matthew rhetorically heightens the punishment in verse 22: liable to judgment in the local court, liable to the Sanhedrin (the highest court), liable to the Gehenna of fire (hell). The heightened punishment is meant to clash with the obvious lack of ascending seriousness in the crimes of being

---

[17]For an explanation of the antitheses in a context of spirituality and homiletics, see my article, "Celebration of the Word in Communal Services of Penance," *Worship* 50 (1976) 413-420.

[18]While this process of radicalizing is often referred to globally as "internalizing," there is no need to understand the anger as merely internal. *Pas ho orgizomenos tō adelphō autou* ("everyone who is angry with his brother") would include those who display their anger in action.

angry, of calling one's brother empty-headed, and of calling him a fool.[19] To ask which wrongs against one's brother are truly serious is to remain in the legalism of the Pharisees. All acts of anger and injustice toward one's brother are, for the true disciple, equally serious, and are as grave as murder. One might well ask whether our neat distinctions between mortal and venial sin can really hold up in the face of this radical morality of Jesus.

And, just as it breaks down the comfortable distinctions of the theologian, so too radical morality breaks down the sacred precinct of the liturgist. Only for particular cultic reasons could the ritual of sacrifice in the Temple be interrupted once it was begun. But, in a parable-like saying (vv. 23-24), Jesus demands that personal reconciliation take precedence over liturgical rubrics. Thus Jesus foreshadows by his teaching the attitude he will inculcate in the disciple's own prayer: "Forgive us our debts, just as we also have forgiven those indebted to us" (6:12). In a sense, Jesus' basic teaching on the union of love of God and love of neighbor is summed up in this parable. An alienated brother alienates us from God, no matter how splendid be the liturgy we perform. Liturgy reconciles us with God only when we are reconciled with our brother. The need for reconciliation with our brother before we approach God is continued in a second parable (vv. 25-26), which shifts the image from a liturgical to a judicial context.[20] With the final judgment about to break in on our lives, we disciples must use the little time we have left, while we are "on the way," to come to a speedy reconciliation with our enemy (the *antidikos*, the legal adversary). Otherwise we face a most stringent reckoning on the last day (v. 26).

---

[19]Once this mocking rhetorical technique of crescendo is recognized, there is no need to seek out deeper religious meanings for the insults (e.g., fool = rebel against God).

[20]Notice how to the core of the antithesis Matthew has appended two parables, both concerned with the allied theme of reconciliation. The first parable (vv. 23-24) at least preserves some connection with the original antithesis by keeping the key words "your brother." Even this verbal link disappears in the second parable (vv. 25-26). The first antithesis (the longest of the six) is thus a fine case study in the diversity of material Matthew welds together into one antithesis.

(b) The antithesis on adultery (5:27-30) again clearly follows the "not only-but also" pattern. Jesus obviously does not revoke the prohibition of adultery; rather he affirms that lustful looks, lustful thoughts, and provocative, lustful touches are equally serious. And against the tendency of his day to place the burden of fault on the woman, Jesus clearly places the responsibility on the man guilty of lustful desires and glances. A woman has a dignity which a man may not violate even in the privacy of his thoughts and looks. Here indeed we have a radicalizing which is internalizing. So decisive and complete must be the decision to remain pure in body and spirit that one must be willing to suffer the loss of any temporal good—symbolized by the right hand and the right eye[21]—rather than risk the eternal damnation of the whole person.

(c) The antithesis on love of neighbor (5:43-48) belongs to those antitheses which merely radicalize the Law without annulling it. At first glance, we might think there is an element of abrogation in the statement: "You have heard it said: 'You must love your neighbor, but you may hate your enemy[22] . . . but I say to you: Love your enemies." The words seem to indicate that Jesus revokes permission to hate one's enemy and enjoins positive love of one's enemy. But the situation is not so simple. While the words, "You shall love your neighbor," are taken from Leviticus 19:18, there is no precise Old Testament parallel to the command or permission, "You shall hate your enemy." This fact naturally creates a problem, since this is the only time in the antitheses that Jesus does not quote the exact words or a paraphrase of the Torah before his own "but I say to you." Various commentators have come up with various explanations of the

------

[21]Rabbinic texts also speak of adultery of heart, hand, and eye; adultery of the hand may refer to masturbation, and this may be the meaning in the Matthean context.

[22]Both future tenses are modal. "Thou shalt love thy neighbor" means: you are obliged to love your fellow Israelite in the cultic community. "Thou shalt hate thine enemy" means: you are not obliged to love, you are permitted to hate, a foreigner, a non-Israelite, especially a national enemy.

origin of "thou shalt hate thine enemy": a popular maxim, a scribal commentary, an expansion of the text in its Aramaic translation (Targum), a reference to fiery nationalistic positions of the Zealots or the Qumranites. Whatever the correct explanation, Jesus is not quoting here the words of the written Torah; and so we cannot, strictly speaking, designate the sixth antithesis as one that annuls the Law.

And yet it certainly comes close to that. While we can find no one command in the Old Testament which enjoins hatred of enemies, such an idea is certainly in line with Old Testament texts which speak approvingly of such hatred (Pss 139:19-22; 137:7-9; the commands in the Pentateuch to exterminate the populations of Canaan). And, since the Old Testament understood neighbor in the restricted sense of the fellow member of one's cultic community, and since the Old Testament instilled a sense of obligation to fight the enemies of God and his people, a command to love one's neighbor would almost necessarily be understood as permission not to love the "non-neighbor." This would especially hold true of the uncircumcised foreigner or the evil Israelite who persecuted God's people or the individual just man. To attack God's people or God's servant is to attack God himself, and hatred was the only proper response, in the eyes of Old Testament man, to such sacrilegious arrogance.

Although such hatred was not strictly a command of the written Torah, it was and is a prevalent attitude among many "good" men, who see the very point of religion as the upholding of the distinction between, and the different sanctions for, good and evil men. And notice, even Jesus himself does not do away with the category of enemy in this antithesis. There is no pious sentimentality about all men being neighbors, brothers, or sons of God. With bracing biblical realism, Jesus recognizes the distinction between neighbor and enemy, good and evil. All the more shocking, in the face of this realism, is Jesus' demand that we love our enemies and do good to evil men. The reason given for this topsy-turvy morality which subverts law and order is: that is the way God is and God acts. The Father loves without limit, the Father shows mercy without measure, the Father extends compassion without customs-barriers—and precisely to the undeserving, to the evil men who persecute God's people. True sons must prove their legitimacy by their resemblance to the Father, by imitating the squandered mercy of the prodigal Father. Imitation of the Father by those made sons in the Son means first of all imitation of his mercy. The Father shows his even-handed mercy to the evil as well as to the good in a million little ways, from sunrise to raindrops. The sons must show the same even-handed love to the unloving and the unlovable—otherwise they are no better than those moral monkeys who scratch each other's backs, the tax collectors and the pagans. There must be something more, an eschatological plus (*perisson*, v. 47)[23] in the morality of Christ's disciples. This plus is the limitless love of the Father, which, for Matthew, is embodied in the life, death, and resurrection of the Son. Every disciple of the Son must tread the same path.

III. RADICAL MORALITY THAT ANNULS THE LAW

(a) *The antithesis on divorce* (5:31-32) is the most hotly disputed of the three antitheses which seem to revoke some command, permission, or institution sanctioned by the written Torah.[24] One reason for the dispute is that the statement of Jesus on divorce is one of the most widely reported sayings of the Lord in the New Testament—but each passage give us a somewhat different form. A Markan form exists in Mark 10:11-12, which Matthew takes over with some changes in Matthew 19:9. The Q-document also carried the saying, which occurs in different forms in Luke 16:18 and Matthew 5:31-32. An independent form is cited by Paul in 1 Corinthians 7:10-11.

---

[23]*Perisson*, "more," harks back to the *perisseusē*, "be more abundant" in 5:20—a good example of Matthew's technique of inclusion.

[24]This is what I mean when I use phrases like "annulling the Law" or "abrogating the letter of the Law." Obviously, the entire moral content of the Law seen as a whole is not being rejected; 5:17 made that clear. But, contrary to impressions gained from a superficial reading of 5:18-19, various important socio-religious institutions sanctioned by the Law (divorce, oaths and vows, legal retaliation) are being rescinded.

A welter of interesting questions, such as which form comes closest to the original form spoken by the historical Jesus,[25] must be set aside, since our precise question has a very narrow scope. We are asking whether Matthew 5:31-32 involves a revocation of the Mosaic Law. If we were dealing with the Markan, Lukan (Q), or Pauline forms, the question would be readily solved. All these forms seem to involve a revocation of the Law. But Matthew has complicated the situation by adding what are commonly known as "exceptive clauses" in 5:32 and 19:9. Matthew 5:32 states that a man who divorces his wife *parektos logou porneias* [except on grounds of *porneia*] forces her to commit adultery [*moicheuthēnai*]. Matthew 19:9 states that anyone who divorces his wife *mē epi porneia* [except because of *porneia*] commits adultery [*moichatai*]. Do these exceptive clauses take the "sting" out of Jesus' prohibition and prevent these words from constituting a revocation of the Law?[26]

Those who answer yes to this question usually explain the Matthean form of the prohibition against the background of the dispute over divorce between the rabbinic school which followed the Jewish teacher Hillel and the rabbinic school which followed

---

[25]The original form might well be reflected (with perhaps slight modification) in Luke 16:18.

[26]Some would try to forestall any revocation of the Law simply on the basis of the key text on divorce in Deuteronomy 24:1-4. (1) It is sometimes pointed out that the Old Testament text may simply mean that a divorced woman may not later return to her first husband if she has entered into a second marriage. But, even granted that interpretation, Mark 10:3-4 and Matthew 19:7-8 understand the text on the giving of the bill of divorce to constitute a command or permission. And what we are concerned with is the understanding and teaching of Matthew, not Deuteronomy. (2) Deuteronomy 24:1-4, taking the institution of divorce for granted, tries to regulate it and protect the woman by stipulating a written bill of divorce, acknowledging her right to remarry without being stigmatized as an adulteress. But this means that Jesus' prohibition (a) *directly* rescinds the Law's institution of the bill of divorce and the command to give it and (b) *indirectly* rescinds the whole institution of divorce, presupposed and legitimated by the Torah. In a sense, Jesus is following through on the humanistic thrust of the Deuteronomic legislation, but in radicalizing that thrust he rescinds the letter of the Law. More than one yod or stroke (Matt 5:18) is passing away here.

the Jewish teacher Shammai. The dispute centered on the ambiguous phrase in Deuteronomy 24:1 which gave the grounds for the divorce: *'erwat dābār,* literally, "the shame of a thing," "a shameful thing." The followers of Hillel stressed the vague word *dābār,* "thing," and came to the conclusion that practically anything (burnt food, finding a prettier woman) constituted sufficient grounds for divorce. The followers of Shammai stressed the word *'erwat,* "shame," and demanded that the reason for divorce be a serious one, something that involved shame, e.g., adultery.[27] To stress this point, the school of Shammai would even invert the phrase of Deuteronomy 24:1 to read *debar 'erwâ,* "the thing of shame." Some commentators on Matthew interpret this "exceptive clause" as reflecting this rabbinic dispute. Matthew (or his church)[28] is supposedly espousing the strict view of Shammai when he inserts into the prohibition of divorce *parektos logou porneias,* "except on the ground of impurity." Indeed, the Greek phrase *logou porneias* (literally, "a word of impurity") is a surprisingly close translation of the Hebrew *debar 'erwâ* (literally, "a word of shame"). Matthew would thus not be teaching revocation of the Law but simply would be siding with the stricter position among the rabbis.

This view, though widespread, runs into a number of difficulties if we examine the evidence closely and ponder its consequences. For one thing, the philological data are not all that

---

[27]However, it may not be quite correct to restrict the grounds allowed by the school of Shammai to what we understand as adultery. Other immodest conduct short of actual adultery might have come under the rubric of "shame" (*'erwâ*). For all this, see the Mishnah tractate *Gittin* 9, 10, and the Babylonian Talmud's commentary in the Gemara, *Gittin* 90 a-b.

[28]Since it is unlikely that Matthew, on his own authority, would be introducing a major change in his church's discipline on divorce, the "exceptive clauses" probably represent the tradition of Matthew's church, which had already modified the injunctions of Mark and Q. Given the varied witness from Mark, Q, and Paul, it is most unlikely that Matthew or his church preserved the original form of Jesus' teaching. For bibliography on the whole complex question, cf. my *Law and History in Matthew's Gospel,* 140-150; for another view, see B. Vawter, "Divorce and the New Testament," *CBQ* 39 (1977) 528-542.

clear-cut and the reference to *'erwat dābār* in Deuteronomy 24:1 is not all that certain. It is strange that the phrase supposedly parallel to *'erwat dābār, logou porneias,* occurs not in Matthew 19:9, where Jesus is supposedly being asked to choose between Hillel and Shammai, but in Matthew 5:31-32, where no such clear-cut choice is indicated by the context. Moreover, the inversion of *'erwat dābār* to read *debar 'erwâ,* which is supposed to parallel *logou porneias,* is not very common. *Parektos logou porneias* in Matthew 5:32 does not have to be taken as a literal translation of *debar 'erwâ.* It makes perfectly good sense as ordinary Greek: "except on grounds of impurity." In fact, the Greek Septuagint translation of Deuteronomy 24:1 uses nothing like *logou porneias* to translate *'erwat dābār.* Instead, the Septuagint renders the Hebrew phrase quite nicely by *askēmon pragma,* a "shameful thing." How was Matthew's Greek-speaking audience supposed to recognize the allusion? Of course, none of these linguistic considerations disproves the reference to the dispute of Hillel and Shammai. But we do see that the reference is not all that certain.

More damaging to the Hillel-Shammai interpretation are considerations drawn from an investigation of the meaning of *porneia* (in general: any illicit sexual activity) in Matthew 5:32 and 19:9. If we take *porneia* to refer to what seems to have been the Shammai position, we must give *porneia* a rather wide meaning: not only impure sexual activity, but also social immodesty. This seems a bit strange in the mouth of the radicalizing Jesus. If, on the other hand, we hold that Jesus is being stricter than the school of Shammai and is restricting the ground for divorce to adultery alone, we run into another difficulty with *porneia.* Given the wide range of meanings the word can have in Greek, *porneia* could mean adultery (unlawful sexual activity involving at least one married person) instead of fornication (unlawful sexual activity between unmarried persons). Yet a survey of Greek usage in the Septuagint and the New Testament shows that, in general, "adultery" is designated by various forms of the verb *moicheuō* and the noun *moicheia.* The Septuagint indeed has passages where *porneia* is applied to married people, but usually this can be explained by some further idea present in the context (e.g., prostitution, religious infidelity). More specifically, Matthew quite plainly employs words like *moicheuō* and *moicheia* when he wants to refer to adultery. This is clearly the case in Matthew 5. He uses *moicheuō* in 5:27 (from the decalogue), repeats it in 5:28 (to broaden the concept of *moicheuō* beyond visible acts of sexual intercourse), and uses it for a third time in the antithesis on divorce (5:32, where *moicheuō* and *moichaomai* stigmatize the divorce allowed by the Torah as adultery). Granted this context, if Matthew wishes to name adultery as a reason for divorce, he would be almost forced to employ some form of *moicheia* to express the concept. Suddenly to interject a vague word like *porneia* into a context which has spoken of *moicheia* would be a strange procedure if the writer is intent on specifying adultery as the only grounds for divorce. Moreover, Matthew knows and uses the noun *moicheia* in 15:19, in clear contrast to the noun which immediately follows, *porneia*. Clearly, then, Matthew knows both words and distinguishes between them. Whatever *porneia* means here, it does not mean "adultery."

There are further reasons for rejecting the Hillel-Shammai interpretation. Matthew 19:3-12 is often read as a story depicting a challenge to Jesus to choose between Hillel and Shammai. Yet Matthew, following Mark, introduces the Pharisees as coming to Jesus *peirazontes* —testing or tempting him. In the Synoptic gospels, this verb *peirazō* always refers to an action with a malicious or evil intent. Usually it is employed only of the devil or of the enemies of Jesus in their attacks upon him (cf. Mark 12:13-17 = Matt 22:15-22). But, if the Pharisees are simply asking Jesus whether he favors the opinion of Hillel or Shammai, how does this constitute a malicious attempt to force him into a dilemma whereby one choice or either choice would involve a damaging statement? After all, both rabbinic opinions were perfectly respectable. Instead of reading Matthew 19:3-12 as though it were a video-tape replay of what happened in A.D. 30, we should realize that Matthew is writing Christian theology for a Christian audience, and is writing the beginning of a story with full knowledge of how the story will end. Matthew knows that the Pharisees' question will climax not with a choice among legitimate rabbinic opinions but with Jesus' abrogation of an important institution of the Mosaic Law. Hence the *peirazontes* at the beginning of the story.

That this is Matthew's understanding of Jesus' teaching is confirmed by Matthew's addition of the exclamation by the amazed disciples in 19:10 (no parallel in Mark): "If this is the case of a man with a woman, it is better not to marry." This is not a reaction to the well-known position of Shammai, which would hardly lead a Jew or anyone else to such a conclusion. Matthew has the disciples react all too humanly to Jesus' total prohibition of divorce. This presentation of Jesus is perfectly in keeping with Matthew's overall portrait of Jesus as the great eschatological "radicalizer" of the Law. Making Jesus simply echo Shammai would hardly fit the theological view of our anti-casuistic, anti-rabbinic Matthew.

And, as a final aside, we might point out that, if Matthew were espousing adultery as grounds for divorce, he would soon run up against grave practical difficulties. In this hypothesis, Matthew would allow divorce and remarriage for a husband and wife who had committed adultery. But a husband and wife who remained faithful to each other would not be allowed to divorce; indeed their attempt at divorce would be considered adultery. Obviously, the only thing to do for a faithful Christian couple who wanted a divorce would be to commit adultery, after which a dissolution of the marriage would be allowed. What we wind up with is divorce on demand, with a technical proviso of committing adultery. This all constitutes a strange church discipline, one in which adultery seems encouraged and fidelity discouraged. Unless our radicalizing Matthew was extremely obtuse when it came to practical consequences, this arrangement of church discipline would not be acceptable to his line of thinking.

But if the Hillel-Shammai interpretation is wrong, and if *porneia* does not mean adultery in Matthew 5:32 and 19:9, how should one understand *porneia*, the exceptive clause, and Matthew's view of divorce? Perhaps we would do well to turn from rabbinic sources (which, in their written form, stem from a couple of centuries after Jesus) and concentrate on the New Testament documents which, like Matthew's gospel, were written in the second half of the first century A.D. If we attend to certain marriage practices of the eastern Mediterranean region and to New Testament references to *porneia* which may reflect these practices, we may come to an explanation of *porneia* which fits better with the Matthean text and the situation of the Matthean church.[29]

In the eastern Mediterranean world of the first centuries B.C. and A.D., the Jews were almost unique in their strict prohibitions of incestuous marriages. Leviticus 18:6–18 clearly forbade marriage within various degrees of consanguinity and affinity. Many other peoples in the eastern Mediterranean region did enter into such marriages, a fact which sometimes created problems for a Gentile who wanted to convert to Judaism. If, in good faith, he had entered into a marital union which Leviticus 18 judged to be incestuous, he had to face the prospect of dismissing his wife. Jewish authorities, however, were divided on the issue. Some taught that the incestuous union had to be dissolved. Others pointed to the belief that circumcision (and proselyte-baptism?) made the convert like a new-born child. Since he was a new-born child, all his previous blood-relationships had ceased to exist, and he was free to keep his wife, for the union was no longer incestuous.

Matthew's church, as we know, had originated as a markedly Jewish church, in or around Antioch in Syria. As the decades passed, an increasing number of Gentiles sought entrance, an event which forced the Jewish-Christian church to face a problem not unlike the one faced by Jewish authorities. Did Christian baptism efface all former blood-relationships, so that the Christian convert could retain his wife, despite the degree of relationship forbidden by Leviticus 18? Indeed, the "liberals" might argue, could not one appeal in this matter to the Lord's prohibition of divorce? Nothing less than the command of Jesus himself forbade the convert from sending away his wife-relation. But Matthew's Jewish-Christian church spoke a firm no to what it no doubt considered a lax approach. Accordingly, the church put into Jesus'

---

[29]For what follows, see especially H. Baltensweiler, "Die Ehebruchsklauseln bei Matthäus. Zu Matth. 5,32; 19,9," *TZ* 15 (1959) 340-356; and his *Die Ehe im Neuen Testament* (Zurich: Zwingli, 1967).

prohibition of divorce the clarification that this prohibition was not to be used to countenance an incestuous marriage contracted before a convert's baptism. The reply of the church was: true, Jesus forbade a man to dismiss his wife. But this prohibition does not apply in the case of an incestuous union (*parektos logou porneias*), for that is no true union, being forbidden by Leviticus 18. To use later terminology and distinctions not worked out in Matthew's day: the incestuous union was null and void from the beginning, and so did not fall under the Lord's prohibition of divorce, which was concerned with genuine marriages.

This explanation fits in well with all that we know of Matthew and his church (its Jewish-Christian origins, its radicalizing tendencies). But can we say anything more than that this explanation is possible, along with many others? The word *porneia* can mean so many kinds of illicit sexual activity that we need some justification for restricting the meaning in 5:32 and 19.9 to "incestuous union." Fortunately, there are two key texts in the New Testament which supply a justification for the restriction, since they seem to address similar situations. In both passages *porneia* definitely or most probably has the meaning of "incestuous marriage."

The first text is Acts 15:29 (cf. 15:20; 21:25), the so-called "Apostolic Decree." Speaking to Gentile Christians living with Jewish Christians in the area from which Matthew's gospel stems (Antioch, Syria, Cilicia), church authorities (supposedly the "Council of Jerusalem") state that they will not impose circumcision or complete observance of the Mosaic Law on Gentile converts. The decree does, however, prohibit four practices: eating animals sacrificed to idols, eating meat with its blood, eating animals killed by strangulation, and *porneia*. These four practices were especially objectionalbe to strict Jewish Christians, since they were prohibited both to Israelites and to resident aliens in Leviticus 17-18 (precisely in the order listed in Acts 15:29).[30]

---

[30]It is possible that another reason operative here is that these four stipulations were counted as part of the "Noachide Laws" which were obligatory for all men, not simply for Jews. Luke, however, does not appeal to Noachide Laws but to "Moses" (Acts 15:21).

Now, the sexual practice forbidden in Leviticus 18 is incestuous sexual activity. Therefore, granted this context of levitical purity and kosher laws, *porneia* in Acts 15 probably refers to incestuous unions. And, significantly, this meaning of *porneia* occurs in an ecclesial context and problematic very similar to that of Matthew's church. In both cases, a traditionally Jewish-Christian group is beginning to undertake a mission to the Gentiles. But common life in one church is proving difficult for Jewish sensibilities. The solution to this difficulty is the imposition of certain ritual laws from Leviticus (but certainly not the whole Mosaic Law!) on the Gentile Christians. Among the levitical laws imposed is the prohibition of incestuous unions. In both Acts 15 and Matthew 5, the incestuous union is called *porneia*, and in both cases it is forbidden—notwithstanding the Gentiles' basic freedom from the ritual elements of the Mosaic Law (the problematic of Acts) and notwithstanding the Lord's prohibition of divorce (the problematic of Matthew).

One link in our argumentation may, however, still seem weak. Since the word *porneia* does not occur in the Septuagint translation of Leviticus 18:6-18, do we have definite evidence that *porneia* was in fact used by Christians to designate an incestuous union during the New Testament period? Fortunately we do, and this brings us to our second passage, 1 Corinthians 5:1: "It is actually reported that there exists among you *porneia*, and such *porneia* as does not even exist among the pagans, that a man should have his father's wife." The clear sense of the text shows that *porneia* here carries the sense of incestuous union. The precise union seems to be a case of marriage with one's stepmother, a practice explicitly forbidden in Leviticus 18:8. Unfortunately, it is not entirely clear why the Corinthians had been so complacent in allowing such a union to continue. Some might point to supposed gnostic or antinomian tendencies at Corinth. Freedom from the Law meant literally freedom from everything in the Mosaic Law, including the prohibition of incest in Leviticus 18. Another possibility, one I think more likely, is that Jewish or Judaizing views had influenced the Corinthians on this point. Since Paul himself had emphasized that faith and baptism made the Gentile convert a new creature, what was wrong in adopting the rabbinic view that the convert had wiped out all his previous blood-ties and was not living in an incestuous marriage? Paul, like Matthew's church and like the "Apostolic Decree," rejects any attempt to open the door to incestuous unions brought into the church by converts.

If all this be true, then the meaning of Matthew's "exceptive clause" is anything but a watering down of strict moral demand in the face of practical necessity. By inserting the proviso, the Matthean church rejected any lax position on the question of converts coming into the church with incestuous unions. Once the "exceptive clause" is understood in this light, Matthew 5:32 becomes just as much an abrogation of Deuteronomy 24:1 as is Luke 16:18.[31]

(b) The antithesis on oaths and vows (5:33-37) also concerns the revocation of an important Old Testament institution. The quotation in 5:33 is a paraphrase and meshing of a number of passages from the Torah: Exodus 20:7; Leviticus 19:12; Numbers 30:3; Deuteronomy 23:22. The actual wording of the command also borrows from the Septuagint of Psalm 49:14. As an examination of the various Old Testament passages will show, the noun

---

[31] I have presented Baltensweiler's approach to the exceptive clause, since it seems to me that it satisfies the New Testament data better than any other explanation. If one were to prefer the "classical" view of J. Dupont (i.e., separation from bed and board is allowed in case of adultery, but remarriage is not allowed), it would make no difference in my major position: Matthew 5:31-32 does involve a revocation of Mosaic Law. For Dupont's view, see his Mariage et divorce dans l'évangile (Abbay de Saint André: Desclée, 1959). Similarly, I do not bother to present here other interpretations of the exceptive clause, such as the "inclusive" or "interpretative" explanations. They are much less likely on philological or redactional grounds, and moreover would not make all that much difference in my major thesis. All these interpretations run into difficulty with some part of the data: defining the exact sense of porneia and justifying its restriction to one precise meaning, explaining the relationship of porneia to moicheuō, and giving a convincing Sitz im Leben for the rise of the exceptive clause in Matthew's church, as opposed to the churches of Mark and Luke.

horkous in Matthew 5:33 probably covers both oaths and vows.[32] While divorce was permitted or tolerated by the Mosaic Torah, oaths and vows were positively esteemed and in certain circumstances were commanded or imposed by the Law. For example, if a neighbor promised to safeguard another man's goods, and if the goods then disappeared, the neighbor had to take an oath as to his innocence in the matter (Exod 22:6-7, 10). An oath could also be imposed on a woman suspected of adultery (Num 5:19-22). And Numbers 30 closes its treatment of oaths and vows with a general statement about statutes commanded by Yahweh (v. 17). Thus, when Jesus revokes the institution of oaths and vows, he is also necessarily and concomitantly revoking specific commands of the Law.

Attempts to avoid seeing revocation here exist as they exist in the case of divorce. The general approach is to claim that Matthew is substituting, for all direct or indirect invocations of God, a very simple oath which does not refer to God at all— namely the "yes, yes, no, no" of Matthew 5:37. Arguments for this position stem from such diverse sources as the parallel in James 5:12 ("let your yes be a genuine yes and your no a genuine no") and the supposed parallel in a non-biblical work, *Slavonic Enoch* 40:1 ("let men swear by the words yea, yea, or else nay, nay"). But what these parallels are supposed to prove is far from clear. Granted that the wording of Matthew 5:37 differs from James 5:12, there is no need to take the Matthean text as a mild oath. The use of a double yes or no was known in the ancient world, and their use signified nothing more than a clear or emphatic answer, certainly not a form of oath. At any rate, that the

---

[32]We must not impose later canon law distinctions concerning oaths and vows on ancient texts where the usage is more fluid. We might say roughly that oaths look more to the past or present (what was or is the case) and are more common in a judicial setting, while vows tend to look to the future (what will be the case) and are more common in daily life. Another distinction, made by the rabbis, was that an oath required the naming of God, directly or by a substitute, while a vow did not. If this distinction is operative in Matthew 5:33-37, the statements would be mainly concerned with oaths. And, even apart from rabbinic parallels, oaths rather than vows seem to be the main scope of 5:33-37.

anti-casuistic Matthew, who mocks the Pharisees for their hair-splitting, would take such a route is unlikely. As for Jewish parallels, we run into the old problem of dating and exact interpretation. To take but one example: *Slavonic Enoch* might be as late as the seventh century A.D., though a first-century date is also possible. The manuscripts on which we depend come from the sixteenth and seventeenth centuries, and may reflect Christian influence. Moreover, one of the key manuscripts lacks the passage about swearing by a double yea or nea. And even that passage says such "swearing" is not an "oath."

Instead of interpreting Matthew by such dubious parallels, we should take him at his word—which is the categorical prohibition of 5:34: "Do not swear *at all*!" The "at all" stands out all the more because it is lacking in James 5:12. Everything which follows only exemplifies, but does not narrow down, that absolute prohibition. As we move through the subsequent verses (34-37), we slowly realize that Matthew sees something intrinsically wrong in all oaths and vows, something which could not be remedied by a milder oath. Every oath, to be an oath, must refer however indirectly to God; one "pays" one's "oaths to the Lord" (5:33). And this is precisely what Matthew finds wrong with oaths and vows. They infringe on God's transcendence and majesty by presuming to drag the Almighty into man's petty affairs, by presuming to make the all-truthful God the guarantor of man's sometimes truthful statements. Oaths are objectionable to Matthew not because they infringe on our neighbor's right to have the truth but because they infringe on God's right to be God.[33] Oaths

---

[33]This reason for rejecting oaths reminds us that Matthew's theology in the antitheses cannot be simply reduced to the rubric of love of neighbor. Nothing is said about our relation to our neighbor in 5:33-37. A great deal is said about our relation to the Creator who alone has absolute control of our existence (cf. the prohibition involving one's hair in verse 36). The formulas in verses 34-35 are rejected because they try to have it both ways: they skirt naming God directly (and thereby skirt an absolutely binding formula) and yet try to involve God as the guarantor of their affirmations.—Needless to say, after the absolute prohibition of 5:34a, the list of oaths in 34b-36 are to be taken as samples or examples, and not as an exhaustive list of the oaths that are forbidden. Nor should Matthew 23:16-22 be called upon to counter 5:33-37. Matthew 23:16-22

create the illusion that man may control God. But the entire message of the Bible is that God is God and man is not God, and that therefore God does not stand under man's control or at man's disposal. Every oath is a hidden act of impiety in that it makes a subtle claim on God. Therefore, for Matthew, all oaths, no matter how indirect, are to be avoided. And, accordingly, the whole Old Testament institution of oaths and vows and the law governing them are to be revoked. Nothing is to be used but an emphatic yes or no—which, given Matthew's whole reason for rejecting oaths, cannot be understood by him as a milder form of oath.

(c) The antithesis on retaliation (5:38-42) supplies us with the clearest example of revocation. The law of retaliation (the *jus talionis*) is clearly enunciated, in a variety of forms, in Exodus 21:24, Leviticus 24:20, and Deuteronomy 19:21: eye for eye, tooth for tooth, hand for hand, foot for foot, burning for burning, wound for wound, stripe for stripe. We should not speak here of revoking a permission in the Law, because the Law was quite firm about the obligation of the judge and the community to see strict justice done. After all, the only alternative conceivable to ancient man was rampant injustice, judicial corruption, and social chaos. It is for that reason that such texts as Deuteronomy 19:21 sternly enjoin: "And your eye shall show no pity." The three passages have cited are suffused with a sense of strict obligation, not optional practice.

It is quite true, of course, that the *jus talionis* was in its origin a humanizing institution which limited unregulated situations of private vengeance. Some who would want to exclude revocation even in this antithesis claim that Jesus is simply following the ultimate humanizing thrust of the Law. In a sense, that is correct. But such an insight cannot wipe out the real difference between a simple radicalization (such as we saw in the first, second, and sixth antitheses), and a radicalization which involves the abroga-

---

expresses a mocking, *ad hominem* polemic against the hair-splitting casuistry Matthew sees in the Pharisees. Presupposing the Pharisaic rules for oaths, Matthew holds them up to ridicule. This hardly tells us about what Matthew considers legitimate for his own church, especially when 23:22 includes an oath Matthew firmly rejects in 5:34b.

tion of the letter of the Torah. In the case of the *jus talionis*, we have the latter.

Nor will it do to object that, by the time of Jesus, the *jus talionis* had been softened to allow monetary compensation in place of compensation in kind, and that therefore Jesus was simply following this tendency. We should note, in reply, that the possibility of monetary or transferred compensation was already known in ancient Israel, and so Jesus would still be rescinding the letter of the Law as it had been understood in Israel from ancient times.[34] And what Jesus is rescinding is not simply retaliation in kind as opposed to a more humane monetary compensation. What Jesus is forbidding is any seeking of retaliation, retribution, or compensation *whatsoever*.[35] It is this basic system of retribution set up by the Torah which Jesus rejects for his disciples.

The ramifications of this revocation are astounding. For any human legal system, not just the *jus talionis* and not just the Mosaic Torah, any human legal system rests on the basic insight that, in order to insure order and balance in society, crimes must be punished in a way commensurate with the offense. The fifth antithesis is in a true sense the great antithesis, for it is antithetical to all human law systems. Here the "otherness" of the eschatological life-style Jesus brings and imposes on his disciples shines through most clearly. Not just esoteric, arcane, or superstitious rituals are abolished by Jesus. Reasonable, human systems protecting reasonable human society are likewise abolished for the life of the disciple, simply because the eschaton has come.

Our survey of the six antitheses thus confirms our view that the first, second, and sixth antitheses (on murder, adultery, and love of neighbor) simply radicalize the Law, while the third, fourth, and fifth antitheses (on divorce, oaths, and talion) actually

---

[34]It might also be noted that statements by Josephus and Rabbi Eliezer ben Hyrcanus leave one with the impression that the literal observance of the *jus talionis* was not unknown in the first century A.D.

[35]In the judicial context of 5:38, the difficult phrase of 5:39, *mē antistēnai tǭ ponerǭ*, probably means: do not contend at law with your legal adversary, the same idea which is present in verse 40a, *tǭ thelonti soi krithēnai*, "the one who wishes to contend with you at law."

abrogate the Law in the act of radicalizing it. What is especially astounding here is that Matthew does not approach this question of the retention-yet-abrogation of the Law as did some of the Fathers of the Church. The latter distinguished between ceremonial or ritual laws which were abolished, and the moral laws (especially the decalogue) which were retained and perfected. Instead, Matthew constructs the antitheses to proclaim abrogation not simply for ceremonial or ritual rules, not simply for esoteric or antiquated customs of ancient Semites, but for ethical, social, and religious institutions of the greatest significance, not only for Jews but also for many of the other religions and societies of this world. To abolish totally and at one fell swoop the institutions of divorce, oaths, vows, and legal retaliation would be unthinkable not only to zealots for the Mosaic Torah but equally to the upholders of many other religions and cultures.

IV. FINAL SUMMARY

Reviewing all we have seen in Part III, we can see that what Jesus enunciated programmatically in 5:17-20 he then fills out consistently, with concrete examples, in 5:21-48. In 5:17, Jesus forestalls any false interpretation of the coming antitheses. Despite the astounding revocations about to take place, Jesus tells his disciples that his mission vis-à-vis the Law and the prophets is not one of complete dissolution. His mission has rather the positive scope of giving the Law and the prophets their eschatological fulfillment, a prophetic fullness which rescinds the letter of the Law even as it completes its meaning. Jesus is the Messiah who brings consummation, not the revolutionary who brings desolation. As he assures his disciples in 5:18, not the slightest part of the Law will fall away until all prophecy is fulfilled in his own life, death, and resurrection. Only then will his eschatological teaching be proclaimed to all nations, for only then will the end-time have definitively broken into this age—bringing with it a new people, a new initiation rite, a new understanding of God, and a truly "new morality." Jesus is therefore inculcating anything but a light-hearted and negligent approach to the teaching and doing of the commandments of the Law. Teachers in particular must avoid any negligence which would betray their office now and would lower their status in the final Kingdom (5:19). Indeed, to enter that final Kingdom, one's justice, one's doing of God's will, must far transcend the casuistry and formalism of the Pharisees; it must overflow with all the eschatological fullness and newness Christ brings (5:20).

It is to describe in greater detail what this new eschatological justice is that Matthew then draws up the neat pattern of the six antitheses. The strange mixture of simple radicalization with a radicalization which revokes is a perfect reflection of the eschatological fullness Jesus brings: a new age breaks into and fulfills all the promises of the old age of prophecy, while it necessarily brings that age of prophecy to a close. Continuity yet discontinuity: the theme struck in Matthew's Christology from the genealogy of 1:1-17 onward finds its resonance in the Christian's moral life. The eschatological note of fulfilling yet transcending which characterizes Jesus naturally characterizes the morality of his disciples as well. For the believing Christian, prophecy has come to pass, even in the area of moral teaching. The letter of the Law must give way to the eschatological fulfillment of God's will. As we saw throughout Part II, this radicalized Christian justice, which can even rescind important elements of the Law, is understood and grounded Christologically: this justice is simply all that Jesus ever commanded (28:20a). And the living of all he commanded is made possible by his own victory over sin and death in his death-resurrection (chaps. 27-28). It is the mission of *his* church, the new people of God, to spread, interpret, and observe this radicalized will of the Father—a mission that is possible for the church only because its risen Lord is ever with it to sustain it. The exalted Son of Man, who of old exercised authority during his earthly ministry, and who now exercises all authority over heaven and earth (28:18b), has not ascended *from* his church, as in Luke 24 or Acts 1. In Matthew 28, the Son of Man comes *to* his church in proleptic parousia, to be with it and support it in its mission all days, until the old world is completely abolished (28:20).

At the end of Part II, we saw that the specificity of Matthew's gospel was the nexus between Christ and his church. At the end of Part III, we can see that this nexus between Christ and church is the foundation on which Matthew builds his presentation of Christian morality. During his earthly ministry, the Son of Man inculcated his eschatological morality, promised his eschatological community authority to enforce his demands (18:15-20), and spoke of the leaders of the eschatological community, to whom he would give the authority to teach and interpret his eschatological morality (16:18-19). By his death-resurrection he both fully founded this eschatological community and fully grounded the possibility for every disciple to live the eschatological morality he taught. Thus, out of the death-resurrection of the Son of Man proceeds not only the existence of his church, invested with his authority to teach his commands, but also the ability of individual members of his church to live those eschatological commands he once taught on earth—those eschatological commands according to which he will judge his church when he comes on the last day. It is this rich combination of Christology, ecclesiology, and eschatological morality which gives Matthew's gospel its special—and perennial—relevance to the church. Matthew's gospel continually presents the church and the individual Christian with a salutary shock. The radical demands of Christ in this gospel summon both institution and individual believer out of the "reasonable" life-styles of this world, including this world's religions. The uncompromising radicalism of Christ's moral message in Matthew is a challenge to all of us to realize, in our own lives, that the word "eschatological" is more than theological jargon. It is the designation for the total change the Son of Man brings anytime he comes, in proleptic parousia, into his church and into the lives of individual believers. For anyone who hears Matthew's gospel and believes, the foundations of the earth are shaken, tombs are rent asunder, the dead rise, and the Son of Man comes in power, to remain with the believer all days, until the end.

TOPICAL INDEX

AUTHOR INDEX